HERGÉ

HERGÉ

THE MAN WHO CREATED **TINTIN**

pierre assouline

TRANSLATED BY
CHARLES RUAS

OXFORD
UNIVERSITY PRESS

OXFORD
UNIVERSITY PRESS

Oxford University Press, Inc., publishes works that further
Oxford University's objective of excellence
in research, scholarship, and education.

Oxford New York
Auckland Cape Town Dar es Salaam Hong Kong Karachi
Kuala Lumpur Madrid Melbourne Mexico City Nairobi
New Delhi Shanghai Taipei Toronto

With offices in
Argentina Austria Brazil Chile Czech Republic France Greece
Guatemala Hungary Italy Japan Poland Portugal Singapore
South Korea Switzerland Thailand Turkey Ukraine Vietnam

Pierre Assouline's text copyright © 1996 by Pierre Assouline and PLON
Originally published in France under the title *Hergé*

Translation copyright © 2009 by Charles Ruas

This first English-language edition retains the core
but not the totality of the original French edition.

Published by Oxford University Press, Inc.
198 Madison Avenue, New York, NY 10016

www.oup.com

First issued as an Oxford University Press paperback, 2011

Oxford is a registered trademark of Oxford University Press

Library of Congress Cataloging-in-Publication Data
Assouline, Pierre.
Hergé: the man who created Tintin / Pierre Assouline;
translated by Charles Ruas.
p. cm.
"This first English-language edition retains the core but not the totality
of the original French edition."
Includes bibliographical references and index.
ISBN 978–0–19–983727–4 (pbk.)
1. Hergé, 1907–1983. 2. Cartoonists—Belgium—Biography. I. Title.
PN6790.B43H47264 2009 741.5'092—dc22 [B] 2009022411

9 8 7 6 5 4 3 2 1
Printed in the United States of America
on acid-free paper

To you three

What if I told you that I put my whole life into Tintin?
—Hergé, 1982

contents

part iii: recognition

preface

HERGÉ BECAME SO COMPLETELY IDENTIFIED with Tintin that whenever he arrived at a reception it was as if Lewis Carroll were making an appearance at a children's tea party. His easy serenity and friendly manner, the gentle magnetism of his presence, made everyone forget that the character he created inhabited only a paper universe. I have to confess right at the start that until I began my research I was also guilty of this illusion, because, like so many others, my childhood and adolescence were conditioned by my passion for Tintin. It's still difficult to overestimate the impact of his work on several generations of Europeans. Countless numbers of people claim to be complete strangers to the world of comic strips and never read comic books, then add, "Except for Tintin!"

I first considered doing a biography of Georges Remi, alias Hergé, as a result of a conversation with my friend André Versailles, an editor in Brussels, who managed to plant a serious doubt about the true nature of this creative genius.

Sometime later, after appearing on the television program about books called *Bouillon de Culture*, I was backstage talking with panelists and members of the audience over a glass of wine when guests from Wallonia—French-speaking Belgium—said, "You understand that Simenon and Hergé are our two sacred monsters ... but if both are admired, Hergé is also loved. Belgians would not stand for your treating Hergé the way you did Simenon." I wondered why. The journalist in me suddenly became curious.

The following month at a book signing in Brussels a distinguished-looking elderly gentleman handed over a book to be inscribed and said, "May I suggest that you devote your next work to Hergé? The subject is prodigiously interesting, and in portraying his life you would be telling the

story of Belgium in the twentieth century. And as Belgium is on the verge
of disappearing, it would be timely."

That's when I understood that Hergé was the personification of Belgium.
He remains one of the last great myths of a Belgian Federation.[1]

Finally, when Philippe Goddin of the Hergé Foundation offered to place
his archives entirely at my disposal I no longer hesitated. The keepers of this
temple have such a reputation for secrecy that their encouragement was an
"Open Sesame." I stated my terms: my critical focus on the man and his work;
my desire to know everything, with complete freedom in my writing; and my
refusal to allow any outside control of my work. This was necessary because I
fully intended systematically to go through the thousands of unpublished
letters that comprised Hergé's private and professional correspondence.

FANNY RODWELL of the Hergé Foundation assisted me in every way, as if
there had been an institutional decision to dispel all misunderstandings or
doubt about any aspect of his life and to clear up any confusion about the
origins of his work. For the duration of my research, I had their full support.

Questions about World War II, colonialism, and misogyny arose during
the course of my research. These skeletons in the closet could no more be
dismissed than allowed to take over as the focus of this work. Sensationalism
obliterates the major trajectories of a life and obscures the original motivation:
the body of work. If there is no Tintin without Hergé, Hergé is of no interest
without Tintin. By now Hergé's creation has outpaced his creator and pulls
him along in his continuing evolution. Today some speak with some justifica-
tion of "a Tintin century," signifying the twentieth. But what about Hergé?

They owe everything to one another. That is not always the case. For
example, his contemporary Georges Simenon had another life as a writer,
an even richer one, independent of Inspector Maigret, who had assured
his fame.

If there is an example of the work as a life, it is that of Hergé. But his life
cannot be divided into as many chapters as there are volumes of Tintin's
adventures. Even if the series as a whole forms a coherent coming-of-age novel,
in a life it is the breaking points that count. Nothing is more rewarding than
identifying those rare moments that are exceptionally and intensely pivotal; a
destiny has come to an abrupt stop, pausing there before restarting. Generally
these pivotal moments can be identified only much later. There's a Chinese
saying that a fish is in the worst position to judge the existence of water.

There were four critical moments in the life of Georges Remi, and
starting from there in the works of Hergé. They correspond to four dates:

1927, 1934, 1945, 1960. They represent decisive encounters: Father Wallez, Germaine, Chang, Fanny.

IF THE CHARACTER OF TINTIN is clear-headed and upbeat, that of his creator is contradictory and inscrutable. It is difficult to take at face value this extraordinarily creative person who, after revolutionizing his art form and leaving an indelible mark on his age, can say in the most unassuming way, "N'exagerrons pas"—"Let's not exaggerate … I was just happy drawing little guys, that's all." Such a claim suggests, perhaps disingenuously, a total inability to explain what he created: a cast of characters whose stories have sold millions of volumes in dozens of languages for many decades, without any sign of letting up. Biographers of someone like Hergé pursue an impossible chimera: to discover the sources of creative genius and then to reveal them, even though they cannot possibly be explained. It's not that they cannot be found, but that the life and work cannot be separated.

The adventures of Tintin and his friends reflect not only a world, its history and geography, but a whole society with its codes and rituals. That they come to constitute an international language is their great accomplishment. Even more, I would say, that is their great triumph.

No other body of graphic work has given rise to so many books, articles, and monographs. This is all the more impressive since they feature a hero who remains fifteen years old for half a century and a talking dog.

I never met Georges Remi, which I do not regret. I found him in his drawings and his letters, the comments noted in the margins of his proofs, and the doubts jotted down on the back of his notes. He probably would have told me little, given that the bridge between his work and his life had been built and rebuilt with great care. Toward the end he played down everything, as illustrated by the interviews he gave to Numa Sadoul in 1971. Regretting having let himself open up before a microphone and speaking freely, he immediately censored the interviews severely. In the same way, he wrote interesting but aseptic memoirs. This present work, which referred to the original typescript of his interviews, with corrections marked, reveals the distance of autobiography from biography.

As might be expected, Hergé was in the weakest position to speak about his lifework. When asked how a book for children could also be a work for adults, he generally answered with a vague, self-deprecating remark about how his work was intended for young people between seven to seventy-seven.

Great men are often surpassed by what they have given us, for better and for worse.

part i: **truths**

1.

A Life in Gray
1907–1925

IF IT'S TRUE that we are as much the product of a childhood as of a country, then Georges Remi's childhood has neither flag nor frontiers, but only a color: gray. As far back as he could remember, these were years of a monochrome gray. More than the sign of Gemini, which would become increasingly important to him, the color influenced his birth and development.

May 22, 1907, at 7:30 A.M. Nothing much happened in Belgium that day except for one more birth in Etterbeek, a parish in greater metropolitan Brussels. The father, Alexis Remi, was an employee in a candy factory. Elisabeth Remi, née Dufour, was a homemaker. They were twenty-four and twenty-five, respectively. Georges was their firstborn. A second child, Paul, would arrive five years later. The father was absent during childbirth; Dr. Schovaers had to sign the birth certificate. Two formalities, you would say. Just like the baptism on June 9 in the local parish church. The family was Catholic, but not devout.

In the Remi home the parents were not demonstrative; affection was there but without any sparks. They were proud, without ostentation, of their heritage. Georges's father was Walloon and his mother, Flemish. All his life he would consider himself a "synthetic Belgian," a pure product of that third region, the crucible of Brussels. An unquestionable Francophone, he also knew Flemish. As well, he was marked by the loud, jovial Marollian accent of his maternal grandmother, who always spoke the Franco-Flemish jargon of the common people from the neighborhood behind the courthouse.

Georges was five years old when the Socialist deputy from Charleroi, Jules Destrée, published in his local newspaper a letter to the king, which

became famous, affirming that there were no Belgians, only Walloons and Flemish. Although Destrée was a patriotic advocate of a unified Belgium, he recognized that there were two communities that made up the country, in which French was the language of the elite and Flemish the dialect of the people.

In Georges's family, as he later recalled it, everything was average: the setting, the place, the people. Even the slices of buttered bread topped with grated chocolate had a bland taste. Everything was colorless, scentless, tasteless, and of no interest. In the Remi home, there was no one to admire, no books to read, no plays to attend, no discussions. (Music was reserved for Sunday, and in one place: the music pavilion of the park in Brussels opposite the Royal Palace. The music was martial.) There were no crises or scenes; the father and mother were equally reserved. There was nothing to say. Parents and children lived side by side rather than together. They loved each other but without any outward manifestation or exchanges. They were neither happy nor unhappy. They were simply there.[1]

If the Remi family was without mystery, that does not mean they were without secrets. The family had only one, but its specter dominated them. The absolute discretion that it imposed may have been the cause of their laconic way in all things. Ever since he was old enough to understand, Georges knew that he must never question his parents about the identity of his grandfather on his father's side. You just didn't talk about it. Looking at the portrait of his paternal grandmother, he would wonder about the secret behind the sad, pensive expression on her lovely face.

"Your grandfather? He was from here," they would say to put him off. Or if he was too insistent they would say, "If you knew you would become swell-headed."

Toward the end of his life, Hergé repeated this, word for word, to his cousin Marie-Louise to brush off her curiosity. To some of his coworkers he often mentioned that his family originally came from Chaumont-Gistoux, without any further details.[2] The subject was taboo.

In 1882 Marie Dewigne left her family home in Uccle to take up residence in Anderlecht. Within the year she gave birth to twin boys, Léon and Alexis, of an unknown father. Until then the young mother had been a chambermaid in the service of the Countess Hélène Errembault de Dudzeele (1849–1900). The count was a collateral descendant of Louis Errembault, president of the Council of Flanders, who acquired the fiefdom of Dudzeele in 1664. A century later the family was ennobled by Maria Théresa, Empress of Austria.

On the family estate of Chaumont-Gistoux in Brabant, just outside Brussels, the twin boys grew up with the two daughters of the house, Germaine and Valentine (who would later wed Count Sforza, the Italian minister of foreign affairs). The countess educated the twins as if they were her own children. Every Thursday the two boys, impeccably dressed, left the chateau in a carriage with the countess to pay their weekly visit to the pastry shop in town. Eventually Marie Dewigne was married off to Philippe Remi, a much younger man, a printer by trade. It was a white marriage; the boys were recognized by him and took his name.[3]

The boys were shadowed by a rumor. People would whisper after them, "Be polite when you speak to them, they are from a very important family." The implication was that their father was someone from the chateau, and for some time it was simply rumored that they were of royal descent. After all, King Léopold II, a friend of the family, often stayed at Chaumont-Gistoux. Alternatively a more reasonable aristocratic origin was attributed to them. The master of the house, Count Gaston Errembault de Dudzeele (1847–1929), a career diplomat, wasn't always away on a mission.[4]

FROM HIS CORNER little Georges watched, his favorite pastime. When he was not observing, he imitated. Every time he started mimicking, his mother reproved him, "Stop acting like a monkey!"[5]

As an adolescent, turning inward, he joined a paper family in the attic, where a trunk filled with books was stored. He would retain an abiding love not for authors but for certain novels and characters: *Huckleberry Finn, Treasure Island, The Pickwick Papers, Three Men in a Boat,* and *Robinson Crusoe.*

French authors did not have as important a place in his pantheon, though there were exceptions: *General Dourakine* transported the adolescent from Brussels to a strange land; Dumas's *Twenty Years After* and *The Viscount of Bragelonne* never ceased to interest him, along with Hector Malot's *Without a Family*, which had a special place in his imagination. By thirteen his critical sense made him reject *Twenty Thousand Leagues under the Sea* as not credible enough and lacking any sense of actual experience. His disappointment would keep him from exploring other works of Jules Verne.

The trunk of books contained not only the classics of several generations but also illustrated books. His first artistic revelation came from discovering Benjamin Rabier's illustrations for the *Fables of La Fontaine*, which amazed him, especially "The Fox and the Crow."[6]

By October 1914 Belgium had been occupied by the Germans for several weeks. Prussia had trampled on the Treaty of 1831 that had guaranteed Belgium's neutrality. Regrouping at the River Yser, the Belgian army launched an attack to stop the invaders from reaching the sea.

Two men embodied the resistance of a whole people from the very beginning, never giving ground nor compromising: Albert I, "the Soldier-King," who elected to stay among his people in their hour of need, and Cardinal Mercier, archbishop of Malines, who encouraged resistance. But the Occupation Forces had only to revive the old language divide between French and Flemish to win over the Flemish extremists.

Georges was a good student who had many friends. He was sociable everywhere but at home. His parents found only two ways of controlling the hyperactive boy: giving him a sound spanking or handing him paper and pencils to draw with. When out in restaurants he kept himself from being bored by drawing on the cardboard beer coasters. Very soon he went from making scribbles to stick figures and then to scenes drawn with a story line, some of them inspired by the war and the German occupation.[7]

His schoolbooks have a curious appearance. The upper three-quarters of each page is filled by a conscientious student who applies himself, whereas in the bottom part he sketched stories. They seem all the more modern because the text of these little tales is not always contained in captions but sometimes is placed in balloons coming from the lips of his characters, which was not done at the time. The illustrated books by Rodolphe Töpffer (1799–1846), a pioneer of the genre, are firmly planted in the conventions of an earlier century. Bécassine, the Breton housemaid often called the first female protagonist in the history of comics, had appeared since 1905 in the pages of *La Semaine de Suzette* with the text under the illustrations.

Georges and his parents rarely spoke; they communicated through drawings. Hergé remembered it was by this means that he understood what he had in common with, and how he was different from, his father. One day both were drawing airplanes; his father gave his the lightness of dragonflies, while Georges's versions carried the whole weight of the aeronautics industry. From that Georges deduced the fact his father was an idealist and that he was a realist, and with that understanding he came closer to outgrowing his adolescence. In the same way, when Georges undertook to draw a picture of a large battle scene from the War of 1870, he asked, "In your opinion, Papa, in the battle are the French on the right and the Prussians on the left or vice-versa?"

"It all depends on where you stand," was the reply.[8]

At school his drawing teacher, Mr. Stoffijn ("Fine Dust" in Flemish), gave his students an uninspiring subject for a contest: an iris seen against wrought-iron grillwork. Georges finished the assignment and received a below-average grade. He was all the more disappointed because he was good at drawing—at least better than his classmates. In 1918, on the eve of the signing of the Armistice, when a martyred Belgium, a member of the League of Nations, signed a pact with France, Georges drew a large patriotic picture in color of German soldiers being destroyed by the Belgian army. This time Mr. Fine Dust was truly moved. The euphoria of the victory had something to do with his indulgence: "Remi, I will go over your drawings from the test." Georges still wound up with a below-average grade.[9]

Georges had two means of escape: Scouting and the movies. At the age of twelve in 1919 he was still too young to appreciate the great pacifist lyrical epic by Alfred Machin, *Cursed Is War*. Georges preferred a revolutionary film in another style, *Gertie the Dinosaur,* a ten-minute animated film by Winsor McCay, who drew all ten thousand distinct frames. Georges also delighted in film shorts featuring Charlie Chaplin, Harry Langdon, and Buster Keaton, whose burlesque qualities had a greater influence on him than any book. Indeed film would determine the internal structure of his future work: the invention of the visual gag. Coordinating image with music to celebrate humor in motion was more than a technique, it was an art in itself.

But it was as a Boy Scout that Georges came into his own. By 1920, a year after making his First Communion in the church of Sainte-Gertrude in Etterbeek, he began attending Saint-Boniface School and became a member of the troop of that religious institution. Saint-Boniface was under the auspices of the archbishop, which meant that all the teachers were priests. They were in charge of his secondary studies, known as the Cycle in the Humanities, in two curricula, Latin and Modern.

Georges started in the fifth form in Modern. To his peers he appeared both steady and cheerful, good natured with a touch of the mischievous, and with broader views than the majority of his fellow students. He was as passionate about history and geography as his teacher, Father Pirotte, who was also the person in charge of the projector and who managed to show films at least one afternoon a week.

But what distinguished Georges from his peers was his mania for drawing: he scribbled on everything all the time—in his textbook margins,

in his notebooks, and on any scrap of paper at hand. He doodled whatever came to mind. When Father Raty lectured on Hannibal, elephants storming up mountains surged from Georges's pen. When Father Pharsazyn selected Dickens for the exercise in translation, Georges sketched the characters from *David Copperfield*.[10] Landscapes, sketches, figures, and portraits—he was talented and already could capture action. The essential was all there, not just as potential. Techniques he would acquire with experience. It would come, his new friends had no doubt about it; they already had started saving his drawings.

Georges was a brilliant student. At the end of each school year he was awarded a prize for academic excellence. In July 1925 he finished his secondary studies, taking first place with an average of 83 out of 100. Paradoxically it was in drawing that he performed the least well: 34 out of a possible 50. The academic constraints of that class were too narrow for his talent. When Father Proost assigned his students to draw a pistol, Georges refused because the mechanism seemed too detailed and fussy. This cost him points.[11]

Later Father Proost announced that the drawing prize would not be awarded that year. Georges's classmates did not hide their disappointment. The teacher tried to reassure them: "Of course Remi deserves better! But he had to draw diagrams, prisms, and other objects with their shadows. Another type of drawing is innate in this boy."[12]

For Georges the philosophy of Scouting was the alpha and omega of his moral sense. The students of Saint-Boniface were proud of their double allegiance as students and Scouts; they could not conceive of being one without the other. His neat appearance, his determination, his composure, and his skills as a Scout (he became an Eagle Scout) made Georges popular. He was named troop leader of the Squirrel Patrol and was known as "Curious Fox." This enabled him to make trips abroad, to summer camps in Italy, Switzerland, Austria, and Spain. In July and August 1923 his troop hiked two hundred miles on foot across the Pyrenees by way of Lourdes.

The Scouts also liberated Georges. At the end of the term the Scout troop divided into two teams, the Maccabees and the Gargoyles, of which Georges was a member. They improvised gags and created outlandish scenes, which were so good that the boys were invited to perform them on festive occasions.[13]

This period would remain an ideal for the rest of his life, giving him a value system all the more effective because it did not appear as such, a way of looking at the world, a social attitude. More than giving him a taste for

camping and a love of nature, his years as a Scout would give him a moral compass for the rest of his life, teaching him friendship as a natural virtue and generosity as an everyday act. Scouting stressed the importance of giving your word and staying true to it. It alone permitted him to travel, to make friends for life, and to leave behind an atmosphere whose vacuity and inertia threatened to smother him.

Even more than school, Scouting gave George a push forward by offering an opportunity to publish his drawings. His Scoutmaster, René Weverbergh, was the first person with enough faith in his talent to give him a break, in *Jamais Assez* (Never Enough), the newsletter of the Saint-Boniface Scouts. The dynamic Weverbergh was soon working on *Boy-Scout*, the publication of the Federation of Scouts, and brought Georges along. As early as 1922 the fifth issue carried a drawing signed "G. Remi." The pages of *Boy-Scout*, which would soon be transformed into *The Belgian Boy Scout*, served as his testing ground. Georges was learning, and he tried everything. He would fondly recall this monthly as the privileged place of all his great efforts. In these pages he would publish his first cartoon, his first drawing for a cover, his first woodcut, and his first illustration for a story. Less than two years later "G. Remi" would disappear into "Jérémie" which in turn became "Jérémiades." A self-respecting artist needed a pseudonym. His initials, G. R., were not inspiring, and he dropped them shortly after using them; by reversing his initials he found Hergé (R. G.), which he first used in the December 1924 edition of *Boy-Scout.*

In addition to the drawings he did on a regular basis for such articles as "On Patrol," "The Cub Scouts' Corner," and "Strings and Things," he also executed his first true comic strip: "The Adventures of Totor C.P. of the June Bugs." It begins as the hero, a Boy Scout patrol leader, leaves to join his uncle in Texas. The lines are awkward, hesitant, incomplete, but the movement, rhythm, and, above all, the humor is apparent. The text of three to five lines is in the captions. Very soon the text would seem to him redundant with the drawings. Indeed Georges Remi daringly introduced a speech bubble in his picture. Traditional techniques seemed incapable of expressing his thoughts. An exclamation point expressed the characters' amazement or puzzlement, and onomatopoeia was used to underline jubilation ("Hip! Hip! Hip! Hurrah!"). An exclamation borrowed from Archimedes expressed the sudden illumination of an idea ("Eureka!"), and others expressed an action or its effect ("Bang!" "Aie!"). Some speech bubbles continued dialogue ("Hands Up!"). The story was very Boy Scout in spirit and clearly a prefiguration of Tintin.

If he wanted to draw, let him draw, thought his parents, though they could not imagine that he could become an artist without learning how to be one. Georges Remi, who had already become Hergé for some, left one school behind for another, abandoning humanities for the graphic arts.

His very first evening at Saint-Luc was enough for him to realize that there had been a terrible misunderstanding. He had expected life drawing and instead he was assigned to faithfully reproduce a plaster Corinthian column. It was more than just a gap between him and his teachers at Saint-Luc, it was a world. A living model is a nude, and for the virtuous Catholics of Saint-Luc, you might just as well conjure Satan and Beelze-bub.[14] He was the student, they were the teachers, so he complied. For the first time since he began following his passion, he was bored—and that was unforgivable. He spent only one evening in an academic art class.

2.

Scoutmaster in the Twentieth Century
1925–1929

DISENCHANTED WITH ART SCHOOL, Hergé started thinking of making posters or becoming a graphic designer in advertising, a job with a future and obviously more lucrative. Drawing was secondary to his passion for typography and composition. His attention to details, his precision and discipline made him conscientious. He admired the Swiss graphic artist Léo Marfur, the Art Deco elegance of the French fashion illustrator René Vincent, and the artist Cassandre (Adolphe Mouron), famous for his stylized posters "Le Nord Express," "L'Étoile du Nord," and "La Route Bleue."

These interests indicated a possible vocation, but they did not provide an eighteen-year-old with a salary. Once more René Weverbergh, now a journalist on the staff of *Le Vingtième Siècle* (Twentieth Century), came to his assistance. The old Scoutmaster got Curious Fox hired through the back door in the autumn of 1925, as part of the subscription department.

He may have been on the wrong floor, but Remi was in the right place. In August 1926 he was called up for military service. Being a soldier was another way of being a Scout, but holding a rifle in one hand didn't prevent his holding a pencil in the other. On his discharge in August 1927, Hergé returned to *Le Vingtième Siècle*, this time as a reporter-photographer and illustrator. His three-year contract specified that he would take photographs, work in the darkroom, and provide illustrations for both editorials and advertising. The terms for his employment were 600 francs (current equivalent, $255) a month, a railway pass, and an allowance for expenses. Under no circumstances could he work for another newspaper.

Everyone in Brussels knew the headquarters of *Le Vingtième Siècle*. Located in a large building at 11 Boulevard Bisschoffsheim, a main thoroughfare in the fashionable area of town, it was more than a newspaper. It was a gathering place. For businessmen and speculators it offered political and financial news; for the conservative middle class it was the main platform for Catholic doctrine and information. For Georges Remi, twenty years old, it represented the chance of a lifetime.

Remi was Catholic by birth, habit, and tradition. In Belgium at the end of the 1920s three ideologies defined the political landscape: liberalism, socialism, and Catholicism. The more the first two pushed their anticlerical agenda, the more militant became the stance of the third. The Catholics were both members of a political party and followers of the faith. This faith was the only real ancestral link binding together the Flemish-speaking and the French-speaking populations, and *Le Vingtième Siècle* favored a permanent bond between them. Nationalistic, it was hostile to Communists, Jews, and Freemasons, as might be expected, and critical of politics, the money-is-king outlook, the advent of mechanization, and modernism in general. *Le Vingtième Siècle* also never printed anything related to mores, customs, or behavior condemned by the bishop. In its pages no one ever committed suicide, which it called "an unexpected death." If a conservative notable had a child out of wedlock or was caught in adultery, scandals that were feasts for the other presses, for the editorial staff of *Le Vingtième Siècle* they simply never occurred.

The newspaper was presided over by a man who didn't have to pound his fists on the table to be obeyed. Norbert Wallez was the one man of whom Remi would say to the end of his life, "I owe him everything." Designated simply as "Father," as if there were only one priest in all of Belgium, Wallez is one of the keys to understanding the inner world of Hergé.

Forty-five years old at the time, of massive build and a bellicose personality, in another age he would have been a warrior monk. He was the declared enemy of Freemasons, who paid him back in kind. The son of wealthy farmers from the region of Ath, he did nothing by half, and it's difficult to dismiss him as simply a nationalist, a conservative, a representative of rural opinions, critical of parliamentary democracy. If temper and aggressiveness were second nature to him, they were often attenuated by bursts of laughter and his sense of humor. If he was a feared polemicist, he was also extremely sincere, even toward the opposition. He was one of those rare individuals with the gift to get things and people moving, to

push events and history. Such a forceful personality would always be controversial, to its credit. His opponents, and they were numerous, called him either a "rustic Walloon," "a vain village cock of the walk,"[1] or "the worst type of fascist."

Before the Great War, while Wallez was still a teacher, he had started writing for the conservative Catholic daily of Antwerp, *La Métropole*, and was won over to journalism. After the war and while Wallez was a seminarian at the Seminary of Bonne Espérance in Mons, Cardinal Mercier sought him out and placed him at the head of *Le Vingtième Siècle*. He quickly transformed the moribund Christian Democrat newspaper into a fighting force with a huge circulation and supported by powerful industrialists.[2]

His *Vingtième Siècle* was administered by the conservative wing of the Catholic Party and closely linked to the weekly *Catholic Review of Ideas and Events*. They often shared the same editors and were in lockstep in their political intransigence, corporate sympathies, and criticism of democracy. For both, the only nationalism was Catholicism.[3] For Father Wallez, Belgian political unity was a given.

The situation in Italy offered a new way of looking at things. At first Wallez had shown his solidarity with the People's Catholic Party, who were badly treated by the new masters of Italy. But starting in 1923, when Benito Mussolini carried out his first educational reforms by placing crucifixes in schools and public buildings, Wallez's newspaper enthusiastically supported all the measures of the new regime. In the autumn of 1923, a year after the "black shirts" march on Rome that brought Mussolini to power, Father Wallez decided to make a trip to Italy to study the situation. He returned completely won over, especially as he had been able to interview Il Duce. He would never recover from that meeting, one of the great moments of his life. Afterward a number of his articles would directly or indirectly allude to the experience, captured in an autographed portrait of Mussolini that Il Duce dedicated "to Norbert Wallez, amico dell'Italia et del fascismo, con simpatia di camerita, 1924."[4] Under Wallez's pen, more lyrical than proselytizing, the new Italy became the champion of Catholicism, the most sublime of religions,[5] the incarnation of a strong, authoritarian order, alone capable of ridding Europe of democracy. Even as he praised the more spectacular successes of the regime, he failed to recognize its other side.[6] His blindness was shared by all Belgian ultra-Catholics, who seemed to hold to the illusion of some sort of "platonic fascism."[7]

Father Wallez became the herald of this new order, obsessively denouncing the members of Parliament and their connivances and criminal

activities, for which he blamed foreigners, Jews, and Freemasons. He had great hopes for his country, and his political philosophy was laid out in his book *Belgium and the Rhineland*, in which he denounced the Treaty of Versailles, attributing it to the scheming of international high finance, guilty of profiteering from supplying the aggressors on both sides. The political errors in the treaty between France and its allies were the results of stockbrokers' monstrous calculations. Those responsible—the despots, scoundrels, and criminals—could be lumped under one name: Israel. In other words, the Jews, specifically those who, since the Berlin stock market crash at the end of 1912, controlled the world's precious metal market. Father Wallez devoted a section of his book to an anti-Semitic diatribe in the polemical mode of the extreme right; he pilloried the financiers of the stock market. Also, in the pure Germanophobic tradition of the old Belgian Right, he exalted the Catholic Rhineland, damning the militaristic Prussian heretics and calling for a Belgium-Rhineland Federation.[8]

Wallez attracted either devoted followers or rabid detractors. He was more drawn to political activism than to the practice of religion; dismissed by the clergy, he was admired by journalists. He had only one known vice: a love of candy. Intelligent, cultivated, erudite, and always eager for more knowledge, he was energetic to the point of brutality, yet always ready for a laugh. He was resolutely a Walloon, as his name suggested, meant to enjoy life, and he transformed Hergé's destiny.

Wallez was old enough to be his father, and indeed Georges Remi already considered him his spiritual father. For the young man, Wallez became the teacher he always longed for and whom he desired to emulate. He inspired Georges, whom he pushed into opening himself to other people, reading more, and acquiring some culture.

The young man knew he tended to be cautious, which he ascribed to his Gemini temperament. But with the example of Father Wallez before him, he felt a need to strive for perfection, to find the very best in any situation. It was as if the priest had helped him to reject earthbound realism for a fuller utopian vision.

Father Wallez's influence was not restricted to Georges's spiritual life, nor to the strictly political. It had both a moral and an intellectual dimension. Wallez helped him become conscious of his abilities and put color into his life. Thanks to him, Georges no longer felt inadequate and could overcome the mediocrity of his education, which otherwise could have led him straight to a life as a bank clerk.[9] Father Wallez was like a revelation to him, and Georges Remi was becoming Hergé.

"TEACH WHILE ENTERTAINING" was Father Wallez's motto. To hold his younger readers' attention and to secure their future loyalty, he conceived of producing a separate section within the newspaper devoted exclusively to them. This idea was part of an overall plan that followed the example of American dailies.

Georges Remi had already had some experience with photogravures before Wallez called him in to discuss the project. This experience was important for the young man, whose determination always to strive for greater clarity and simplicity in his art coincided with the evolution of printing. His penchant for line drawing paralleled the new methods of reproduction.

The priest decided to give this beginner an opportunity. Remi didn't as yet have much of a curriculum vitae, but what there was in his slender dossier spoke for him in its content and spirit. Included were numerous illustrations for *The Belgian Boy Scout,* the journal for the Federation of Catholic Scouts. Georges also brought out his drawings for *Youth,* the Red Cross review. But most important was the work that had appeared in *The Wheat in Bloom, The Effort,* and *Little Belgians,* the official publications for the Catholic Action of Belgian Youth, a lay movement inspired by Cardinal Mercier. He produced his first book jacket for *The Soul of the Sea,* a novel by René Weverbergh, his former Scoutmaster, published by the Colonial Library. Everything bore witness to the fact that he was a right-thinking boy on the right track.

Father Wallez, who owed his position to Cardinal Mercier, asked Remi to work on the illustrations for the Monday supplementary section of the paper, *Vôtre Vingtième Madame,* and made him the graphic designer for the Sunday supplement, *Le Vingtième Siècle artistique et littéraire.* Remi was the right choice: he was less an illustrator than a graphic artist. He had a sense of rhythm and motion, as well as of spatial relations, and a good eye for typography and proportion in a layout. He discovered that he was as passionate about the text as the accompanying illustrations.

In addition to doing the layout, selecting typefaces for titles and leads and ornamental capitals, and designing the tailpieces, Remi had to submit for the Sunday section a hundred illustrations of every sort. These were mostly ink drawings, but some were done in the style of woodcuts, to go along with Andersen's fairy tales, or the *Thousand and One Nights,* or the war memoirs of Maurice Genevoix, or the narratives by Henri Lavedan, or even to launch the publicity campaign for Café Castro. All this was secondary to the new supplement to the newspaper, which Wallez planned

to entrust to Georges, in terms of both graphics and text. *Le Petit Vingtième*, as it would be called, would appear every Thursday, a school holiday in Belgium. Remi had the opportunity to prove himself.

At the beginning there were certain problems, starting with the first issue of *Le Petit Vingtième* on November 1, 1928. Remi was ordered to publish and illustrate "The Extraordinary Adventures of Flup, Nénesse, Pousette and Cochonnet" in the supplement. He thought the story, signed "Smettini," the pseudonym of a certain Desmedt, an editor at the paper working in the sports section, boring and stupid. Yet he still had to deliver two plates, each containing three comic strips, to appear every Thursday for the next ten weeks. He completed it so as not to disappoint Father Wallez.

The unhappy experience made him understand that he was not made to work in tandem with anyone. Henceforth he was convinced that he had to provide his own scenarios and only in exceptional cases use ideas and stories by other people. He had the feeling that he could do it all, from beginning to end, conception to realization, dialogue and music included. "The Adventures of Totor, Troop Leader of the June Bugs" had been entirely his creation, his first work in a narrative sequence with continuity, and deeply influenced, as we've seen, by silent pictures, in which the image is self-sufficient and free of all extraneous explanations.

The title of this series, which would continue to run in *The Belgian Boy Scout* until the summer of 1929, was always preceded by the title "United Rovers presents a great comic film" and followed by the caption "Hergé, director," or closed with "Hergé Moving Pictures." If his readings were fodder for his stories, films were the source of his drawing for the comic strips. Film techniques influenced the action, pacing, and sequencing and were always in the service of the "gag." The film community had taken this English word for "comic remark" to designate a "comic visual effect," whose secret was speed of execution.

Charlie Chaplin was the master. The film persona of Charlie Chaplin was created out of whole cloth, as he had explained in interviews. Mack Sennett had needed some gags for certain sequences and asked Chaplin to devise a comic character. Chaplin found a pair of pants that were too large and big shoes, a derby hat, and a cane, making sure that from the largest to the smallest, all these elements were in contradiction. Then he pasted a mustache on his face. Chaplin continually explained that in staging a comedy, the chase was only a pretext for humor, and that action without a gag was doomed to failure.[10]

Hergé, "director," understood the lesson, inasmuch as he knew that humor was the way to present the absurd. He looked for a visual equivalent to paradox, nonsense, and understatement. He would never forget Chaplin's often-repeated tenet of faith: (1) Give the public a character who finds himself in a ridiculous and embarrassing situation; (2) it's even funnier if the ridiculous person, in spite of everything, refuses to admit that anything extraordinary is happening and stubbornly maintains his dignity.

Since 1921 Chaplin had appeared as a comic strip in French publications. Film animations and comic strips were complementary forms of pictorial narratives. Walter Elias Disney grasped this better than anyone when he created his Hollywood studio in 1923. He invented his art as he went along, extending the comic strip into animated films. This development between the two media of expression was not surprising, considering one of the first films by the Brothers Lumière, *L'Arroseur Arrosé* (The Sprinkled Gardener, 1896), in which a gardener gets sprayed full in the face by his own hose.

Toward the end of 1928 in Brussels, the young editor of *Le Petit Vingtième* had no model to either intimidate or paralyze him. In art as in literature he was a novice; he took from everywhere, without apprehension. The weekly deadline of *Le Petit Vingtième,* and continuing the adventures of Totor for *The Belgian Boy Scout,* brought him close to the spirit of the serial. Increasingly he passed from the narrative to the illustration to the comic strip, which is to say a narrative in which text and illustrations were combined within the same panel.

The editorial offices of *Le Vingtième Siècle* were in a permanent state of ferment. Everything seemed to pass through them, via the editors, the calls and telegrams, and the foreign press. Léon Degrelle, a correspondent sent by *Le Vingtième Siècle* to Mexico to cover the martyrdom of twelve thousand Catholics by revolutionaries, was not satisfied simply to send back his reports; he always included several local newspapers. Going through them, Hergé discovered to his delight Spanish-language versions of syndicated American comic strips: "Bringing Up Father" by George McManus, "Krazy Kat" by George Herriman, and "The Katzenjammer Kids" by Rudolph Dirks. Though he missed the linguistic nuances in the translation, the essential for him was the discovery of a technique.

At the time, unlike in the United States, the systematic use of bubbles to indicate speech was little used in France and Belgium. It was in a 1928 issue of *Le Sifflet* (The Whistle) that Hergé published his first comic strip

with the dialogue integrated in the bubbles. "I thought basically that it was much better to tell a story this way than putting the captions under the picture."[11]

Hergé singled out "Bringing Up Father" and its author, George McManus, whose influence can be seen in his drawings starting in early 1928, as particularly key. He was fascinated by its spirit and its humor and even taken with the way McManus drew noses: small, round, or oval, they gave dimension to his characters. They were irresistible but not inimitable, and Hergé appropriated them. He even admitted to having taken certain characters nearly line for line.[12]

More than McManus and his work, it was the entire scope of American comic illustration that Hergé took on. Rather than its mythical universe, he would retain only its organizing principles, the composition of the story, and the sequence of scenes. In a word, its great clarity.[13]

It would take half a century, twenty-three books, and tens of thousands of drawings to illustrate this simple idea.

3.

The Many Births of Tintin
1929–1934

TINTIN AND SNOWY WERE BORN on January 10, 1929, in *Le Petit Vingtième*. On that day the supplement for young readers in *Le Vingtième Siècle* first published a comic strip under the title "The Adventures of Tintin, the 'Petit Vingtième' Reporter, in the Land of the Soviets," the first two plates of a weekly comic strip that would eventually number 121 in all.

These are the bare facts, but we are left with the question of why and how Tintin and Snowy came into being. According to Hergé, it was very simple: "The idea for the character of Tintin and the sort of adventures that would befall him came to me, I believe, in five minutes, the moment I first made a sketch of the figure of this hero: that is to say, he had not haunted my youth nor even my dreams. Although it's possible that as a child I imagined myself in the role of a sort of Tintin."[1]

Tintin has a prehistory. Hergé made a sketch of a character resembling Tintin in the Totor series, which was a sort of trial run. This period of trial and error in the creation of a character is far from exceptional. To cite only two examples, Mickey Mouse was first called Mortimer, and Inspector Maigret in a previous life was Agent No. 49.

Hergé never denied it. When pressed to explain the origins of Tintin, he admitted that he was conceived of as the younger brother of Totor, the troop leader of the June Bugs. Tintin wore plus fours because Georges Remi sometimes wore them, and they might distinguish Tintin as easily as Chaplin's vagabond's baggy trousers did him. Hergé also gave him a tuft of hair that stood straight up on his forehead (first seen during a car chase in *Land of the Soviets*), drawing it as seen full face. If Tintin is shown in profile

or three-quarters to the left or to the right, the facial features are only barely sketched in. The figure is in harmony with the face, the result being neutral, without dissonance. Everyone can identify with him because he is everyman.

Tintin was born at fifteen and therefore never had a childhood. What did Georges Remi look like at that age? Probably like Tintin—like him he had the appearance of an intrepid Boy Scout—except that Remi combed his hair flat, he was thinner and taller, and his face was not as round. It has been said that Hergé had unconsciously taken the traits, attitudes, and gestures of his younger brother, Paul.

In terms of graphics, there is nothing simpler than Tintin. He is as uncomplicated as the story line. Tintin is a journalist or, rather, a reporter, which means the contrary of sedentary. He is less often shown writing at the typewriter than out in the field. In his eyes, the investigation of something, not the resolution, is the basis of his profession. Tintin seems to suggest that he is in fact a great reporter, a member of a select group of legendary journalists such as Albert Londres, Joseph Kessel, Édouard Helsey, Henri Béraud, and others. Of course Remi himself had wanted to become one of them—and he would, by proxy. Tintin would accomplish his dream.[2] For one of the youngest people on a newspaper's staff, belonging to this select group represented the ultimate promotion.[3] For Remi it also symbolized a quest for adventure.

The transformation of Totor to Tintin would continue. Though a reporter, Tintin never loses the spirit of a Scout. On the contrary, he expresses it in his face, his attitudes, and his actions. It could be said of Tintin, as Voltaire said of Candide, that his face revealed his soul. Hergé's constant dilemma was how to make Tintin lose his naïveté while remaining pure.

Here are Tintin's vital statistics: he is Caucasian, lacks a first name, an orphan, without a past, a native of Brussels (as opposed to Belgian), about fifteen years old, obviously celibate, excessively virtuous, chivalrous, brave, a defender of the weak and oppressed, never looks for trouble but always finds it; he is resourceful, takes chances, is discreet, and is a nonsmoker.

Remi and Tintin had quite a few things in common. First of all, both were middle class. But what distinguished one from the other is equally remarkable. The reporter was always getting caught up in what was none of his business. He had the character, the temperament, and the instincts of Remi but none of his ideas. Also, he had a dog, while Remi liked only the company of cats.

If Tintin was in many ways a Don Quixote, Snowy was his Sancho Panza. Our hero needed a companion because according to Scripture it's not good for a man to remain alone, and there is no better companion for a man, especially for a traveler, than a dog. Wire-haired fox terriers were popular at the time.[4] Hergé saw Snowy as a real character, with a short fuse, a tendency to grumble, preoccupied by his comfort but courageous when circumstances called for it. His love of good food, his curiosity, and his cantankerous nature were weaknesses, but he kept himself under control when loyalty to his master demanded it. Finally, Snowy had the gift of speech, which isn't a negligible advantage for the creator of a comic strip. To Hergé's way of thinking, Tintin could only engage in a monologue when Snowy was absent. Still, even at a distance, they had to be able to communicate.[5]

There are those who claim that because Tintin didn't grow up, he is "the Belgian asexual Peter Pan."[6] Even his family name was the subject of speculation. It was not a last name, because he did not have any family. Nor was it a given name, even if it appeared to be a diminutive of Augustin or Constantine. Hergé chose it because it sounded heroic, clear, and cheerful and, he thought, was easy to remember.[7]

The origins of Tintin may be discovered in Hergé's tribute to the genius of Benjamin Rabier (1864–1939), the creator of Gideon the Duck, whom he always claimed influenced the way he drew animals. However, he never mentioned another creation, *Tintin le Lutin* (Tintin the Goblin), cosigned by Benjamin Rabier and Fred Isly, published in 1898 by Félix Juven Editions. It's the story of a mischievous goblin, named Artin but called Tintin by his mother. The resemblance is startling, beginning with the tuft of hair. The shape of the face is reminiscent of Tintin as he might have looked at eight years of age. Nonetheless Hergé always swore that he did not know of Artin's existence until 1970, when he was informed by an obliging reader.[8]

His word must be taken on faith because, in a way, the catalyst for the creation of Tintin was none other than Norbert Wallez. Wallez had commissioned his young employee to create an adolescent and his dog imbued in the spirit of Catholic virtues (which he did not have to spell out, so great was his influence on the illustrator).[9] Hergé recognized this debt among so many others that linked him with Father Wallez. To those who asked about the origins of Tintin, he never failed to mention his name.[10] In the dedication of his book he would thank him for having "carried Tintin at the baptismal fount."[11] On the other hand, Father Wallez

would never have imagined for a moment that he would be remembered by posterity for having taken under his wing a young illustrator of whom he was mildly fond.

LE PETIT VINGTIÈME, always seeking to satisfy its readers and to keep them abreast of world events, sent one of its best reporters to the Soviet Union: Tintin. They would be able to follow his adventures every week. (The editors of *Le Petit Vingtième* guaranteed they would rigorously screen for authenticity all the photos taken by Tintin, by himself or with the help of his sympathetic dog, Snowy.)

The initial panel of the first comic strip, under the title "The Adventures of Tintin, the 'Petit Vingtième' Reporter, in the Land of the Soviets," is not a picture but a panel full of texts, words instead of drawings. It was edited and reedited. At the time Hergé did not feel that he had started on a long-term project. Later, in going back over the past, he would consecrate the moment to the point of altering the chronology. Even when readers pointed out that drawings of Tintin and Snowy first appeared on January 4, 1929, in issue number 10 of *Le Petit Vingtième,* Hergé would continue to insist that Tintin and Snowy were born on January 10, in issue number 11, traveling to the Soviet Union and nowhere else.[12] By the eighth panel he would differentiate among Soviets, Bolsheviks, and terrorists. Every character was immediately typecast by his uniform, impossible to miss even at first glance. He used a style he would call *la ligne claire* (the clear line), consisting of simply drawn characters against a minimal background. Events largely follow from pursuit to gags, and from gags into full-blown fights. Tintin was unaware of his future. He was never again so free; nor was his creator. From his trip to the Soviet Union, the special envoy from *Le Petit Vingtième* would bring back a Dantesque vision of poverty, famine, terror, and repression.

In retrospect it would become clear that he was not wrong. In January 1929, the moment when Tintin the reporter takes the train for Russia, Leon Trotsky had just been banished and was traveling in the other direction. Stalin threw himself into the gigantic enterprise of systematically liquidating the kulaks. The same year, on his fiftieth birthday, he launched the campaign of his personality cult. Consider what Hergé would have made of this detail had he been on the spot to research his story. Only he never left Brussels. The author was under the influence, for better or for worse, of his reading and of Norbert Wallez. The priest's anti-Communism was unrelenting: Communism was the Antichrist. Tintin's adventures

conjured up the priest's books, as well as the works of Albert Londres and Joseph Douillet, whose *Moscow Unveiled* was replete with living witnesses' accounts and dire warnings about education, health, religion, terror, and the Komintern. Hergé drew liberally from the most spectacular events recounted in these sources, and the influence can be seen in the tone of cynicism and derision mixed with irony. However, equally important was the classic children's book author the Countess de Ségur, whose recollections of her Russian grandfather, *General Dourakine*, inspired the episodes on the Russian Steppes.[13]

In this beginning Tintin feels little sympathy for humanity. Only the spectacle of human misery tempers his tone, particularly when it is caused by atheist Bolsheviks. The reporter's travels through this Communist hell is a tale of impostures and mystifications, of deceit and treachery; nothing escapes his eye. When an airplane goes into a nosedive, Snowy concludes that in this country even the propellers aren't solid.[14] Some judgments made by Tintin are harsh, if not cruel, despite all the gags. This is redeemed, not to say moderated, by his naïveté and humor. When Tintin seems on the verge of dying he exclaims, "Quick!" When Snowy thinks of something to save his master he cries out, "Idea!" Hergé's sense of the understatement is a teaser; after an explosion on his train, Tintin thinks, "Something unusual must have occurred." Hergé's taste for spoof and mockery was equally efficient: the KGB agent in charge of shadowing Tintin hopes to be awarded "the order of the unsheathed aluminum sickle."[15]

"In reality my early works are books by a young Belgian filled with the prejudices and ideas of a Catholic, they are books that could have been written by any Belgian in my situation. They are not very intelligent, I know, and do me no honor: they are 'Belgian' books."[16] For Hergé, "Belgian" meant self-satisfied and narrow. It's true that in their early adventures, his heroes are very Belgian. A reader learning the history of Belgium between the wars through the works of the two eminent writers Hergé and Simenon would come away with the impression that all their fellow citizens were nationalistic, anti-Semitic, and anti-Communist.

Nonetheless Hergé did not lend himself to categories. It would be too easy to judge him by his first Tintin book. Starting in January 1930 and for the next six years he would publish every Thursday, on pages 12 and 13 of his *Petit Vingtième*, another series under his name. It was a comic strip completely opposite in spirit to the first adventures of Tintin, utterly lacking ambiguity or cynicism. Quick and Flupke ("Quick" was the name of a friend; "Flup" in Flemish is the diminutive for Philip, and "Ke" means little),

who have been unfairly eclipsed by Tintin's fame, have a lightness of touch, a charm, a tenderness and poetry that can be found nowhere else in the works of Hergé. In these comic strips he seemed freer and more of a rebel, but he did not spend much time on them, as if he considered them of secondary importance, generally beginning work on them the morning of the day when the pages were typeset. He worked in a rush for an hour or two. They were no sooner drawn than set, and by the end of the day *Le Petit Vingtième* had gone to press and was on the stands.[17]

"The Exploits of Quick and Flupke" views the world through the eyes of two street urchins of Brussels, an update of the nineteenth-century German characters Max and Moritz by Wilhelm Busch. But Hergé's "kids" are at the same time pranksters and hapless, scatterbrained and shrewd, naïve and cunning. They are resourceful without being Boy Scouts. They are always ready to play a joke behind the back of Police Officer No. 15, their nemesis.

Most often they become victims because of their good nature. The street is their turf and Brussels their kingdom. They are types both in their personalities and their appearance. Both wear short pants. Flupke, short and blond, wears a cap and has a scarf around his neck; he is always asking questions. Quick, tall and dark, with a beret on his head and a turtleneck sweater, always has an answer ready. Each episode is a self-contained gag in the consummate art of taking a fall. The policemen are straight out of Charlie Chaplin; only the uniforms are different. Hergé's sense of the comic is fully displayed and refines itself. He gives full vent to his play on words, especially in the names of the characters: the veterinarian M. Moraurat (Death to Rats), the boxers Sam Suffy (I've Had Enough) against Mac Aronni (Macaroni).

The publication of "The Adventures of Tintin in the Land of the Soviets" would come to an end on May 8, 1930. To celebrate the event, Charles Lesne, a colleague of Father Wallez, suggested rallying the young readers of the supplement to welcome Tintin in person on his return from the Red Hell. It was shrewd but risky. How many adolescents would come to see a hero who doesn't exist? Even on a Thursday without school, rallied by the newspaper and *Le Petit Vingtième*, it was far from being a sure bet. The editors were willing to take the gamble, however. Meanwhile they were planning the cover of the next edition of *Le Petit Vingtième*.

Lucien Pepermans, a fifteen-year-old Boy Scout, member of the Kapelleveld in the town of Woluwe, was hired, for one hundred francs (current equivalent, $45) and a bouquet, to play Tintin. He was too tall and his hair

was too long, but he would have to do. They sent him to the barber, and in the men's room of the Louvain train station he put on the costume of a Russian (red boots, a stand-up band collar with buttons). His hair was plastered with Argentina Gel to make his tuft stand up. He was accompanied by Snowy on a leash, and he embarked on the Cologne train for Brussels.

The platforms of the Gare du Nord train station could not contain the eager crowds. The moment the faux Tintin stepped off the train, he became the victim of a gag Hergé himself might have perpetrated. A young mother placed her baby in the arms of the hero of the day to be kissed, and then disappeared, swept away by the crowd. For a while the young Scout wondered what to do. There was no question of Tintin returning from Russia with a baby in his arms. Father Wallez would be furious. The surge brought back the mother, just in time. The enormous esplanade in front of the massive train station was solidly packed with people. Hergé stayed close to the side of his creation made flesh and bone. They got into a Buick driven by a friend of Hergé's, who had borrowed it from his father. Then the procession slowly wended its way across town to the offices of the newspaper. Stepping onto the balcony, Tintin delivered a speech the crowd could not hear because of the noise.

It was a blinding success. Tintin had existed but a year and was known only to the readers of *Le Petit Vingtième*, yet he was launched. Hergé and Father Wallez would do everything possible to transform this trial run into continued success by presenting a sequel, by selling the rights to "In the Land of the Soviets" to foreign periodicals, and by publishing the adventure as a separate book.

HERGÉ CAME TO COMIC ILLUSTRATION the year that silent films began to speak. In 1930 Charlie Chaplin had just screened *City Lights,* unanimously acclaimed as his masterpiece. Hergé had obviously been among his admirers. "The Lovable Mr. Mops," eight comic strips drawn for the Bon Marché department store in Brussels, were entirely conceived around gags dealing with romance and flirtation. The main character is a short, mustachioed man, wearing a derby hat a size too small, a shabby jacket, and pants abnormally short, and sometimes carrying a cane. He is touchingly awkward and luckless. The resemblance goes beyond coincidence.

For Walt Disney it was also a decisive year. Unlike Otto Messmer, the creator of "Felix the Cat" in a partnership with Pat Sullivan, who took care of the business, Disney was both creator and entrepreneur. His third animated film starring Mickey Mouse, *Steamboat Willie,* was a success. But

it was only the beginning. His new series of musical shorts, *Silly Symphonies*, would be received with popular enthusiasm and would have influence worldwide, ranging from the works of Hergé to those of Osamu Tesuka, the precursor of Japanese mangas.

In France illustrated adventures would have an enormous impact on the press. Messmer's Felix the Cat and Disney's Mickey Mouse would be serialized in numerous newspapers. At the same time, three new publications for young readers made their appearance: *Benjamin*, edited by Jean Nohain; *Rick and Rack*, created by the publisher Fayard; and *Coeurs Vaillants* (Brave Hearts), launched by L'Union des Oeuvres. In 1930 Father Courtois, the editor of *Coeurs Vaillants*, traveled to Brussels to win the exclusive serial rights to Tintin in France.

In October *Coeurs Vaillants* started publishing "Tintin in the Land of the Soviets." The motto of this paper, whose roots were ecclesiastic, pleased Hergé: "For Brave Hearts Nothing Is Impossible." However, there was an immediate conflict between the editors and Hergé, who would never tolerate anyone touching his illustrations. To better explain the action, the editors added a narrative caption beneath his drawings, a throwback to the old "Bécassine" format. Hergé protested vigorously, but the editors turned a deaf ear. The publication would prove decisive for the international career of Hergé.

After Russia, America? Hergé was considering it seriously, because the Scout in him was passionate about the lore of the Indians, and he was drawn to exoticism.[18] However, Father Wallez saw things otherwise, and he made all the decisions.

Having sent Tintin off among the Bolsheviks for his edification and that of his young readers, Wallez intended to send him to the Congo. The Congo was studied by every schoolchild in Belgium. Sending Tintin there could inspire colonial and missionary zeal in his readers. The spirit of this adventure was the opposite of Tintin's trip to the Soviet Union: where the Soviet Union was hostile to Tintin, the Congo welcomed him with open arms.

Long after decolonization, people still said of Zaire (the former Congo) that it was "the only country in the world where they still believe that Belgium is a great power." The particular relationship between the two countries began in 1908, when Léopold II, King of Belgium and personal ruler of the Congo, had Parliament formalize his bequeathing it to Belgium. This independent state in the heart of Africa was his private property and was recognized as such by the European colonial powers.

Hergé had had a foretaste of what Father Wallez asked of him. Three years earlier he had to furnish two drawings for the newspaper illustrating articles celebrating the fiftieth anniversary of the discovery of the Congo by Stanley. One of them showed a native kneeling before the white father. The symbolism was clear and representative of the spirit of the times, but that would not be enough to hold the interest of young readers for weeks on end. For "The Adventures of Tintin in the Congo" Hergé needed documentation, the kind that was in the news every day as well as abundantly present in popular literature and propaganda booklets. As noted, Remi never read the works of Jules Verne, yet Tintin gets promoted to "great white medicine man" by curing a native with a large dose of quinine, exactly as Dr. Châtonnay does in *The Astonishing Adventures of the Barzac Mission*.[19] This was commonplace in adventure novels at the time. Hergé researched visual materials at the Colonial Museum of Tervueren, where he viewed exhibitions of the weapons and costumes of the Leopard Men, or Aniotas tribe. From the André Maurois novel *The Silence of Colonel Bramble* he lifted the hunting expeditions.[20] His animal drawings are freely inspired by the prints of Benjamin Rabier.[21] The opening scene takes place on the train platform in Brussels, and among the people gathered to see Tintin and Snowy's departure for new adventures are none other than Quick and Flupke.

Hergé begins his story in the most inoffensive way. Onboard the steamship taking them from Antwerp to Matadi, the young reporter and his dog absorb the attention of the reader for thirteen panels with the dangers of psittacosis because a parrot has bitten Snowy's tail. The dog is always putting himself in dangerous situations, forcing his master to take serious risks to save him, all so he can then exclaim, "How heroic you are, Tintin!" Hergé was experimenting with cinematic techniques, such as jump cuts, which he would henceforth use. In one panel Tintin leaves Brussels by train and in the next he is clambering up the ladder of a steamship in Antwerp. Hergé's drawing has become more assured in this story without losing any of its spontaneity.

It is not merely a Belgian reporter but a true international personality who is welcomed and carried off in triumph on his arrival in the Congo. His fame has traveled overseas. In fact the representatives of all the major newspapers, English, American, and Portuguese, compete for the right to publish his future news reports, which tests his resistance to the lure of money. He remains a Scout in all circumstances and faithful to his contract with *Le Petit Vingtième* and to his moral debt to Wallez.

To these lazy, childish, dull, but nice "Negroes" who express themselves in French jargon, Tintin comes to speak about the wonders of their homeland, Belgium. When he first encounters the Pygmies he treats them as villains before discovering that they are loyal readers of *Le Petit Vingtième*.

Snowy has come to Africa to hunt big game. Tintin imitates him, firing his rifle point blank at a crocodile, a monkey whose skin he appropriates, a boa, an elephant; he attacks a rhinoceros with dynamite. When he is not shooting at something, a white priest is. "What whizzes, these missionaries!" Snowy exclaims on visiting a hospital with a farm school and a chapel they built where once there was only brush.

The only true villains in this story are not the animals (killed serially) nor the Natives (too childish to be dangerous) but the hidden passengers glimpsed on the steamship and their boss. When Tintin sets foot in Africa he is preceded by his reputation. Al Capone, the gangster king of Chicago, believes Tintin is there to prevent his taking control of the local diamond production. He orders his men to eliminate him. This doesn't hamper Tintin's investigation, even if it makes him more of a detective than a reporter. In the end the guilty will be punished, and morals will be upheld.

The series first came out weekly in *Le Petit Vingtième*, then was brought out as a book by the Editions du Petit Vingtième, and finally was serialized in *Coeurs Vaillants* on July 9, 1931. Father Wallez organized the reporter's return from the Congo. This time a smaller boy was selected; Henry Den Doncker impersonated Tintin at the Gare du Nord wearing shorts, socks, and a white shirt without forgetting the indispensable colonial pith helmet. Snowy was borrowed for the day from the owner of a local café, the habitual haunt of the staff of *Le Vingtième Siècle*. The whole thing was such a success that they had to protect the dog from the hundreds of boys who wanted to give him a piece of sugar. When they came out, the crowds were so dense that people watched from the windows. It wasn't every day in Brussels that you could see Tintin, Snowy, and Hergé riding in an open carriage with an escort of Natives.[22]

The publication of *Tintin in the Congo* stirred no controversy because it reflected perfectly the spirit and mentality of the times; it wasn't racist, but paternalistic. In those days when Hergé was writing the dialogue he did not ask whether he should write "Black" or "Negro" or if, when citing the benefits of Western civilization, he should put "benefits" between quotes. Much later these adventures in the Congo would be accused of racism, of which Hergé tried to absolve himself in a letter to a reader: "It was a period

when it was the most natural thing for a country to have colonies. In Belgium we had a colonial lottery: a lively little black boy publicized it on the screen of every cinema. There was a street of The Colonies, taverns called 'The Colonial,' the staff in hotels were primarily black people, 'Negrita' was a brand of shoe polish."[23]

It was all undeniable, as was Hergé's conformity with the dominant mores, especially as they coincided with Father Wallez's ideology, whether about Christianity, anti-Communism, or colonialism. There was no hint of criticism or of reservation in his drawings. In fact his talent was an anesthetic. It disarmed all challenges to the established order. The newspaper *L'Essort colonial et maritime* praised Tintin for its fantasy by reminding its readers that true propaganda begins in the schools: "You will laugh till tears come to your eyes because the Congo presented by Hergé will make you forget the other one, the one you saw."

The journalist Albert Londres, whom, as we've seen, Hergé considered a model for Tintin, published *Land of Ebony* in 1930, based on a series of articles about the treatment of blacks that appeared in *Le Petit Parisien*. He gives a hallucinatory narrative of the construction of the Congo-Ocean railroad from Brazzaville to Pointe-Noire, a construction site that had already claimed twenty thousand lives, with two hundred miles of rails still to be laid. Londres was not attacking the fundamentals of colonialism; he simply wanted to stop the killing. He wanted to denounce an injustice that no journalist worthy of the name should ignore. Three years earlier André Gide had published *Travels in the Congo,* a literary work with a sincere indignation at the abuses of colonialism. The reaction was a violent campaign by the colonial lobby in the government and attacks in the press.

Even if Albert Londres was an acknowledged model for Tintin, he was French, and Belgium was different. Yet the young Simenon had written ten novels under his pseudonyms J. de Perry and Georges Slim, set in Africa, filled with adventures and exoticism. Needless to say, they also were replete with prejudices and racist stereotypes. But when he was sent to the Congo as a reporter in 1932, Simenon published a series of articles in *Voilà* under the title "L'heure du nègre." He presented not one Africa, but an infinite number of Africas. He did not have enough words to denounce the barbarism of the Congo-Ocean railroad line.[24] He concluded his series, "Yes, Africa tells us *merde*, and it's well deserved."[25]

With Gide and Londres, to cite but two examples, not to mention the African reports by Edmond Tranin, Hergé had the means to know more.

The question remains: Did he want to? Later, looking back, he would give the impression that he had been constrained by his environment. In fact he was perfectly suited to his milieu. He was a man in harmony with the ideas expressed around him. It was neither chance nor necessity that led him to *Le Vingtième Siècle* and to remain in the orbit of Father Wallez. He was like a fish in water; it was the world of his choice, his natural place. At twenty-four his priority was not to politically or morally reform the world; he wanted to succeed.

The initial success of Tintin hadn't altered Hergé's sense of humility. In May 1931 he went to visit the legendary Alain Saint-Ogan to show him his illustrations. In his eyes the French author and illustrator, then thirty-six, was a legend. He wasn't the inventor of comic books, nor the first to use a bubble for speech. But he had created a classic in what had been a despised form when he published "Zig et Puce" and their adventures with their friend, Alfred the penguin, in the mainstream press, characters and a whole universe presented in stories immediately readable. These were the most important qualities for a young man preoccupied with efficiency.

Hergé showed the master his drawings. After examining them, Saint-Ogan congratulated him, which was quite unusual. Most of the time when young colleagues came to him for advice, Saint-Ogan would urge them to pursue another profession: "It's so hard to earn a living doing this!" This time he encouraged his visitor to persevere. He liked his drawings, which he found "very healthy." As proof of his esteem he gave Hergé an original plate of "Zig et Puce" with the heading "Fame and Wealth," warmly dedicated to his "young colleague" who showed such promise.[26]

Hergé didn't have a moment to think of the future. He had no time. Hardly had his hero officially returned from the Congo than, in his mind, Tintin was already on his way to America. No matter what the Father said.

HERGÉ IMAGINED TINTIN as a knight fighting the forces of evil. This time there was an undeniably noble cause at the core of his adventure. Rather than denouncing Bolshevik terror or praising missionary work in Africa, he was defending the American Indians expelled from their ancestral lands. The author and his character would never be such exemplary Scouts as in the America story, which seemed to be a homage to a people who served as a model for so many Boy Scout troops. But no sooner was it conceived than it evolved in such a way that the Indians would no longer be its sole heroes.

The America narrative was more developed and detailed than its two predecessors and would split off in different directions. Hergé was reading *The History and Mores of the Indians of North America* by René Thévenin and Paul Coze, where he found a wealth of information about the daily lives of Indians. He also followed a series of articles in the press by the reporter Claude Blanchard, who traveled from the skyscrapers of New York to the Indians of New Mexico. In Chicago Blanchard reported on the slaughterhouses and the gangsters. The article was illustrated with photos of Spike O'Donnell's armored vehicle riddled with bullets. Another showed Alphonse "Scarface" Capone, the tsar of Chicago gangland, a multimillionaire against whom was issued a warrant for his arrest. Needless to say, Hergé saw many films about the United States but was most impressed by Georges Duhamel's *Scenes from Life in the Future,* which had an indirect influence on the narrative of *Tintin in America.* In his book Duhamel denounced the culture of consumerism, publicity, and standardization—in short, modernism. This was in the context of the economic crisis of 1928. Duhamel compared Europe's prudent policies to America's frenzied capitalism. Hergé set aside the book's cinephobia. Duhamel rejected the concept of cinema as art and even deemed Chaplin's films "entertainment for the illiterates, and idiots."[27] What Hergé did retain was the speed with which cities were built in this country, the invasion of daily life by publicity, the slaughterhouses of Chicago, the unbelievable amount of traffic in the streets. Hergé was in sympathy with the values of a society in which the individual is the essential keystone and rebels against a society driven by the ideal of standardization and mechanization.

"The Adventures of Tintin, Reporter, in Chicago," the serial, would first appear on the newsstands on September 3, 1931. From the first panel the intrigue begins by means of a technique Hergé would use regularly: referring back to previous adventures to reintroduce his cast of characters. The moment Tintin and Snowy set foot in Chicago, they are kidnapped. Then begins the chase, in which they escape and try to track down their aggressors, causing a serious car accident that lands them in the hospital. There they receive a threatening letter from Al Capone himself. (He is the first of only two historical characters whose actual names Hergé would use in his work.) Fortunately one of the gangsters has sought refuge in Indian country. The pursuit and race leads to gags and mistaken identities, dramatic surprises, and trapdoors that will introduce new characters, each more ominous than the last. In the end Tintin defeats the gangsters, sending no fewer than 355 off to jail. The city of Chicago celebrates him as if he were a national hero.

In the segment dealing with the Indians, who are not as prominent as he had first foreseen, Hergé takes a stand against the dominant caricature of the Indian and demystifies the stereotype of the "cruel savage" portrayed in westerns. The incident is not as inoffensive as it seems and would reveal its full significance years later when debated in the courtroom during Hergé's trial for racism.

Tintin in America revealed Hergé's state of mind in the early thirties. His rejection of materialism, violence, and the worshipping of the almighty dollar seemed to carry over to his fascination with the America of skyscrapers and Native Americans. He had been categorized as a visceral anti-Communist, and now he was revealed to be anticapitalist at the moment when Europe was economically and politically shattered by the aftershocks of the Wall Street stock market crash. The Belgian extreme right was against both New York and Moscow. There was only one difference between the two: Moscow was officially evil, and New York was insidiously evil.

The book *Tintin in America* would remain Hergé's greatest success for a long time. Because of his experience and know-how, and his inspiration, his illustrations were superior. Still, he felt his graphic technique suffered from awkwardness and naïveté. He didn't believe that he had mastered all the codes of the comic strip. He didn't place his characters in space when they were in motion. Chaplin, to whom he referred often, spoke of having understood the importance of scenic staging from the start: "I had only to distinguish my left from my right for entrances and exits. If I left on the right at the end of a scene, then I entered on the left in the following scene. If I left facing the camera, I entered with my back to the camera."[28] In this third work Hergé makes the error of drawing his character in contradiction to what he is saying. In the episode inside the underground tunnel, he shows Tintin walking up when he was supposed to be going farther down into the tunnel. In the next panel, when he should be returning above ground, Tintin appears to be going in deeper. Hergé seems not to have grasped the elementary rule of the direction of the reading. When a character goes up, or advances farther, it's always from the left to the right, in the direction in which one reads. It's as much about readability as logic. He gives the impression that Tintin is walking backward or tripping over himself.

LE *PETIT VINGTIÈME* had its own office in a large space on the third floor of the building on Boulevard Bisschoffsheim. By now Hergé had a small team

of part-time helpers. Among them was Germaine Kieckens, a spectacular redhead, as elegant and popular as she was untouchable because she was none other than the secretary of Father Wallez. To say she admired the priest would be an understatement. There was no one she admired more in the world, even to the point of adopting his uncompromising political opinions. Meanwhile she had cast her eye on Georges Remi.

A year older than he, Germaine was more mature and self-confident, more determined in her attitudes than Georges Remi, who was timid, quiet, and still somewhat juvenile. When she first met him he was working in the subscription department. They had known each other for four years and had been dating for a few months before they became engaged. Naturally Father Wallez brought this about. The energetic director of *Le Vingtième Siècle* had decreed one day that all single employees of the newspaper must find someone to marry. Father Wallez brought Germaine and Remi together when he had the brilliant idea of sending fifty Tintin books in a numbered edition to the leading personalities of the day. He spread them out on the floor of his office and asked Germaine to make a paw-like signature for Snowy while Georges signed for Tintin.

Wallez was the man Remi most respected, the only person to whom he still could not say no. But before he made up his mind, Georges spent three days meditating on his decision during a retreat in an abbey. For Germaine, Wallez was at the same time her boss, her idol, and a father figure, the only person this young woman of strong character could not refuse. Indeed Remi was jealous of Germaine's veneration for their boss; she talked constantly about him. Worst of all, she never missed an opportunity to let Georges know that he would never measure up to Wallez. He would never have his intellectual abilities, nor his combative spirit, nor his strength of character. It was not a question of age but of personality. If only he were a man like any other rather than a priest!

Georges made every effort to broaden his views and be more mature. But Germaine always demolished him by comparing him to the man they both admired. There was nothing he could do. Georges consoled himself by writing out his grievances in his sketchbook and scribbling down his thoughts in drafts of letters to his fiancée. He knew that she was superior to him in many respects, but at twenty-four he couldn't envisage his future without her. "I won't be happy in my work, I know it. I will be happy with you, or without you in God. Nothing in between."[29]

On July 21, 1932, at last they both said yes to Father Wallez, who married them. Much later Germaine would realize, "We got married because of

Father Wallez. Our two lives were similar. But I wasn't madly in love with Georges. He wasn't my type. I would have liked an older man, someone more mature."[30]

Maturity would come later, with fame and the tribulations of life. But Germaine would become her husband's main collaborator. Every week at the press she would fill in his drawings, do the retouching, and correct proofs and galleys, playing a vital and invisible role. She urged him to devote himself to comic strips when he hesitated and succumbed to advertising work. She tried to make him see that unlike advertising, Tintin was not ephemeral. Material rewards and artistic satisfaction would come in time, and would be lasting. She somehow managed to convince him, though advertising paid better and more quickly and the graphic artist and his character found greater expression there. When Germaine was not lending a hand with the drawings, she was answering mail under the pseudonym of Tantine or editing snippets for the women's page.

Germaine was his principal model. Lying down or sitting, more often dressed than nude, she appeared everywhere in works by Georges, who was not the same as Hergé. In lead pencil, pastels, oils, or watercolors, the features of her face and the contours of her figure filled pages and pages of his sketchbooks and drawing papers during the early thirties: it was the laboratory of a man who could not stop drawing.

Aside from Germaine, the pillar of *Le Petit Vingtième* was Paul Jamin ("Jam"). From Liège, he was a jovial fellow, a prankster who saw himself as a Voltairian spirit with a touch of Swift and Twain. Humor, satire, and mockery were his trademarks. In his drawings his temperament tended toward political caricature rather than illustration for young readers. Knowing this, Hergé, who first met him as a Scout at Saint-Boniface, nonetheless made him an offer. Jamin agreed to join the staff and for six years would enjoy the atmosphere of the place: Wallez's fits; the bizarre people permanently housed in the attic; the parade of colorful characters who haunted the place, including the drunken bishop; Count Perovsky, a White Russian who spoke a perfect eighteenth-century French; the filler-copy employed out of pity rather than necessity, which was an endless source of jokes. Jamin was never bored, and he relished working with his friend Remi to produce a publication.

The pay was terrible for everyone except Hergé, who enjoyed royal treatment by Wallez. The priest understood the illustrator's value. All the others worked as much for love of the Infant Jesus as for *Le Petit Vingtième*.[31]

Georges was the boss but never behaved as such. Making the deadline was all-important, no matter how it was accomplished. Readers were unaware of the cooked-up articles, the crises, the failures; they saw only the results, produced by friends who were equals. The Scout connection contributed a fourth member to the gang, following a three-month stint doing photogravures. Eugène Van Nijverseel, who would soon sign his work "Evany," had arrived before Jam and therefore claimed the right to a drawing table next to Georges.

Even with the relaxed working conditions, Georges took his obligations seriously, feeling personally responsible for the integral contents of *Le Petit Vingtième*. He was scrupulous in the extreme, supervising every detail and rarely absenting himself from Brussels, unless Father Wallez sent him to Paris to meet with *Coeurs Vaillants*. Hergé placed great importance on his relations with *Coeurs Vaillants*, although he was to remain alert to the liberties they took with his drawings, for they presented the opportunity of being known outside the narrow confines of Belgium. With *Le Petit Vingtième* Tintin could win only the loyalty of young Belgians. With *Coeurs Vaillants* he had access not only to the French Catholic public but to the entire francophone market. In September 1932 *L'Écho illustré* contacted him from Geneva about purchasing his series. Owned by the bishop of Fribourg, the weekly served the Catholic families of Switzerland. Two years later *O Papagaio,* published by Father Varzim in Lisbon, made him a similar offer.

The Catholic lobby was simply a continuation of his Scout connections, and Hergé understood the dynamism and efficiency of the system. In the early thirties priests were among the most perspicacious of entrepreneurs. They also understood that entertainment could be as instructional as lessons and therefore saw the potential of the illustrated press for the market of young readers. Hergé was completely at home among these ecclesiastics and soon learned to protect his interests.

One evening in July 1932 at the Café Continental in Brussels, Hergé committed his first act of defiance against Father Wallez. He initiated a meeting with a Monsieur E. Dejardin, the Belgian delegate of the Union for Artistic Property, the Paris-based organization for protecting the rights of artists and writers. Hergé was prepared with clear, specific questions, involving not his wanting to make money but to keep from being wrongfully exploited.

"Can *Le Vingtième Siècle* claim any part of the royalties from my drawings published in *L'Écho illustré* and in *Coeurs Vaillants*? If so, up to what percentage can they claim?"

"I don't know to what extent you have personally committed yourself with *Le Vingtième Siècle* and if you signed any agreement in black and white stamped by a notary. That would be a huge error on your part, but you never know how far these crazy-headed artists can take things! From a moral standpoint, *Le Vingtième Siècle* has absolutely no right to the author's royalties due to you from the reproduction of your work in other newspapers."

Dejardin explained that his union was opposed to these "piratical schemes." He went even further, stepping outside his advisory role and offering to intercede as Hergé's representative.[32] Father Wallez was already worried that his young protégé would be drawn toward horizons beyond Boulevard Bisschoffsheim.

The early success of Tintin had not convinced Hergé to renounce advertising, as we see during an interview he gave to *L'Effort,* the publication of independent Catholic youth. What emerged was Georges Remi the graphic artist rather than Hergé the illustrator. It is sometimes hard to believe that it is Hergé, creator of Tintin, speaking, because he talked only about the advertising campaigns he had worked on and the artists he admired, such as Leo Marfurt and Cassandre. The interview is instructive to the extent that it reveals how he had integrated the canon of the advertising campaign.

"I catch the attention by an outstanding design, simple and very visible. A drawing printed in black and white has to show a lot of white space. Nothing overdone or busy. For the dailies I avoid dark figures, which are better for colored posters or illustrations."

"What is your theory about the uses of colors?"

"I prefer bright colors used harmoniously. But above all: simplicity. In my opinion that's the best way to make something stand out. I try to make the most of the lettering. For an advertising campaign I create a distinct typeface for each brand, such as the twigs for camping equipment, which reappear in all their ads and give it a recognizable look."

In American advertising he preferred the Chrysler poster showing a black Chrysler with white stripes, the black-and-white circle of the wheels flying in the wind; it was, he felt, daring and new. Otherwise the Anglo-American advertising style monotonously stressed complete material satisfaction.

He admired German posters when not too intellectualized, which he thought tiresome. His favorite artist was Ludwig Holbein, "Willrab," who excelled in using lettering such as in his poster for the "Cigarette Problem," in which the letter "O" forms the mouth that smokes the cigarette. Or the

poster for the Advertising Congress, showing a woman whose attention is divided, lending an ear one way while looking the other, symbolizing the two principal means of advertising.

"And what is your ambition, Mr. Hergé?"

"I want to perfect my work, which I enjoy, and to serve to the best of my abilities the Catholic Press of the *Le Vingtième Siècle*."[33]

HE STARTED HIS ADVERTISING WORK in the headquarters of the newspaper at 11 Boulevard Bisschoffsheim with the announcement "Atelier Hergé would be happy to create the trademark, the catalogue, and the poster that will help launch or expand your business." As business took off, Remi joined Adrien Jacquemotte and José de Launoit and rented offices at 9 Rue Rouppe. Created on January 3, 1934, the association took the collective name "Atelier Hergé." Each of the cosigners contributed one thousand francs in the capital. The agency was focused solely on advertising. Hergé reserved the right to use his name on his own drawings published in the press. In exchange his two partners added the clause, "If before the end of the contract for any reason, Monsieur Remi leaves the association, his associates will have the right to continue to use the name 'Atelier Hergé.'"[34] Six months later the association was liquidated, and each partner went his own way. But Hergé kept the title to Atelier Hergé and carried on alone. He was, as he now knew, a loner with a team spirit, but essentially a loner.

By the early thirties Georges was spending most of his time at the office of *Le Petit Vingtième*. When not there he could be found at his drawing table at home. He was bound to *Le Petit Vingtième* by a contract made "in good faith." For a generous salary of 2,000 francs per month (current equivalent, $1,114) and the privilege of working at home whenever he liked, he turned over the exclusive Belgian rights to Tintin and Quick and Flupke. Moreover he had to create the cover of the young readers' supplement, oversee its content, and submit his drawings to meet the deadline every Saturday. To break the contract he was required to give two years' notice.

"His" paper had taken shape, but starting in 1934 he shared it with colleagues in the daily, before withdrawing to devote himself exclusively to his own work. *Le Petit Vingtième* did not form a separate community within *Le Vingtième Siècle;* it reflected the older newspaper's ideas, hopes, and contradictions and was responsible for translating them into a language, written or graphic, that was accessible to children. The contents were very Catholic and practical. In the "Correspondence" columns,

readers were allowed to opine on "the mystery of Tintin." Apart from the adventures of the reporter and his dog, which took up a double-page spread, there was the corner for young ladies (recipes and knitting patterns), a column analyzing your character according to your name, and numerous articles about history and sports. The whole exuded a very Scouting spirit. Good deeds were praised on every page; purity and loyalty, honor and confidence, friendship and fraternity were exalted in all their forms. Young readers, like all Scouts, were to be proud of their faith and to devote their lives to it, to be patriotic and good citizens, and to see that duty begins at home. "Scouting is the resurrection in the twentieth century of the old Christian ideal of Knighthood."[35]

The fact is that in the columns of *Le Petit Vingtième* this ideal progressively went from practicing Catholicism to political proselytizing. Paul Jamin was in charge of editing the columns, and they naturally reflected anti-Communist, anticapitalist, anti-Semitic, antiparliamentarian, and antiliberal stances. For inspiration he needed only to look to the columns in *Le Vingtième Siècle*.

In the "Current Events" column, for example, the young reader learned that to break the embargo on foreign products ordered in reprisal for his racial politics, Hitler had taken measures to attenuate his anti-Semitism: "Wonderful. Let's hope that he will call back to Germany the numerous Jews exiled among us, and that we will hear another language than Yiddish spoken in our good city of Brussels."[36] The viewpoint of *Le Petit Vingtième* was all the more interesting because the embargo against German products was instigated as a result of Germany's refusal to honor its war debt to Belgium.

With an air of complete impartiality, the anonymous editor of *Le Petit Vingtième* (Paul Jamin, most often) defended fascism, praising Il Duce because he decided to abolish homework: "He is owed the sympathy of all schoolchildren.... Students all over the world are envious of their Italian friends."[37] Julius Streicher, a deputy in the Reichstag, was praised as "the great Sachem of the tribe of Nazis." When Streicher proposed to exile all Jews to Madagascar, *Le Petit Vingtième* found it a great injustice to the natives of Madagascar, who hadn't been asked their opinion.[38] The paper justified Hitler's anti-Semitic measures as self-defense, given that the majority of international businesses were controlled by Jews, and denounced the influx of Jewish refugees to Antwerp.[39] In one math quiz installment there is a caricature in profile of a man with a hooked nose and thick lips, the Star of David in his buttonhole. "If Mr. Levy can make one

cigarette out of three butts (he saves them out of economy), how many cigarettes can he make with nine butts?"[40]

It was the most insidious and efficient method of political propaganda because it worked on adolescents, vulnerable to the most simplistic reasoning and lacking critical spirit or tools. *Le Petit Vingtième* fulfilled its role perfectly: young readers were entertained and instructed in perfect harmony with the ideology driving *Le Vingtième Siècle*. Every week there was an editorial that was closely followed, read, and appreciated by its young readers. The column "Words from Uncle Joe" was signed by "Uncle Joe" but written first by Hergé, then by Jam, and finally by others.[41] Generally it reflected the mood of the times. Usually good-natured in tone, when it concerned current events the tone changed. Denouncing Belgians who "Frenchified" their language, rendering it less pure, Uncle Joe began one column, "I am not a political person and I am not going to discuss the benefits of Hitler's regime. But I read that the Reich's Minister of Public Education has just declared war on slang."[42]

Uncle Joe's editorials for young readers clearly reflect the spirit and stance of *Le Vingtième Siècle*:

> In most civilized countries there are severe laws for the protection of minors. In England it is forbidden to sell children alcoholic beverages, cigarettes, certain publications, etc.... Here, children can enter any movie house...children can also go into any theatre. They can buy any publication they please.... Most publications justify blackmail. They praise crime, vice, rape, they exploit scandals. It sells, sells! The Isaacs, Felsenbergs, and other Levys fill their pockets and make fortunes. Slowly they poison the world, by corrupting the young. Christ curse those who cause scandals, especially if these scandals touch the young. They should take all these rotten publications and make a packet of them, tie it up to a millstone and throw it to the bottom of the sea. After also having tied to it all those who live by these shameful and unhealthy activities. —Uncle Joe[43]

This column is exemplary, if only in the way it brings its frightening logic to a crescendo. It begins with moral indignation, followed by an anti-Semitic denunciation, and concludes with a call to murder. You would have to strain hard to discover any trace of Christianity or spiritual mission in it. *Le Petit Vingtième* was not only Tintin and Snowy, it was also a pure product of Father Wallez's notion of journalism: entertaining and Catholic, informative and nationalistic, aggressive in its satire.

Once, however, the priest went too far, and this would prove fatal. In 1933 he began a series of articles vehemently denouncing malfeasance on construction of the Canal Albert. *Le Vingtième Siècle* created a scandal; all of Brussels talked about nothing else. A certain Monsieur Delmer, the director of public works, stormed into Boulevard Bisschoffsheim, demanding to see Father Wallez. Voices were raised; the whole editorial department gathered in the hallway. The man felt slandered and approached the unperturbed priest, who was over six feet tall and weighed more than 250 pounds. Delmer tried to deliver several blows, in vain. The staff ejected him.

A trial ensued, which M. Delmer lost. But those tarnished by the scandal pressed their complaint with the bishop of Tournai, who wanted to resolve the dispute. To appease the people involved, he asked for the resignation of the temperamental priest. With the death of Cardinal Mercier, Father Wallez had no protector within the Catholic hierarchy. He was forced to obey, and by 1934 the deed was accomplished. After six months of depression he was appointed conservator of the ruins of the Abbey of Aulne.[44]

Hergé, who had sided with the priest, had to renegotiate his employment terms with the new administration. In March 1934, without advance warning, he sent notice of his resignation from *Le Petit Vingtième*. Since his contract forbade his working for other publications, he had to turn down an offer from the weekly *Vers le Vrai* (Toward the Truth).[45] Feeling ill used—he had not received any increase in salary from the weekly supplement he had served so faithfully for many years—he nonetheless resolved to leave diplomatically. Several months later his monthly salary was increased from 2,000 francs to 3,000 francs (current equivalent, $1,670).[46] But things had changed. He would henceforth concentrate on his own work, delegating responsibility for the editorial material. His instincts were correct. With the departure of Father Wallez, *Le Vingtième Siècle*'s circulation and influence continued to decline.

Following the first publication in book form of the adventures of Tintin, Hergé had had an understanding with Father Wallez: the newspaper acted as publisher and underwrote the cost of publishing, and Hergé paid for distribution and earned an equal share of the profits. This arrangement had worked satisfactorily until April 4, 1932, when Hergé received a letter from Tournai. It was signed by Charles Lesne, whom he had known as a young man at *Le Vingtième Siècle*. The former journalist was working in publishing at one of the Belgium's oldest houses. Founded in 1780 by the bookseller and printer Donat Joseph Casterman, the Casterman publishing empire

was still controlled by the family. Recently it had expanded into such diverse ventures as the telephone directory.

Assistant to the director, Lesne was in charge of the division dealing with school materials and traditional Catholic texts. He wanted Hergé to design jackets and illustrations.[47] As a test case, Lesne assigned Hergé to update the appearance of *The Year with Mary* by the Jesuit André Prévot. Hergé was delighted with the prospect of working with his old colleague. In his eyes, Casterman was one of the rare publishing firms that was both "up to date" and "with the means to accomplish beautiful work."[48]

Hergé never turned down a job. Four days later a sketch of the cover was ready. Casterman approved of his work: the lettering, the simple design and the color (ceramic blue). When Hergé delivered the mock-up for the cover with an invoice for 225 francs (current equivalent, $125), Casterman informed him that the fee was notably higher than those of French illustrators they dealt with. Nonetheless, they accepted his terms.[49]

Casterman then approached Hergé about a delicate task: sketches for the covers of three books initiating young people to the mysteries of life, one for young men, another for young women, and the third for young married couples. The illustrations could be suggestive but not explicit.[50] Hergé's work found the right balance.

At the end of 1933, just before Christmas, Casterman proposed replacing *Le Petit Vingtième* as the publisher of Hergé's future books. They would give him full author's royalties. Though Father Wallez was on the verge of leaving—in a few months he would no longer be the director of *Le Vingtième Siècle*—he had nonetheless planned to reserve for himself his share of the author's rights for the next three Tintin books. He opposed the idea.

Hergé was paralyzed by the powerful influence Wallez still exerted on him, so Charles Lesne took matters in hand. He traveled to Brussels to negotiate with the priest. Wallez was willing to let Casterman assume the risk of publication and gave the publisher the rights only to a portion of the printing, reserving the rest for himself. He claimed that he had asked Hergé to invent a young character in the Catholic spirit, that he had suggested adding a little dog, that he had made them both famous through his newspaper, and that publishing their adventures in hardcover editions had been his idea. He felt *he* had launched Tintin even though he did not create him. Wallez did not claim to be the author, but the coauthor.[51] Lesne was patient, and Casterman found the means to compensate the former great newspaper editor, now disgraced, who had turned into a disgruntled priest.

The negotiations became all the more urgent because a new Tintin book was in the works. On December 8, 1932, *Le Petit Vingtième* had started publishing the first plates of the serial "The Adventures of Tintin, Reporter, in the Orient." There would be 124 plates in all, a record for Hergé, as extravagant as the story's settings: Port-Saïd, Suez, Colombo, Ceylon, Singapore, Hong Kong, Shanghai. Onboard a ship Tintin lists for Snowy the stops on their itinerary, but their adventures really begin with a sheet of paper snatched by the wind and chased by a scatterbrained character around the deck of the steamship. Except that it is not a piece of paper but a papyrus.[52] In a rapid succession of panels Hergé introduces for the first time several different characters, some of whom would become fixtures of the Tintin family.

The papyrus contains information about the enigma that will confront Tintin: the exact location of the tomb of the Pharaoh Kih-Oskh, an enterprise that has already cost the lives of the archaeologists who had attempted it. Enter Roberto Rastapopoulos, an Italian with a Greek last name, the very personification of cunning and arrogance, with thick vulgar features and flashy clothes and manners. This millionaire introduces himself as the head of the film company Cosmos Pictures, the archetype of the producer who has never produced anything but a bad impression. Given the profession he exercises, his decided traits, and the prejudices of Hergé's circle, Rastapopoulos would appear an anti-Semitic caricature. But his surname suggests that this would be a misleading conclusion. Hergé simply liked the sound of the name, which evoked that of a flashy adventurer, and indeed there is a perfect harmony between name and character. As Hergé explained later in a letter to a reader, "Everything came out of his name. Rastapopoulos, for me, is more or less Greek, a shady Levantine character, without a country, that is without faith or ethical code. Another detail, he is not Jewish!"[53]

Hardly had Rastapopoulos left the scene than in the very next panel the future Thom(p)sons enter. They will never have first names because, according to Hergé, a strict police regulation forbids familiarity among detectives on the force. For the moment they are known as X33 and X33A. They are absolutely identical in appearance (black suits, bowler hats, and canes) but can be distinguished by their mustaches. The mustache tips of Thompson (with a *p*) rise, and those of Thomson (without a *p*) dip. Twinship played a major role in Hergé's imagination. Aside from the significance (to him) of his Zodiac sign, Gemini, his father and his uncle, Alexis and Léon Remi, were identical twins who did everything possible to maintain confusion by dressing the same way. They were vastly different in

character, however. Alexis was a dreamer and loved to take his time, while Léon never wasted a moment. "They adored each other and fought all the time!" recalled a niece and daughter.[54]

The Thom(p)sons are ridiculous, clumsy, and pretentious blunderers who blindly follow regulations. They are not clowns, however. Never in any way mean, and always loyal to Tintin, they are above all functionaries motivated by professional zeal. They are ultimately conscientious men.

On the trail at the Egyptian archaeological site, Tintin and Snowy disappear in the sands while searching for an Egyptologist, the archetypal absent-minded professor who prefigures Professor Calculus. They come nose to nose with their predecessors, I. E. Roghliff and Lord Carnaval (a wink to the historical archaeologist Lord Carnavon, who, with Howard Carter, discovered the tomb of Tutankhamen in 1922). Tintin and Snowy manage to escape—it's not clear how. In any case they emerge from a sarcophagus in midocean, which all seems very natural. Rescued by a writer-smuggler-adventurer in the Red Sea, they again head out into the desert, pursued by local bandits, only to land on a movie set in the middle of the dunes under the suave, monocled eye of Rastapopoulos.

Tintin and Snowy have no idea of what is happening to them, and in truth the story seems caught in the swirls of the pattern in the carpet. It's not clear why Tintin believes that the cigar bands he finds are significant, nor why agents X33 and X33A are obstinately pursuing our intrepid reporter. The narrative divides into three periods, corresponding to the three countries—Egypt, Saudi Arabia, and India—through which Tintin travels without really seeing them. It's not even exploiting exoticism; the backdrop vanishes behind the story and the story behind the cigars. What is on display is the realm of the unreal: during an aerial combat over Saudi Arabia, Tintin and Snowy vanish into a cloud only to reappear a moment later falling out of a cloud . . . in India! A record in the art of the ellipsis that would have left any film editor stunned.

The story is difficult to follow, but the frenetic pace carries the narrative. The sign of Kih-Oskh is the sole meaningful visual element that leads the reader. As for the Egyptologist, he becomes increasingly incoherent and seems to regain his senses only when he is addressed as Rameses II. Unsurprisingly an insane asylum is situated in the periphery of the story. At any moment the reader expects a face to appear at the window of the cell and ask, "Are there many of you in there?" As Samuel Beckett says, "We are all born insane and some of us remain that way." Hergé has included quite a few of the inmates in this adventure.

Meanwhile Tintin disposes of a bucketful of cobras by throwing them a chocolate bar. All this leads to the discovery that the tomb of Kih-Oskh is the hideout of an international gang of arms and drug dealers. (The right-wing press at the time carried stories about trafficking of all sorts.) But the sensational final revelation is that the cigars are fakes; they camouflage opium. The villains are eventually taken to the morgue, the asylum, or prison, the only logical sequence in this fantastic story. "I wanted to attempt a mystery, a detective novel, with suspense, and I inveigled myself into enigmas I almost could never resolve," Hergé admitted in an interview years later.[55]

The Cigars of the Pharaoh was the first hardcover Tintin book to be published under the Casterman imprint. Because of the contract that had been negotiated by Charles Lesne, Remi received three francs royalty (current equivalent, $1.75) per copy up to ten thousand, and two francs (current equivalent, $1.11) above that.[56]

Success did not go to Remi's head. His friends noted that he had changed neither his habits nor his way of life. If Georges sometimes made himself scarce, he was not avoiding them; work would not wait. Commissions were pouring in. In addition to the weekly drawings for the newspaper, the work on his books, and his advertising work, he had also undertaken doing covers and vignettes (small drawings) for publishers. He never refused work and was always grateful to have it.

The day after the death of Albert I, King of the Belgians—the result of a fall from the rocks of Marche-les-Dames—Casterman rushed to print a book commemorating the greatness of the monarch known as "the king knight in armor." Paul Werrie, an author, poet, and collaborator of *Le Vingtième Siècle,* wrote a hagiography under the title *The Legend of Albert I.* Hergé's cover art followed the heroic tone of the book. Inside were colored woodcuts that, rather than showing the king as a soldier, depicted him alone, standing in a rigid pose. The illustrations were immediately criticized, and Casterman—for generations the pontifical publisher, as indicated on their letterhead—turned down Hergé's work. The drawings were not grand enough. Hergé would remember the lesson.[57] When the editors asked him to make another attempt and to enlarge the king, Hergé threatened to resign. "A giant is only a giant in relation to other people of normal stature on the page. Unless I place other people next to him, or a yardstick, I don't see how it can be modified. Even if I increase the stature of the king, he will not look like a giant because there is no common measure between him and a mountain."[58]

Such are the problems of work. These are the rules of the game, and he was resigned to them. But some problems are more sensitive than others. Because he did not know how to say no to his colleague Léon Degrelle, he would unwittingly add another piece of evidence to the charges brought against him much later. Just for the sake of another job. The job would have little significance in itself, but it would reveal Georges Remi's attitude during the thirties.

IN 1932, in the offices of *Le Vingtième Siècle*, Hergé was on friendly terms with Léon Degrelle, who had come up through the Jesuit school and the Catholic University of Louvain and had won recognition for his work in creating *L'Avant Garde*. Degrelle was the correspondent sent to Mexico to cover the republican massacre of Catholics and who sent back copies of Mexican newspapers. He wrote several books about his adventures, all published by Casterman, and would later claim to have been the inspiration for the character of Tintin, which hardly seems likely. Degrelle was avowedly ambitious. He was appointed head of the Catholic publishing house Christus-Rex, which he immediately altered to a three-letter logo: Rex. His motto: "The works published by Rex editions are written by Belgians, printed by Belgians, to be read by Belgians"; the list of publications started with his own works.

After more than five years at the newspaper, it was perhaps inevitable that Hergé would work with Degrelle, without necessarily agreeing 100 percent with his message. In December 1932, right before the general elections, Hergé was asked to work on the campaign material, posters, tracts, and so forth for the Catholic Party. Inspired by the picture of the fist that flourished all over Germany, Italy, and as far as the Soviet Union, Hergé rejected subtlety. He submitted a poster of a little girl praying at the foot of her bed while being stabbed by a Socialist in rags,[59] which was pasted all over the walls of Brussels and Liège. Hergé's propaganda work was very distant from the world of Tintin and Snowy. One poster he did shows a skull wearing a gas mask, a livid image against a black backdrop with waves of ever-deepening green.

One evening he learned that one of his posters was being rushed to press. He protested this, sending a registered letter to Degrelle. His objections were not political but based on purely artistic considerations. He would not sign a product that he had not overseen and approved. Degrelle did not take him seriously, whereupon Hergé threatened to take him to court. Too late: the poster was printed with the slogan "Against the

Invasion, Vote for the Catholics." In place of Hergé's signature there is simply the caption "Studio of Rex Editions."

Hergé was offended by this infringement of his creative rights. "I have decided to teach them a serious lesson," he informed Eugene Dejardin from the Union for Protection of Artistic Property. The case would drag on for months, Degrelle excusing himself, blaming a third party, claiming the work was a contribution and that Hergé's reputation was not affected since his name was not on the poster. The cunning Degrelle proposed arbitration, except that the lawyer he named was on the board of Rex Editions. The case would last a year, and Hergé would receive only 1,500 francs (current equivalent, $845) in an out-of-court settlement. He had asked for a great deal more, stating that his work had been stolen. However, he won in principle and vowed that his copyright would never again be taken for granted.

During rare moments of free time Hergé tried his hand at other projects. He created clones of Quick and Flupke. First there were Fred and Miles, who appeared in the journal for working-class Catholic youths, *Mon Avenir* (My Future), which had the lifespan of one edition. Then came Tom and Millie, who were published in the weekly *Vie Heureuse* (Happy Life). Then, finally, Popol and Virginia.

Popol and Virginia are the names of two bear cubs, obviously inspired by *Paul and Virginia,* the classic pastoral novel by Bernadin de Saint-Pierre. Popol and Virginia emigrate to America, where he makes a fortune in the Far West selling hats to members of the Lapino tribe. This cuts into the business of those making feathered headgear. Popol is targeted for upsetting the balance of trade, and what starts as simple commercial competition ends in open warfare. Popol will save Virginia from being burned at the stake and will have a showdown with the bandit Bully-Bull, from which he will come out the victor.

Hergé was following the tradition of talking animals originating with the fables of La Fontaine and the nineteenth-century illustrations of J. J. Grandville, recently renewed by Walt Disney, and the series seems both a story for children and adult entertainment. Its naïveté and sentimentality appear addressed to children, but the elements of politics and economics are for adults. Hergé seems to have been unable to resolve the story in one direction or the other, and after fifty panels he moved on to other projects.

In 1934, two months after Hergé put the last panel of "Popol and Virginia in the Far West" to press, a weekly appeared that would usher in

a new era for illustrated comics. *Le Journal de Mickey,* the first illustrated publication in France devoted entirely to American comics, appeared on the newsstands in Paris. It started with "Silly Symphony" and " Mickey" by Walt Disney, followed by "Jim of the Jungle" by Alex Raymond, "Touffou" and "Father Lacloche" by C. D. Russell, "All's Well That Ends Well" and "Jacques Beaunez, Detective" by Hoban; it concluded with "Li'l Orphan Annie" by Brandon Walsh and Verd.

Paul Winkler, the director of the project, started out in Paris at a press service, then became the representative of King Features. For years he placed Felix the Cat and Mickey serials in *Le Petit Vingtième,* until he realized that King Features had an endless supply of comic serials and should have its own publication. Hachette financed 70 percent of *Le Journal de Mickey* and Winkler's agency, Opera Mundi, 30 percent. Hergé wrote down the name of Paul Winkler and the address of King Syndicated Features in his notebook, for future reference.

In 1934 "Mandrake the Magician" appeared, and Belgium celebrated the coronation of King Léopold III. It would be difficult to gauge which event had the greater impact on the life of the twenty-seven-year-old Georges Remi. What is clear is that an innocuous encounter would soon transform his life, and therefore his work.

4.

What Chang Taught Hergé
1934–1936

CHINA, AN ENIGMA WRAPPED IN MYSTERY. Hergé had the same commonplace notions all educated Belgian people had about the country: a distant continent of a nation, barbaric, overpopulated, and inscrutable. It had been in the news since the September 1931 Chinese sabotage of the Mukden-Tianjin Railroad, the line connecting Manchuria and China. Whether provoked or not, it became Japan's pretext for invading Mukden and occupying Manchuria, setting up the puppet state of Manchukuo by placing on the throne Pu-Yi, the last emperor of the Manchu Dynasty. Although objecting to the scathing reports of its human rights abuses by the League of Nations, Japan pushed forward with its expansionist policy but stopped just short of quitting the organization.

China was also the subject of a report by the journalist Albert Londres, who never returned from his assignment, having perished when the steamship *Georges Philippar* was sunk. He had spent several weeks in the international zone of Shanghai, where the Chinese and Japanese carried on a fierce if undeclared war. Then he continued on to Mukden. For once he did not confide to anyone the subject of his investigation, not his colleagues, nor diplomats, nor military officials, and especially not the customs officers. It was assumed to involve the shipment of drugs and arms and would have had major political implications, but he took his secret with him to his grave in the Red Sea. Ten years earlier Albert Londres had written articles on China, and these articles were collected into a very popular book with the eloquent title *China Madness*. It helped form Hergé's sense of China as a country of beheadings, a country where incoherence and madness ruled.

Why therefore Hergé decided on China as his next subject is a mystery. It was the first subject he chose without any guidance whatever from Father Wallez, and it had no connection to his long-held Boy Scout ideals. Much later Hergé claimed to have had two intentions: first, to reveal the savagery of the Japanese occupation of China; second, to make China more familiar.[1]

China presented him with an enormous problem of documentation. Every detail had to be exact and authoritative. The story had to be credible: emotionally accurate, factually correct, and exact in terms of settings and situations. Hergé could not pretend to be neutral. Indeed Tintin's ideological position was almost inevitable: he could side only with the oppressed. Hergé knew from the outset that he had to denounce Japanese imperialism. It was the first time that Tintin took sides in a conflict, and in some ways the increasing tensions in Europe in 1933–34 had forced the issue. With Quick and Flupke, Hergé was more direct. After the burning down of the Reichstag and the proclamation of the Nazi Party as the only legal political organization in Germany, Hergé showed the two Brussels scamps listening to a radio blaring with nationalist proclamations from Hitler, Mussolini, Édouard Herriot, Neville Chamberlain, a Bolshevik, and a Japanese before running outside to listen to the sweeter tunes of an organ grinder.[2] He had to risk sacrificing the comic element of the story to a higher purpose, transforming a simple adventure to immersion into a whole world. To succeed he had to combine social realism with the spirit of Charles Dickens or Alexandre Dumas.

Choosing China was all the more complicated because Hergé wanted to do all this without leaving Brussels. He succeeded because three remarkable men, again from the religious community, filled in the blanks. Hergé met Father Édouard Neut right after his studies at Saint-Boniface, on a retreat at the Abbey of Saint-André-lez-Bruges, where lived several monks who had served in China and were versed in Chinese history and culture.[3] As soon as he learned of Hergé's intention of sending Tintin to China, the Benedictine monk lent him two books: Father Thaddée's *On the Origins of the Conflict in Manchuria* and Cheng Chen's *My Mother,* a portrait of daily life.[4] Father Neut annotated newspaper articles that analyzed the differences between the Japanese and Chinese cultures and generally informed Hergé about what Tintin would confront: "Tintin will meet literate Chinese, monks, Chinese Bonzes and Chinese families. He will meet the Japanese military, who have been military for centuries, who are militant about being military, who fight like the Prussians in Belgium in 1914."[5]

Father Neut introduced Hergé to his second guide, Lou Tseng Tsieng, the former Chinese ambassador to Holland and a minister under Sun Yat-sen, the founder of the Chinese Republic. He had renounced the world when his wife died and enrolled as a seminarian in the monastery of Loppem, to emerge as Father Pierre Célestin Lou.

Hergé's third guide was Father Gosset, advisor to the Chinese students at the Catholic University of Louvain. Gosset introduced himself to Hergé, wanting to warn him against Chinese stereotypes that would hurt the feelings of his students, who were all devoted readers of *Le Petit Vingtième*. "The best thing you can do," Hergé told Gosset, "is to find me a Chinese advisor."

ON MAY 1, 1934, a young Chinese of slight stature and wearing a student's cap pulled down over his face made his way to Knappen Street in the Etterbeek neighborhood of Brussels. Georges and Germaine Remi were expecting their visitor, who arrived promptly at 5 PM.[6] Chang Chong-Chen spoke fluent French, though with a strong accent. He was twenty-six years old, a year younger than Hergé. Born in Shanghai, he had lost his mother when he was five. After a brief career on the stage, he received a scholarship to pursue his studies in watercolor at the Royal Academy of Beaux-Arts in Brussels. He had completed his studies and won many medals, but had not the faintest familiarity with comic illustrations.

Hergé informed Chang of his intention of sending Tintin to China. "Why China?" he asked.

"I don't know," replied Hergé. "For a change of continent. He has already been to Europe, Africa, America, and the Middle East. Never to Asia."

Chang said that we would tell Hergé "a story . . . based on what I know, what I've heard, seen, and experienced."[7] Hergé jumped at the suggestion. Having written four books based on his imagination, he was keen to try reality.

They agreed to meet the following Sunday afternoon and every Sunday for several months. They discussed many things and took notes, but drew very little. Chang did not consider it work, as he was not paid for his efforts. He was doing a favor for a friend of Father Célestin, whom he admired, and he was doing it for the sake of his country, crushed by Japanese imperialism. In the course of these exchanges they became fast friends. One day Chang gave Hergé a manual on calligraphy using a brush and ink. "The important thing is to use the brush properly," he patiently explained.

"What matters most are the contours, as this suggests volume. It's working in two dimensions, in which the drawing is reduced to essentials. Think of the whole, and the various proportions will be taken care of later."[8] Chang urged him to choose clarity over light and shadows.

At the same time as they discussed Chinese calligraphy they studied the language. Chang showed Hergé the ideograms, in effect initiating him into a whole culture. Sometimes they went strolling in the neighborhood or took long walks in the park. The least detail of nature was a continuation of Chang's teaching, and if their attention fell on a tree in the garden, Chang threw himself into the subject. He didn't simply explain the tree, he narrated its life story: its destiny, its struggle for life, the courage and will that helped it overcome its failings. Man is one with the universe; he is a universe. Hergé would always be grateful for learning that a small tree he had never noticed was so completely in its rightful place in the garden.[9]

"The Adventures of Tintin in the Far East" began appearing in the *Le Petit Vingtième* on August 9, 1934. Tintin receives a mysterious messenger from Shanghai, but at the moment the messenger is about to deliver some crucial information, he is struck by a dart in the neck that drives him insane. Without losing a moment, the young reporter books passage on a steamer, destination Shanghai, with only one clue, the name Mitsuhirato.

When Tintin eventually meets Mr. Mitsuhirato, who warns him about life-threatening dangers, he trusts this honorable businessman and begins a series of adventures: attempted shootings, kidnappings, poisonings, stabbings. He survives by disguising himself as a Chinese and hiding out in an opium den, the Blue Lotus, where he again catches sight of the mysterious and, as it turns out, treacherous Mitsuhirato.

Tintin jumps into the river in time to save a Chinese orphan named Chang, who is of the same age. They become friends, laughing at each other's cultural stereotypes, and decide to join forces. Off they go to Hukow to run the villains to ground. There they discover that our old friend Rastapopoulos is now the head of an international drug-smuggling cartel. Tintin establishes the link between the drug trade and Mitsuhirato, the Japanese imperialist agent, and earns the gratitude of the Chinese government. Chang finds himself adopted by a family. Tintin reads in the newspapers that Mitsuhirato has committed suicide rather than face exposure. The series ends on a note of pathos as the friends are tearfully separated, their last words drowned out by the blast of the steamship's whistle as it pulls away from the docks.

Even before the series was concluded the newspaper received a visit from General Raoul Pontus, head of the Sino-Belgian Friendship Association. Despite his sympathies with the plight of the Chinese, he had been officially assigned to convey a formal protest over the adventures of Tintin on behalf of the Japanese government. Hergé worried about repercussions and lawsuits, but his friend Chang reassured him, "If the Japanese are angry it's because we are telling the truth."

Hergé felt a deep gratitude to Chang, who had helped transform him from a mere illustrator into a graphic novelist. Thanks to his Chinese friend he had discovered "the wind and the bones," the wind being poetic inspiration and the bones the graphic structure. Without Chang, Hergé would not have come into his own.

Not long after the series was concluded Chang announced that he had to leave Belgium; his family needed him in Shanghai. War was breaking out. The Brussels station was mobbed, and Chang climbed into his compartment searching the crowd for Hergé, who had promised to see him off. Leaning out his window, the whistle blowing, in the smoke and the crowd Chang caught sight of a tall, thin young man waving a handkerchief, running toward the train, but in vain. Hergé, disappointed, also wanted to give him the finished copy of their adventure as soon as it came off the press. In fact he had wanted to give Chang credit as coauthor,[10] though he suspected that Chang would decline, partly out of humility, partly because of the political situation in China. His name appears in Chinese in the book on shop signs, contracts, public notices, and sayings, including the Taoist maxim "The lotus is serene because its heart is empty."[11]

In February 1936, when the plates of *The Adventures of Tintin and Snowy in the Far East* were turned in to Casterman, the publisher sent it to press but personally requested a redesign of the cover. Charles Lesne, who was Hergé's editor, hesitated between keeping it black and white or opting for color. But he believed the drawings inside the book should be in full color to meet the demands of the French market.[12]

Hergé resisted. The black-and-white format was the backbone of his drawings, and he was afraid that if he agreed to color, his book would be lost among the "Mickeys" and "Zig and Puce." He instinctively knew that a book jacket must be a poster. However, he was hesitant about the three-color process, line drawings filled in with colors. For one thing, it would mean extra work, and his calendar was full for months in advance.[13]

Even as he was trying to decide, a title had to be found for the book. *The Adventures of Tintin and Snowy in the Far East* was only a generic

working title. Hergé was struck by a sudden inspiration: "The Blue Lotus!" It was short, it was Chinese, and it was very mysterious.[14]

After many delays Casterman decided to push ahead with three-color process printing for the cover and to insert four or five full-page illustrations in color. Hergé would have to be satisfied with red, blue, and yellow.[15] If he had to agree to these concessions for the interior, however, he would not compromise on the cover, showing a dragon, a lantern, and Tintin and Snowy emerging from a huge vase. Shading and halftones, as well as graduated colors, created an atmosphere of mystery.

The proofs turned out fairly well, except for the gray of the floor and the top of the heads of Tintin and Snowy. These were fixed with a rapid touch-up. In the end Hergé was pleasantly surprised and, despite his initial misgivings, congratulated the photo engraver.[16] The day he received the finished copy he examined it closely. It was, he decided, "too beautiful for kids!"[17]

5.

Eye of the Storm
1936–1940

FROM CHINA, CHANG WROTE to thank Hergé for sending a copy of *The Blue Lotus*. He had been much celebrated on his return and was preparing to move to Shanghai, where he planned to open the first art academy teaching Western techniques of painting and sculpture.[1]

The success of the new book was demonstrated by *Le Petit Vingtième*'s celebration to welcome Tintin's "return" from the Far East. Three thousand readers from Brussels, including numerous Scout troops, turned out at the Cirque Royal. The Tintin impersonator received a great ovation, along with Hergé, the staff of the newspaper, the contortionist Alberto, and the clown Iles, brought up from Paris expressly for the occasion, which was sponsored by l'Innovation and le Bon Marché department stores.

Wanting to take full advantage of the success, Casterman did everything in its power to convince Hergé henceforth to produce his work in color. To support their argument, they showed him letters from booksellers who refused to reorder *Tintin in America* and *Cigars of the Pharaoh* because they did not want to be left holding unsalable stock of black-and-white illustrated books with only the covers in color.

Casterman was not only focused on future editions; their plans included reprinting previous Tintin books in color. Despite Hergé's procrastination about the earlier volumes, Charles Lesne could not imagine that he would refuse to color them before they went into new editions: "I hope that you are not going to refuse to dress your children."[2]

First they asked Hergé's permission to drop the mention "Reporter from *Le Petit Vingtième*" from the title *Tintin in America*. Hergé agreed for

America as well as for *Tintin in the Congo* and *Tintin in the Land of the Soviets*. But he balked when they asked him to design a new cover for *America*. Instead of Indians they wanted Tintin depicted on the running board of a car racing through the streets of Chicago. He refused, saying the American Indians had been dispossessed enough without being driven from his cover.

With only seven days in the week to work, Casterman would continue to pressure Hergé. He was still in charge of covers and the graphic work and for financial reasons carried out these tasks himself, illustrating the covers for their ecumenical titles, such as *Little Pierre's Mass* and *The Golgotha of the Virgin*, on condition that they appear without his name. Casterman understood better than anyone how pressed he was for time.[3] They were already busy launching a Tintin puzzle, a Tintin calendar, and even a cushion embroidered with Tintin and Snowy. Walt Disney was starting to commercialize games, alarm clocks, and bathing suits with Mickey's picture on them, available in department stores. By 1936 Tintin was busily being merchandised.[4]

Presentation copies of the new book were sent to all the leading newspapers, including that of a new political party called Rex, which had decidedly fascist leanings. The election of May 8, 1936, showed a seismic shift in political orientation. The Rex party received 11.49 percent of the votes, seating twenty-one deputies among the 202 in the Chamber, despite being condemned by Belgium's Catholic hierarchy. These results enabled Rex to present itself as an independent political force. Behind its façade of fake ultra-conservative Catholicism and populist rhetoric, it was nothing more than fascism under the national colors of Belgium.

The Rex Party was above all one man, Léon Degrelle, Hergé's former colleague at *Le Vingtième Siècle* and a pure product of reactionary Catholicism. Degrelle had many qualities, notably daring and nerve, but was guided most of all by his unbounded megalomania. His publication, the weekly *Pays réel,* enticed away half the staff of *Le Vingtième Siècle,* and he fully expected Hergé to bring Tintin to the new publication. But in the off-year election of April 2, 1937, Cardinal Van Roey urged all Catholics to join the antifascist coalition by equating Rex with Nazism. As a result Rex saw its twenty-one deputies dwindle to four, and it became more openly extreme.

DURING THIS TURBULENT PERIOD at the newspaper, Hergé sent his young reporter to South America. The story opens with the discovery of a theft at

the Ethnographic Museum in Brussels. A wooden fetish from the Arumbaya tribe has disappeared. Tintin hears this on the news (while doing his exercises in his Chinese pajamas, a link to *The Blue Lotus*). Hurrying over to the museum, he arrives at the scene of the crime only to stumble (literally) on the Thom(p)sons, who for once are on the case before anyone else. But the next day, miraculously, the object reappears, accompanied by a letter from the thief saying it had all been a prank. The case appears settled for everyone except Tintin, who suspects a forgery. The original idol had a broken ear, which was verified by a photo from an old catalogue. Tintin recalls reading about the suspicious death of a sculptor and makes his way to his residence to investigate. Strangely, the victim's parrot did not suffer during this supposed suicide by gas. Thus are all the elements of this convoluted tale set in place.

The young reporter attempts to find the parrot, but a mysterious South American gets there before him. However, in the confusion the bird takes flight and is lost to everyone. Following the trail, Tintin and Snowy find themselves in Las Dopicos, the capital of the Republic of San Theodoros, where they are trapped by their enemies. Suspected as a terrorist, Tintin is thrown into prison and set to be executed when General Tapioca is overthrown by General Alcazar, who also decides to have him shot. Tintin shares a bottle of *aguardiente* with the colonel heading the firing squad, who in his inebriation promotes Tintin to colonel, thus rousing the envy of his men, who are about to set upon him when a sudden storm arises. Lightning strikes the building, hurling Tintin out the window.

Things take a new turn with the appearance of Mr. Chicklett, who represents a company wanting to develop vast oil fields in a bordering area of San Theodoros. He has no trouble convincing General Alcazar to invade his neighbor in exchange for shares of profits from the development. Chicklett is followed by an arms dealer; both are vultures and scoundrels whose business is death and who want Tintin eliminated. After flight, pursuit, escape, and failed attempts on his life, Tintin and Snowy end up in the middle of the jungle searching for the Arumbayas. Now another set of dangers besets them on the trail of the lost fetish, which, they eventually discover, had been offered by the Arumbayas as a token of friendship to the great explorer Walker. But on Walker's departure, a half-caste stole a diamond with magical powers, which he hid in the fetish to escape detection.

Back in Europe Tintin discovers an antiques dealer with hundreds of Arumbaya fetishes; they are being merchandised. Finally Tintin traces the original fetish to the source and to a rich American collector named

Goldwood, who had happily acquired the object with no idea of its value. At that same moment the bandits from San Theodoros snatch the statue, and in the ensuing battle the diamond falls overboard, with everyone leaping into the sea after it. Only Tintin resurfaces; the others are nowhere to be seen. In the end Mr. Goldwood is only too happy to restore the object to the Ethnographic Museum, where it belongs.

In the spirit of Alfred Hitchcock, whom he admired, Hergé playfully drew himself into the picture. This time he appears at the very beginning, in the second panel. His initial inspiration for *The Broken Ear* came from two articles in the illustrated paper *Le Crapouillot* (The Grenade), one about the Anglo-American competition for control of oil and another about the two hundred families who rule the world: the Henry Fords, the Rothschilds, even the Krupps.[5] His South American adventure enabled Hergé to compare so-called civilized cultures and primitive cultures and, in the process, to cast a critical eye on his own society.

In the final days of 1935 Father Courtois and Father Pihan, editors of *Coeurs Vaillants*, made the trip from Paris to Brussels to confer with Hergé. They proposed that he create another series, to run alongside Tintin but geared for their Catholic readers. They liked Tintin well enough, except that he had no family and he didn't go to school. They wanted a series whose hero had a mother and a father, a little sister or brother, and household pets, a dog or a cat.[6] Thus between 1936 and 1939 *Coeurs Vaillants*, in conjunction with *Le Petit Vingtième*, published "The Adventures of Jo, Zette, and Jocko," the only series in which Hergé animated an entire French family.

The boy and his little sister are the children of Jacques Legrand, an aeronautical engineer. This takes readers into the world of inventions and technology, speed and flight. The stories, full of suspense, mystery, kidnappings, and wild chases, verge on science fiction, such as in the tale of "The Mystery Ray." The whole series has a period charm yet never found its audience. The adult characters were really children in grown-up guise, a compromise that satisfied neither child nor adult. It came to an abrupt end after three years. Hergé found portraying a family a burden, restricting his freedom of imagination and limiting the scope of his characters' actions. Now he understood what the author Jules Renard meant when he said, "Not everyone is lucky enough to be an orphan."

If 1936 was the year of *Modern Times,* Chaplin's last silent film, it was also the year King Léopold III announced that Belgium, in the face of

Hitler's occupation of the Rhineland, would return to its policy of neutrality. In Europe at the time the Spanish Civil War divided public opinion. After the military coup staged by the generals, with the backing of monarchists, Catholics, and fascists, Hergé and his colleagues were split in their allegiances. "Here was a war that interested everyone," the author Félicien Marceau wrote, "a war where the opposition was clear, whose passions, ideas, and images corresponded to ours: Democracy versus Dictatorship, the Left against the Right, Civilians against the Military."[7]

SCOTLAND RATHER THAN SPAIN was the setting of Tintin and Snowy's next adventure. The story opens with a mystery, of course. The young reporter and his dog are strolling in the Belgian countryside when Tintin sees an unregistered passenger airplane that had made an emergency landing and now was being repaired by mechanics. As Tintin approaches, he is shot point blank. Fortunately the bullet has only grazed his ribs. While in the hospital he hears over the radio that an unregistered plane has crashed in Eastdown, Sussex. Tintin then flees the hospital for England to further investigate. Once there, he encounters the Thom(p)sons on the train. Two shady characters almost succeed in throwing Tintin off a cliff, but the resourceful Snowy manages to save his master. Arriving at the site of the plane crash, Tintin pieces together from shreds of paper a single name, "Mueller," which, coincidentally, is also the name of Hergé's Portuguese editor. By chance Tintin arrives at the villa of a Dr. J. W. Mueller and on meeting him discovers that he is the director of an insane asylum of an unusual nature, in that you enter sane and leave completely insane.

After a struggle with the staff, Tintin is arrested and incarcerated but manages to escape in the confusion of a fire that engulfs the place. Still curious, he returns to Mueller's asylum to discover sinister clues that electric lines are buried in the garden, lighting beacons that signal airplanes to make a night drop. Tintin appears at the appointed drop site as well as the bandits—counterfeiters whom he puts out of commission, and he grabs the bags dropped from the sky. The counterfeiters manage to escape, and Tintin and Snowy are in full pursuit in a truck carrying a vat of whiskey. Profiting from the occasion, Snowy gets drunk and receives a lecture from his master on proper conduct (as he had in *The Broken Ear*): "You should be ashamed of yourself! A mutt off the street couldn't behave more badly!"[8] This doesn't prevent Snowy from backsliding in a land hardly lacking in pubs.

The trail takes them to Kiltoch in the north of Scotland, where Tintin adopts native dress, exchanging his plus fours for a kilt; a tam-o'-shanter

with a big red pompom covers his tuft of hair. Their destination is the ruins of Ben More Castle on the black island, a sinister place guarded by a monster. All those who have attempted to approach the island have disappeared. The beast is more terrifying than the Loch Ness monster. None of this puts off Tintin, who, after many peripatetic twists and turns, captures the gang, discovers their printing press and the secret landing field, and turns them over to the police. The terrifying monster is a gorilla the villains trained to kill but who turns out to be Ranko, Tintin's friend, who now finds a comfortable home in a zoo.

Hergé settled on *The Black Island* as the title. Despite his vigilance, when he received the first copy of *The Black Island* he deemed it "not very good." Casterman prided itself on being a great printer and had recently acquired expensive, innovative offset presses, but there were glaring errors. For one, Hergé's name did not even appear above the line "The Adventures of Tintin." Henceforth it was agreed that Hergé had to see all proofs for final approval.[9]

In 1938 Hergé was thirty-one years old. He was exhausted by the ceaseless work. He also felt profoundly discouraged. Illustrators were treated as second-class citizens in Belgium.[10] But he didn't have much time even for introspection. Everything was moving so quickly, both for him and for Europe. Even as the democracies of Europe were feeling threatened by the rearmament of Germany, the world of the comic strip was divided between savage competition and protectionism.

In April 1938 the publishing house Dupuis Father and Son launched a new illustrated magazine, *Spirou,* the name of a bellhop at a place called the Moustique Hotel, who then becomes a reporter. Very Belgian in spirit—the name is a Walloon word meaning "malice" and "farce"—its popularity quickly grew. Other Tintin imitators included a new serial, "The Adventures of Blanding and Cirage," by Joseph Gillain, alias Jijé. Then two other series appeared, both clearly influenced by Hergé: "Sus and Flup" (echoing his "Quick and Flupke") and "The Mystery of the Hindou Key," whose hero is Freddy Fred, reporter.

At the same time in the United States the comic book, a small-format magazine containing stories devoted to one or more characters, was becoming a phenomenon. The first issue of *Action Comics* swept the newsstands with the birth of Superman. Less than a year later, *Detective Comics* launched Batman. The market for comics was expanding exponentially. The Organization of Spinach Growers even raised a statue to Popeye. The popularity alarmed self-appointed censors, who banished Betty Boop from the numerous dailies where she had exercised her charms for more than four years.

European authorities also clamped down. In 1935 the minister of popular culture in Italy forbade the importation of American and English comic strips, with the exception of "Mickey Mouse." It was said that Il Duce's children loved Walt Disney's mouse, and Benito Mussolini himself was a fervent admirer of the film *Snow White and the Seven Dwarfs*, which he often showed at home along with *Fantasia*. Italian publishers skirted the law by Italianizing names that were too foreign; thus "Mandrake the Magician" became Mandrache. In Italy, despite restrictions, the weekly *L'Avventuroso* took the risk of publishing American comics, the most popular of which was "Flash Gordon."

In France the landscape of the children's press consisted of two camps, each composed of two rivals. On the Catholic side was the firm Fleurus (*Coeurs Vaillants* for boys and *Âmes Vaillantes* for girls) and "La Maison de la Bonne Presse" (Bayard). The secular press was dominated by Opera Mundi of the Paul Winkler Agency (*Le Journal de Mickey, Robinson, Hop-La*) and La Société d'éditions de périodiques illustrés, or SEPI, run by Cino del Duca (*Hurrah!, L'Aventureux*). The Communist critic Georges Sadoul denounced *Le Journal de Mickey* and *Hurrah!* because 90 percent of the texts and illustrations came from abroad. He believed that Disney equaled Hearst equaled Hitler. The Catholic hierarchy attacked both the imported comic strips and the secular press. The critic Jean Vaillant (the pseudonym of Father Pihan of *Coeurs Vaillants*) urged young readers to make a bonfire of foreign illustrated comics, Mickey Mouse in particular. Auto-da-fés were being conducted in Germany, which made Bertolt Brecht comment that when you start burning books you end up burning men.

The irony is that Mickey is an exemplar of the American middle class whose world is governed by three axioms: respect for property, authority, and security. Nothing could be more conservative and conformist.[11]

Le Vingtième Siècle continued to have exclusive rights to Tintin in the francophone press in Belgium, but not in the Flemish-language press in Belgium and abroad. Hergé's friend Adelin Van Ipersele de Strihou, an advertising executive from Antwerp, proposed becoming his agent in that market. Hergé sent Van Ipersele his thoughts:

1. The stories of Mickey and Donald Duck, etc., are excellent but nevertheless are American. It's undeniable that a series created by a European (such as I am) will be more understandable to European children.

2. Mickey and Donald Duck are known everywhere. Tintin, Quick and Flupke, are really new (I am speaking of the Flemish and Luxembourg Press).

3. If you approach a Catholic newspaper don't forget to cite the Catholic papers that carry Tintin. It's a certification of morality and a guarantee on account.

4. The creator is the greatest artist of modern times, and he has the best understanding of a child's mind.[12]

IN AUGUST 1938 Germany annexed Austria; the Anschluss was ratified by a plebiscite, with 99.73 percent of Austrians in favor. As a province of the greater Reich, Austria was henceforth known as "Ostmark." At the same time, *Le Petit Vingtième* started publication of "The Adventures of Tintin in Syldavia."

This was the second time that Hergé decided to draw on contemporary events, though now there was, as with China, the risk of his story's being overtaken by them. In his notebook Hergé succinctly sums up the plot: "A gang of international anarchists plan to blow up, one after the other, all the great monuments of Europe. Tintin tracks them to their hideout in the Balkans."[13]

While strolling in a park Tintin and Snowy come upon a briefcase left on a bench. Ever the Scout, Tintin returns it to its owner, Professor Hector Alembick, a distinguished sigilographer, a specialist in the study of seals and coats of arms. He is about to leave for Syldavia to study the seals of King Ottokar IV. Tintin decides to accompany him in the capacity of secretary. In midflight on the plane sent by the Syldavian government, the pilot releases a trap door. Hurled into free fall, Tintin lands miraculously in a haystack. He immediately reports to the nearest police station his suspicion of a plot against the reigning king of Syldavia, Muskar XII. There is a conspiracy to steal the king's scepter, since tradition dictates that the ruler must step down if he loses this precious symbol of power.

On his way to Klow, the capital, Tintin meets Bianca Castafiore from La Scala in Milan, the soprano of the formidable and dreaded pitch (witness the mad dash by rabbits along the road). Overcoming infinite obstacles in his quest to alert the king, being denounced as an anarchist and hunted by the police, Tintin by chance comes face to face with Muskar XII. Tintin and the king race to the castle to check the room where the scepter is kept, only to find that it is gone. Professor Alembick, a photographer, and all the guards are unconscious. By unraveling the mystery of how the scepter was

removed from the room, Tintin races to recover it, tracking the gang all the way to the Syldavian-Bordurian frontier. A certain Müsstler, head of a Nazi-like shock troop, is preparing a coup to take over Syldavia and annex it to Borduria. The conspiracy is foiled, the scepter recovered. The king expresses his gratitude by making Tintin a Knight of the Order of the Black Pelican, the first outsider to be so honored.

The serial "Tintin in Syldavia" was published in *Le Petit Vingtième* on August 10, 1939. Less than three weeks later German armored divisions invaded Poland.

The story represents a departure for Hergé, who both invented an entirely new country with its language, history, and traditions and made it reflect current events. To create Syldavia, Hergé drew upon the architecture, landscape, and costumes of Eastern Europe: Serbia, Albania, Montenegro, Hungary.[14] For the language, the syntax is French but the vocabulary is Marollian. Hergé enjoyed playing on words, forging neologisms with a wink to his fellow citizens of Brussels familiar with the dialect. The plot echoes the reportage by Albert Londres, "Les Comitadjis, ou le terrorism dans les Balkans, 1932." The characters are reminiscent of King Zog I of Albania, and the names are taken from the history of Czechoslovakia and Bohemia. The atmosphere is straight out of Franz Lehar's *The Merry Widow*, with added touches from films by Erich von Stroheim and Ernst Lubitsch.

The two totalitarian regimes are mirror images of each other. One ruler wears a mustache like Stalin's, but his uniform has SS insignias.[15] The name of the enigmatic "Müsstler" is a combination of "Mussolini" and "Hitler." In the Europe of 1938–39 it was evident that Germany was the only country that would invade its neighbors. During the occupation, however, Hergé did not push this interpretation and afterward would give a slightly altered version: "Tintin is not the defender of the established order, but the defender of justice, the protector of widows and orphans. If he flies to the aid of the King of Syldavia, it is not to save the monarchy, it's to prevent an injustice: the 'evil' perpetrated here as far as Tintin is concerned is the theft of the scepter."[16]

Because of the gathering storm in Europe, Hergé insisted that his editor publish the book within the year. "If you have followed current events you will see that it is completely based on what is happening now," he wrote. "Syldavia is Albania. They are preparing to annex it. If you want to take advantage of the current events, it's now or never."[17] Later he would deny that he had only one country in mind. He also decided that "reporter"

should be dropped after the heading "The Adventures of Tintin"; its time was over. He changed the title as well, from *Tintin in Syldavia* to *The Scepter of Ottokar IV*. But this was difficult to pronounce, and he agreed to the editor's compromise, *King Ottokar's Scepter*.

In 1939, just as Europe was on the verge of war, Georges Remi was called up to serve his country. His departure caused the sales of *Le Petit Vingtième* to drop precipitously. His friend Pierre Ickx suggested a way to keep things going. If Hergé would establish the plot lines, with drawings and sketches, Ickx would draw the actual comic strip. The work would be signed "after Hergé" or "Hergé Studio," and they would split the author's fee.[18] He little knew Hergé if he thought him capable of accepting such a proposal. Instead, posted near Turnhout, a small town in the north of Belgium, Hergé managed to send two plates of the adventures of Tintin to *Le Petit Vingtième* nearly every week. Army or no, he was committed to the continuation of the series, and in recognition of how valuable he was, they continued to pay his salary.[19] Drawing was his only relief from the monotony of the military. When not working for the newspaper, he filled his sketchbooks with vignettes of military life and portraits.

The situation over the weeks became more and more Kafkaesque. A reserve officer in a francophone division of machine gunners, he was posted as an instructor in a Flemish-speaking infantry division. At one point he was assigned the delicate mission of "requisitioning" bicycles from the farms in the region. But it did not last long. He was suddenly discharged when Belgium called off its military preparations; war did not seem imminent.

During this time he had made friends with Dominique de Wespin, a correspondent for the newspaper *Candide* who was assigned to China and on her way to Peking. "I so desperately want to go to China and find my friend Chang," Hergé confided to Wespin. "Do you believe in astrology? I am a Gemini. I have four paws, two that always want to go forward, and two always going backward. It's not easy making a decision when you are a Gemini."[20] His indecision would be sorely tested when at the end of 1939 he received an invitation from Chiang Kai-shek, president of the Nationalist government of China, who had enjoyed reading *The Blue Lotus*.[21] There was much to please him: the book exposed Japanese imperialism and revealed the great qualities of the Chinese people in their capacity to resist the invaders. He asked his wife, Sung Mei Ling (Madame Chiang Kai-shek), who played a major diplomatic role, to invite Hergé to visit

their country. He would also be commissioned to make drawings for the Chinese government.

Sadly Hergé was forced to decline the invitation. First, Belgium's Defense Ministry sent out a notice that he could be recalled to active service at any moment. The situation in Europe would not permit his getting permission for a long trip abroad. Second, he was bound by his contract to *Le Petit Vingtième;* even if he prepared all his work in advance and let Germaine handle the details, he risked breaking his part of the bargain.[22] His regret was sincere; the reunion with his friend Chang had to be postponed.

IN THE CHARGED POLITICAL ATMOSPHERE of 1939 the United States declared its neutrality. In France the government assumed emergency powers, and Russia invaded Finland. Hergé wanted to be neutral, like his country, like King Léopold III, who declared, "Belgium with the other neutral states constitutes a bastion of peace and an element of conciliation which, alone, will save our civilization from the abyss toward which a general war would plunge it."[23] He believed Monsignor Van Roey when he preached, "If she remains outside this conflict Belgium can become the instrument of Providence, first in relieving the misery that a prolonged war will inevitably bring, and then, becoming a platform for the voices of peace."[24]

Neutrality is not a passive attitude. True neutrals proclaim themselves as such. Yet nothing was more alien to Georges Remi than an act of commitment; he maintained his position in private. Thus his name does not appear on the Pacifist Manifesto of September 1939 signed by leading intellectuals and journalists.[25] Hergé believed he was supporting the cause in his own way by publishing drawings in the newspaper *L'Ouest* (The West), a weekly that claimed to support Belgian neutrality and consequently was hostile to all political views advocating military aggression. It recognized only one political party, that advocating a new Europe. In actuality it had been founded by Raymond De Becker, with support from Max Liebe, an attaché to the German embassy in Brussels and a protégé of the Nazi's foreign minister, Joachim von Ribbentrop (later executed at Nuremburg for war crimes).[26] Hergé had known De Becker for years, having illustrated the covers of his books *For a New Order* and *Christ the King of Business,* as well as various pamphlets.

For the comic strip published in the early issues of the paper in December 1939, Hergé created Mr. Bellum, who was well named.

He seemed like the typical petty Belgian Francophile, with the appearance of an absent-minded professor, but was in reality a rabid warmonger and a complete coward. The paper was short-lived; ten thousand copies were printed, although it had only five hundred subscribers and newsstand sales of a thousand a week. You don't make war on war without being compromised. One day it was revealed that since the beginning the paper had received financial support from the German ambassador.[27] Who would have suspected it? The Thom(p)sons perhaps, but apparently not Tintin.

On April 10, 1940, as the German army invaded Denmark and Norway, Georges Remi was demobilized for reasons of health and given a three-months' sick leave. This was due to the intervention of the former minister of transportation, Charles de Bus de Warnaffe, closely allied with *Le Vingtième Siècle*, who had intervened for him before. Two months earlier he had contacted Colonel Servais, the commander of the unit in which Hergé was serving, to ensure that he would receive an exceptional leave of two consecutive days in order to complete his work.[28] While he was accomplishing this task, Hergé received a letter from the management of *Le Vingtième Siècle* terminating his employment: supplies were too uncertain, the income from advertising inadequate.[29] The paper continued publishing, but as a precaution the management had sent this advance warning to all employees.

Against all odds, and despite the unforeseen problems, Hergé had continued working on "The Land of Black Gold" for eight months, at the rate of two plates a week. Tintin, intrigued by the explosions every time the Thom(p)sons tried to use gasoline, initiates an investigation that leads him, naturally, to the country of black gold. In the middle of the desert he's imprisoned by Sheik Bab El Her, who mistakes him for an arms dealer supplying his worst enemy, Sheik Ben Kalish Ezab. Managing to escape along with the Thom(p)sons, Tintin discovers the harsh reality of the desert and finds an old acquaintance, Dr. Mueller, who headed the counterfeiting ring in *The Black Island*. Mueller gains the upper hand and is about to execute Tintin by shooting him at point blank range when ...

This time the dramatic resolution does not come from Hergé's imagination but from Hitler, who launched his troops against Holland, Belgium, and Luxemburg on the way to his ultimate destination, France. By stopping the presses of *Le Vingtième Siècle* and its supplement on May 8, including Tintin's adventures on the fifty-sixth plate, the Germans had created narrative suspense.

Two days later Georges Remi returned to his division but was judged unfit for service.[30] Neutral Belgium was invaded by the Wehrmacht. After the shock of the total defeat of the army, the Belgians felt an almost physical sense of relief.[31]

On May 12, back home, Hergé received a telephone call from the management of *Le Vingtième Siècle* informing him that German paratroopers had launched an assault on Fort Eben-Emael, which guarded the road to Brussels, barely fifty miles distant. Brussels would be occupied, they told him. He should leave as soon as possible.[32]

He didn't have to be told twice. Most Belgians of Hergé's generation and that of his parents remembered the occupation during the First World War. Germaine was prepared, waiting with her suitcases and Thaike, their two-year-old Siamese cat. They drove off in the car and became part of the exodus. Belgians by the tens of thousands headed toward France to find refuge, streaming from the Northern Department to La Rochelle, in the middle of the country, where there was a refugee center run by Georges Simenon, who had lived in the area for several years. They stopped to rest at the Abbey of Saint André les Bruges, where Father Neut and Father Lou, who assisted him with *The Blue Lotus,* warmly welcomed them. They were completely taken with Thaike. "I congratulate you on not abandoning her," said Father Lou.[33] Outside the abbey walls, it was the end of the world.

On May 15 the Germans suddenly altered course and breached the French line of defense between Sedan and Namur, enabling their armored vehicles to reach the Somme and Oise Rivers. The Remis were now in Paris, having stopped at the offices of *Coeurs Vaillants* to settle accounts with Father Courtois, who owed Hergé money. Then they started off again, this time headed toward the Auvergne region. Their destination was Saint-Germain-Lembron, where the illustrator Marijac had lent them his house. They were soon joined by their sister-in law-and niece. With Marijac mobilized, his wife and mother lavished their attention on the Remi family. They all followed the harrowing advance of the German war machine and speculated about what the king, the cardinal, and the prime minister would do. Above all the Belgians looked to the king. Would he submit to the occupation of his country as Albert I had been forced to do in the face of the carnage of the First World War? Georges Remi, like most of his fellow citizens, waited for their beloved king to decide their destiny.

On May 25 a dramatic meeting took place at Wynendaele between the king and the government ministers, resulting in mutual recriminations.

Both parties broke off relations. King Léopold III had decided to stay in Belgium. He would remain with his soldiers, but in his residence, the Laeken Palace, which would become his jail. Renouncing all the prerogatives of a head of state for the duration of the occupation, he hoped his mere presence would limit the damage to his country, despite being enmeshed in what later would appear to be a complex web of concessions and compromises. It was the beginning of accommodation. The government ministers, for their part, chose exile, causing a divorce between legality and legitimacy that would create a fault line in Belgium.

On May 28 Léopold III, as the supreme commander of the army, signed the military surrender. Although this was difficult for many Léopoldists to accept, public opinion was solidly behind the monarch. Out of loyalty, Belgians closed ranks behind him. Much later Hergé would confide to Colonel Rémy, secret agent for Free France, "As for me, my feelings and my reasoning placed me completely and without hesitation, on the side of those who approved the decision of May 28."[34] Hergé would never allow anyone to say in his presence that the king had willingly surrendered, arguing that he had done what any individual driven to the limit would have done. In his eyes, Léopold III had shown nobility of character by remaining with his people to share their suffering. His motive was beyond question, and a thousand times more honorable than the London exile of Queen Wilhelmina of the Netherlands. The subject of the king was one of the few topics about which Hergé would remain intractable, if not intolerant, his whole life. It was not a matter for discussion.[35]

Prime Minister Pierlot, head of the government-in-exile, declared the surrender "without legal basis." His cabinet resigned in protest.[36] By June 10 the administration of the country had reorganized. An agreement was reached between the College of Secretary Generals, who represented the nation, and the Military Authorities of the Occupation. Four days later the Wehrmacht entered Paris, and on the seventeenth of June Marshal Pétain asked for the terms of an armistice. Only Churchill's England remained to continue the struggle.

On June 28, out shopping in the village of Saint-Germain-Lembron, Remi learned that the roads were open again. That afternoon, with all their luggage packed and the family in the car, they were on their way back to Brussels. They felt a sense of urgency, as they had been without news of his brother, Paul, an officer on active duty. Letters sent to him had remained unanswered. His parents had been without a word from either son, Paul or Georges, and must have been at their wits' end.

On June 30, due to the occupation, the publishers of *Le Vingtième Siècle* still did not know if it could stay in business. Hergé's duties would come to an end in three months, but his mind had already been made up. For a year he had been trying to break his contract, and the management had always persuaded him to stay. Now he was only waiting for a sign to leave.[37]

His house was requisitioned by the occupation; an officer of the Propagandastaffel was temporarily quartered there. When Georges suffered an abscess to his foot, the officer put his car at his disposal to drive him to the hospital. Nazi, but polite.[38]

On August 10 Hergé wrote his editor, "'Le Vingtième' is dead. 'Le Petit Vingtième' also. Let's see what happens."[39] He did not have a long wait.

6.

The Golden Age
1940–1944

TO HERGÉ, THE KING was the personification of Belgian resistance, and it was in this light that he understood the speech given by Léopold III the day after the surrender. The war was over, the Germans occupied the country; horrible as it was, the situation could not last forever. In other words, let's be practical and adapt while waiting for better times. "That was why," Hergé said later in an interview, "I had no scruples about working with a newspaper such as *Le Soir*."[1]

This spirit of compromise also marked the first step on the path to passive collaboration. From the start Hergé had wanted to stay in print under the occupation. The crisis of conscience that had led some of his colleagues to break their pens, so to speak, was alien to him. "I worked, period; that's all. Just like a miner works, or a streetcar ticket taker, or a baker. While everyone found it normal that a mechanic made trains run, they thought that people of the press were supposedly traitors."[2] He objected to the very idea that writers and journalists should be more responsible. His attitude revealed denial, which in turn masked an unstated emotion. During the occupation a number of friends from his youth had attained positions of power in the press. From Hergé's perspective, there was no reason he should deprive himself of working with them. Politically there was no great gap between them and him. The Germans had to leave someday. *Le Vingtième Siècle* was shut down for good. Remi waited four months before the Occupation Authority lifted the sequestration and he could get at the money the paper owed him and settle his taxes.[3] Fortunately for him, Casterman was late in settling its accounts and advanced him 10,000 francs (current equivalent, $3,300).[4]

There were now three categories of newspapers: those that continued to publish under their own initiative (a total of eleven), those that appeared for the first time (nine), and those labeled "stolen" because they had been confiscated and published against the will of their owners or board of directors (thirteen).

By the end of summer 1940 Hergé had come to an agreement with the Flemish press of Belgium, *Het Algemeen Nieuws*, for exclusive rights to "Quick and Flupke," and with *Het Laatste Nieuws* (a stolen paper) for exclusive rights to Tintin.[5] Against the advice of Casterman, he chose to publish a volume of "Quick and Flupke" rather than *Popol and Virginia among the Lapinos*, which involved arms dealers—"innocuous in normal times," as he put it, "but these days could cause us problems if not the outright refusal of permission to publish."[6] Hergé also approached *Le Nouveau Journal*, a new daily of questionable merit that was launched in October 1940 with the team from the weekly *Cassandre*. It was under the direction of Paul Colin, a collaborator, whom Hergé described as "a first rate man, very sympathetic."[7]

The Belgian press under the German occupation was in a paradoxical position: it was read, but not believed. Although the papers were too servile to have any credibility, people nevertheless bought them and devoured every line. Despite the logistical problems of printing and distribution, newspapers had roughly the same circulation as before the war. The hardships of life transformed people into avid readers. They consumed everything, books and pamphlets, yet without surrendering judgment. The majority listened to the BBC, which reestablished the balance, corrected errors of point of view, and removed any doubts about the origin of specific information. A great mistake of the occupiers was not to have confiscated all radio sets, as they had in the Netherlands.

Among French-language newspapers *Le Soir* still retained some authority. For the staff of the Propaganda Abteilung, who wanted to maintain the illusion of a Belgian newspaper made by Belgians for Belgians, it was their favorite vehicle for forming public opinion. The daily sold an average of 250,000 copies per day for the duration of the occupation. Eggert Reeder, the head of the military Occupation Authority, acknowledged, "*Le Soir* neutralized public sympathy for England, and countered anti-German sentiments in the bourgeoisie." Its purpose couldn't be more succinctly stated.[8] The Rossel family, the original owners, had tried to recover their property by negotiating with the Occupation Authority, in vain. The Germans consented to return the newspaper only if they retained editorial control. This was unacceptable for the Rossels.[9]

As 1940 was coming to an end, Raymond De Becker, editor of *Le Soir*, came across Paul Jamin (the illustrator Jam) at a meeting and asked if he was still in contact with Hergé. Jam said that he was. Hergé was delighted to meet with De Becker. The two had worked well together on *L'Ouest*. Hergé's first paycheck was 2,000 francs a month (current equivalent, $670), a tidy sum at the time.[10]

The illustrator was obsessed with the need to recover lost ground in newsstands and bookstores. "As for me, I don't think it's the moment to let myself be forgotten," he wrote his editor, Charles Lesne, on September 5. "On the contrary, I must take advantage of the absence of French competition to dominate. *Le Soir* has asked me to start up an illustrated weekly for children on the model of *Le Petit Vingtième*. Everything is set. We are only waiting for the authorization."[11] Hergé was eager to return to Tintin, and the new management equally so. Belgians read collaborationist newspapers not only for practical information but for the comic strips.

Hergé's impatience was sharpened by the reappearance of French competition. After the shock and confusion of defeat, the editors of the French press rapidly adapted to the new conditions. Having suspended publication following the general collapse, *Le Journal de Mickey* reappeared on the newsstands with great fanfare on October 22. It was printed in Marseilles and, as before, with the authorization of Walt Disney. However, it was no longer under the direction of the Jewish Paul Winkler, who had sought exile in the United States. The first page united Mickey and Pinocchio. Inside was a collection of some of the most attractive comic strips available: "Jim of the Jungle," "The Eagle Patrol," "Pim Pam Poum" (the Katzenjammer Kids), "Cora," "Bernard Tempest," "Marc Luron," "Richard the Reckless," "Prince Valiant," and the serialized story "Phantom River." Some were new, others not. The editorial deserved attention. Titled "Club Mickey" and signed "Your old uncle Léon," it evoked the painful times France had lived through and answered letters from readers:

Marshal Pétain, in granting you the support of his prestige and confidence, which you must strive to earn, has designated the path you must follow: great things need to be accomplished to rebuild a better France, and this duty befalls you. . . . You know, my dear nephews and nieces, that the *Journal de Mickey* is not simply a publication made to amuse you, and it is in this spirit that we will continue now, when more than ever France needs the vitality and the enthusiastic drive of all its children.[12]

Shortly after this introduction, French-German collaboration became a fact when old Uncle Léon told them about Marshal Pétain's triumphant visit to Marseilles: "There you could see the immense adherence of a people who recognized their leader. Affection, joy, and respect united their voices."[13]

"Tintin and Snowy are back!" This triumphant announcement on a strip across the cover of the first number of *Soir-Jeunesse* on October 17, 1940, showed the young reporter, wearing a backpack, walking energetically with Snowy along a road with the sign "Toulouse-Brussels." The spirit of *Le Petit Vingtième* had been resuscitated. Hergé's assistants on staff were Paul Jamin and a newcomer, Jacques Van Melkebeke, a talented painter and illustrator who also served as the art critic for *Le Soir*.

In the first issue De Becker set the tone. He called on the children to seek the purity and the strength they needed were they to help rebuild Belgium so that it could find its place in the New Europe. In the second issue the political moralizing was set aside; the focus was the death of Tom Mix, the King of the Cowboys. The article was not signed by Hergé but could have come from his pen. His tone is recognizable in the praise of this American Don Quixote who wanted to revive, in an age of dull conformity, the spirit of chivalry, adventure, and generosity.[14] If the venture was an undeniable success, the enthusiasm was not unanimous. As soon as Tintin's return was announced, Hergé received an anonymous letter:

> Permit me, sir, as the father of a large family, to express my sorrow and disappointment at seeing "Tintin and Snowy" appear in the new "Soir." Have you thought about the responsibility that you have assumed? Without Tintin, the new "Soir-Jeunesse" would fall flat in six weeks. With your friends it will continue because we know them, we like them and will buy the paper to follow their adventures.
>
> Then little by little children will come under the new influence. Insidiously and deceitfully the venom of their neo-pagan religion from beyond the Rhine will be introduced in the margins of your entertaining drawings. They will no longer speak of God, of the Christian family, of the Catholic ideal.... Can you agree to collaborate in this terrible act, a real sin against the Spirit?[15]

Hergé was touched, if not shaken, by this letter. He saved it among his papers. But two days later he proudly announced to a friend that *Le Soir* had doubled its usual sales of 300,000.[16] That's what mattered to him.

Did he have any choice? Without a doubt, as with all citizens of occupied Belgium and colleagues in Europe, every position was possible. Jijé continued to produce his serials for the newspaper *Spirou* ("Don Bosco," "Jean Valhardi," "Christophe Colomb," "Spirou"), proving that one could continue working without compromising. In Italy, in the paper *Il Vittorioso*, Kurt Caesar committed the heroes of his series on Roman Legionnaires to the fascist cause in their struggle against the Allies. In the Netherlands the illustrator Alfred Mazure refused to collaborate; the Germans tried to force his hand, but he obstinately refused to place his character, "Dick Bos," in the service of their cause. At the same time, in France, André Lachenal, alias André Daix, continued in the direction he had pursued before the war, illustrating for publications of the extreme right, such as *Le Franciste*. He would henceforth publish the series "Professor Nimbus" and "The Baron de Crésus" in *Le Matin*, a collaborationist paper. They all had a choice; Hergé also.

On October 17, 1940, *Le Soir-Jeunesse* began publishing the latest adventures of Tintin and Snowy, "Tintin in the Land of Black Gold." After a slow start consisting of a series of incidents that leave trails and clues along the way, Tintin sums up the situation as follows: "A tin can + a drowned man + five forged coins + Karaboudjan + a Japanese man + a letter + a kidnapping = a famous headache of a Chinese puzzle."[17] In any event, he sails away on a cargo ship and soon discovers that the shipment of cans of crabmeat in reality contain opium. To escape the smugglers who are in charge of the ship, he pushes off in a launch with Haddock, the depressed captain of the ship. The two somehow manage to board and gain control of a hydroplane, only to crash in the middle of Morocco. Sun, heat, thirst, mirages, physical exhaustion—only Snowy is happy because of the abundance of generously proportioned bones. They are rescued by Méharistes, members of the camel corps of Lieutenant Delcourt, commander of the base at Afghar. They continue their journey, trying to locate the boat. After countless races and pursuits, Tintin finally exposes all the activities of the gang and puts the smugglers behind bars.

Many deem this adventure unsuccessful because it seems to yoke two different stories together. But there is a certain charm to the whole, stemming from its exoticism and colonial nostalgia—for the French especially, evoking their holdings in North Africa. It remains important among the works of Hergé for introducing a new member of the Tintin family, one who enters and becomes completely and immediately absorbed into Tintin's universe. In subsequent books he would become increasingly

central and so popular that Hergé eventually had to insist in public that Tintin "was the hero of these adventures, not Captain Haddock."[18]

Physically he is easily identifiable: black hair and beard, wearing various suits, a blue turtleneck sweater with an anchor on the front, a merchant marine's cap on his head and a pipe clenched between his teeth. There is no mistaking him. He is immediately recognizable. He is more complicated than Tintin, perhaps because Hergé gave him a face that was much more expressive of an intense inner life.

Haddock seems manic depressive, alternating from being enthusiastic and impulsive to being sunk in a state of profound melancholy. In his despair he resembles Hergé himself when he was discouraged. In his euphoria he resembles his brother, Paul Remi, who had a tendency to brag. Haddock evolves in the course of several books, but his personality remains essentially the same: irascible and clumsy, rough but big-hearted, funny but never a clown. On the whole he is a touching character, who does and says too much and suffers accordingly. He is the personification of a sailor. Yet he is also a descendant of Falstaff and Sancho Panza, as well as reminiscent of the captain in "Katzenjammer Kids," which had so impressed Hergé.

Hergé's captain had the title "ad hoc" and was supposed to evoke the sea. He had appeared in Hergé's sketchbooks a number of years before his debut. Germaine maintained that she chose the name because smoked haddock was one of their favorite dishes, and Hergé had fond memories of eating it during a visit to England.[19] He wanted his character linked to Perfidious Albion and His British Majesty's Navy, in which there was no lack of Haddocks on boats in every latitude.

The two traits that most distinguish Haddock are his love of swearing and his love of alcohol. Haddock's vocabulary seems inexhaustible, although he is often rendered speechless. His expletives fall into two categories. The first is of a professional order ("landlubber!"), the second, of a moral or philosophical order ("guzzler!"). From his first adventure, as if to initiate the reader, Haddock gives a sample of his range. He happens to be chasing hostile Berbers in the middle of the desert: "Scoundrels! Boobs! Guttersnipes! Troglodytes! Nougat chewers! Savages! Little squirts! Embezzlers! Carpet peddlers! Iconoclasts! Rascals! Ectoplasms! Landlubbers! Bachi Bouzouks! Zulus! Jerrys! Cowards! Macaques! Parasites! Dopes!"[20]

With the captain, the imagination reigns; in this he is the opposite of Tintin. But despite the fact that they are worlds apart, or perhaps because of it, Haddock respects Tintin. From the very beginning Hergé has them

address each other as *vous,* the formal address, and it would remain thus. "The *tu* is the counterfeit currency of friendship."[21]

Finally Haddock is an alcoholic, inseparable from his bottle of whisky. This explains his depressive tendencies, his states of confusion and euphoria, his irascibility and its inevitable outcome. Yet it also doesn't. Captain Haddock is not to be judged; he is part of the family, front and center.

On November 19 of that year, with the presses ready to roll, Hergé and his colleagues were in the pressroom waiting for a dispatch announcing an accord between Léopold III and Hitler. The king went with "feet of lead," in his words, to a meeting at Berchtesgaden, going as prisoner to his jailer. He went to be informed and to plead the cause of the Belgian people. But one didn't interrupt the Führer to discuss such irrelevancies as the difficulties in finding basic supplies for a nation. The so-called dialogue became a monologue, Hitler's. Until then the king had complicated the occupation with his presence and attitude; afterward he was not an issue.[22]

The question of what was to become of Tintin, now that Nazi Germany had imposed itself on Europe, was much on Hergé's mind. The cub reporter with the soul of a Scout was out of his league. Either he went forward and grappled with his times, or he left the real world for an imaginary universe. Hergé chose both: confrontation and escape. One adventure would go in one direction, the other in the opposite. Hergé was a Gemini for life.

Shortly before Christmas 1940 the publication of *Tintin in the Land of Black Gold* in *Coeurs Vaillant* was suddenly stopped. Tintin was replaced by another tale. "Did Anastasie use her scissors again?" everyone asked. "Anastasie" was what they called the censor, the fear of all editors. (She was named for St. Anastasia, whose tongue was cut out for refusing the advances of the Emperor Valerian.) A dour spinster all in black, wielding an enormous pair of scissors to keep sensitive material out of the French press, she was the personification of censorship during World War I. The satiric review *Le Canard enchainé* (The Chained Duck) resurrected her at the start of World War II.

The only pages of the *Catholic Weekly* in which she used her powers carried the comic strips. Tintin had pride of place. His adventures had suffered several severe cuts by Anastasie: the allusion to Jews fighting Arabs in Palestine, the replacement of the word "rebels" with "combat troops," and the transformation of "Salomon Goldstein" into "Durand."[23] *Coeurs Vaillants,* which would remain Hergé's distributor in France during the occupation, offered Pétain unfailing support.

On January 1, 1941, Raymond De Becker called a meeting in his office of all his most important colleagues, Hergé among them. In a solemn tone the editor of *Le Soir* read them a letter from the palace: "I know that your position is not easy. You will have to struggle, you will be misunderstood, you will perhaps even be attacked, but you have to affirm Belgian sovereignty wherever necessary."[24]

Despite the changes in the actual situation, the king would not deviate from his position, whatever the impact of his mute protest. There was no unanimous opinion at *Le Soir*. There were in fact two worlds rubbing shoulders, and they tended to avoid each other. On one level, literally, was the editorial staff, and on the level above, the typesetters. Hergé was one of the few to walk up the ten steps separating them, which he did to help prepare the *Soir-Jeunesse* supplement. Hergé loved the atmosphere of the printing shop, the smell of nitric acid and of glue. Every time he appeared, the printers guessed that there was a storm brewing in editorial. There he would find Henri Lemaire, an old acquaintance from *Le Vingtième Siècle*. "What the hell are you doing here?"[25]

Henri Lemaire was convinced the Germans would eventually be defeated. "The day they [the Americans] decide to step in, you'll see your little pals take to their heels," he yelled out to Hergé.

"So, why haven't you enlisted?" Their exchange inevitably ended up with doors being slammed.

These scenes were repeated on a regular basis. Lemaire's colleagues warned him against saying too much lest he be reported to the management. Then there would be real trouble. Lemaire shrugged them off. He believe Remi would never turn him in. Hergé was a good guy who had simply gotten involved with the wrong people.[26]

Hergé was intelligent and cultivated, but he was not a deep thinker. Intuition and a keen sense of observation were his strengths. Aware of his limitations, he had always turned to others, such as Father Norbert Wallez, for guidance. Now it was Raymond De Becker whose encyclopedic knowledge, shrewd arguments, and lively wit impressed him, and whose editorials reflected what he felt in a confused way. It almost seemed as if Hergé had abdicated all critical sense; he could not foresee the consequences of De Becker's vanity.

De Becker was a man of action, teaming up with Édouard Didier and the journalist Pierre Daye to launch the publishing house Les Éditions de la Toison d'Or (Golden Fleece Editions). In reality they were the front men, as the capital was provided by the German trust Mundus, tied to

von Ribbentrop. According to internal memoranda, the Toison d'Or's mission was to disseminate German culture in Wallonia and France through the means of the French language itself.[27]

The launch of Toison d'Or coincided with the distribution of a document listing hundreds of books in French and Flemish that were to be removed from circulation and forbidden in Belgium. Drawn up in cooperation with Belgian professionals of the literary world, it had the imprimatur of General-Baron Alexander von Falkenhausen, the military governor of Belgium and the French departments of the Nord and the Pas-de-Calais. Its goal was to eliminate all works deemed anti-German. In other words, books by Communists, dissidents, Freemasons, and Jews. Interestingly the number of Belgian anti-German works was insignificant. The vast majority, 80 percent, of them were imported from Paris. Belgians complained that they were victims of French and English propaganda.[28]

Starting in May De Becker began holding regular meetings that were less about the newspaper than about the future of the nation. He was building a platform for "the One Party of the French Provinces of Belgium." Squeezed between France and Germany, Belgium had to become strong in order to avoid being absorbed. The tenets of the new party were fourfold: support the European Revolution; uphold the interest of the Walloons in the spirit of friendly existence with the Flemish within a federal state; respect the authority of the king in building an authoritarian and corporate state; and establish a policy of protecting the family, and the Belgian race, by statutes against Jews.[29]

De Becker and his friends were persuaded that they represented a vital political force. It was not a complete illusion, to the extent that as journalists they could influence public opinion on a daily basis. They were in conflict with Rex, the fascist party of Léon Degrelle, whose ambition was to be the head of the sole Walloon party. He accused them of confusing their readers with voters.[30]

On August 5 the embryonic One Party of the French Provinces of Belgium died. De Becker's initiative was judged premature by the German authorities. He announced to his staff, "Given the attitude of the German authorities toward all new political initiatives, it appears inopportune, until new orders come down, for us to continue our meetings."[31]

Conditions in Belgium continued to worsen, between the fear of a severe winter and the dire economic crisis of the country. There was talk of famine. Hergé would not suffer from this during the entire occupation. His solution was to make practical arrangements. The illustrated paper of

Lisbon, *O Papa Gaio*, continued to publish Tintin, and he asked his editor to take his royalties, deposit them, and every month use the money to buy provisions. For the duration of the war Hergé received parcels of figs, almonds, cans of fish, dried fruits, and sardines. He built up a stock in Portugal in order to help his family, and he was able to get Father Varzim, editor of the paper, to send packages of food through the Portuguese Red Cross to his brother, Paul, a prisoner of war in the stalag in Prenzlau, Germany.[32]

He seemed to have been spared the hardships of the occupation when suddenly, in the autumn of 1941, growing dissatisfaction with the king took a turn for the worse. The Belgian people were devoted to the memory of his late wife, the beautiful Queen Astrid, who had perished in an automobile accident. His popularity plunged suddenly with the announcement of his marriage to Mary-Lilian Baels, daughter of the former minister and governor of Western Flanders. Hergé's reaction was a desire to send copies of his latest work to the royal princes, printed on deluxe paper. His brother, Paul, had written of seeing a photo of Prince Baudouin reading the adventures of Tintin. Casterman had to explain to Hergé that this was not the time for such a gesture. Baudouin and Albert were nonetheless sent warmly dedicated books with special red endpapers stamped with the royal coat of arms. Hergé would do the same with all the subsequent volumes.

The new restrictions affected the newspaper *Le Soir* as much as Casterman. With paper in short supply, the supplement had to go. For a moment Hergé believed that they would ask him to bring Tintin's new adventure to a rapid conclusion. In fact they asked him to continue it, not on a weekly but on a daily basis. It appeared next to the stock market report.

The new arrangement forced Hergé to modify his narrative structure since he had to deliver twenty-four comic strips instead of twelve.[33] He acquired a new discipline in his work, relating to the rhythm, the position of the gags, ways to keep his readers in suspense, and the art of making them turn the page once they came to the last picture.

For Casterman the paper restriction also created serious problems. They never considered stopping publication of the books, but they asked Hergé to limit the number of pages. He immediately understood the special commercial requirements, especially in the French market, but he was worried that they would be to the detriment of the quality of the narrative. Abridged in this manner, his stories risked becoming brief vignettes, attractive in the format of a daily newspaper but less interesting as a book. He

worried that he would have to find a different subject every day, running the risk of diminishing his narratives to resemble Ricardo Gomez's Buffalo Bill comic strips, which represented the most elementary form of expression.

He especially did not want to compromise because for the first time the sales figures for his books had risen sharply, topping the 100,000 figure that had previously been his record. To help Casterman obtain the necessary quota of paper, Hergé intervened personally with the Occupation Authority. He returned several times to 39 Rue du Commerce, the Brussels headquarters of the Propaganda Abteilung, to plead his cause with those who controlled the paper supply. His hope was to obtain twelve tons of paper of the thirty he requested.[34] His new Tintin book was ready to be published, and he wanted to take advantage of the demand.

Hergé wanted a new title for the book based on the serial *The Land of Black Gold*. At first he thought of calling it "The Red Crab," which would fit with the titles of the previous books, *The Blue Lotus* and *The Black Island*. He wanted readers to feel that each book was part of a series. But it was too late, because he had provisionally used *The Crab with the Golden Claws*, and this title appeared on the back of the other reprinted volumes. At least he did manage at the last minute to change the type for his name at the top of the cover, from cursive to block letters.[35] Hergé never stopped fighting with the printers at Casterman over his covers. He had submitted a bright and vivid image, only to see proofs of a pale sky, washed-out sand, camels without contrast. He went into a rage, demanding that they reprint.[36]

Three weeks before Christmas his efforts were rewarded. Casterman's edition was sold out, and the presses could not meet the demand: the stock of paper was gone. Casterman even had to cancel the advertisements in *Le Soir* for the latest book.[37] While waiting for their copies of *The Crab with the Golden Claws*, readers bought up copies of the previous Tintin books.

Hergé was constantly working on new projects. Only Simenon could compare in sustaining such a level of work. In 1941, at the end of one book and before starting his next, Hergé agreed to work with Robert du Bois de Vroylande, illustrating a volume of his fables. De Vroylande was a collaborator and former editor in chief of Rex Editions. Hergé would receive 10 percent of the sale price of each book, for which he did both the cover and the illustrations.

Two of the ten fables in the collection reflected their moment. In one the main character is an Englishman who is unrelentingly ridiculed. In the other the Jews are the target. In the autumn of 1941 Jewish residents of

Belgium—whether Belgians, foreigners, or stateless—were all second-class citizens. They no longer had the right to work as government clerks, lawyers, teachers, journalists, or administrators. Confined to four cities (Antwerp, Brussels, Liège, and Charleroi), they were not allowed to go outside between eight in the evening and seven in the morning.

Hergé's view was that this was all part of the so-called human comedy. The fable and his drawings were meant to be satirical. So what if they were offensive to some?[38]

He would pursue the same logic in Tintin's new adventure, *The Shooting Star*, which began to appear in *Le Soir* on October 29, 1941. In the first panel Tintin becomes intrigued by the unexpected presence of a large star in the constellation of the Big Dipper. He heads for the observatory, where, with the help of Decimus Phostle, he discovers that a fiery comet is headed straight for Earth. The end of the world is imminent: packs of rats flee the sewers, car tires burst, and the asphalt melts beneath an abnormally torrid sun. Meanwhile a self-declared visionary calling himself Philippulus the Prophet blames Tintin and predicts worse catastrophes.

In fact there is only a mild earthquake, and the comet misses by 25,000 miles (45,000 kilometers). But a piece of it falls into the Arctic Ocean, enabling Decimus Phostle to verify a new metal he has named Phostlite—if he can recover it. An expedition is organized by the scientist, including Tintin and Captain Haddock, now promoted to the Society of Sober Sailors, as commander of the SS *Aurora*. A huge crowd gathers to see them off, including the Thom(p)sons and Quick and Flupke. It is clear that the journey will not be a restful cruise.

An American banker named Blumenstein has outfitted a rival expedition with the same goal, but from motives that are far from scientific. A caricature of New York capitalism, underhanded and arrogant, Blumenstein plans to make huge profits from this new metal. He will stop at nothing to achieve his ends. Despite all sorts of setbacks, Tintin succeeds in planting the flag of the European team on the meteorite first. Due to mechanical troubles, the boat is immobilized, but the brave reporter and his dog stay with the meteor. Tintin witnesses amazing phenomena: giant mushrooms that grow before his eyes and then explode; apple cores that sprout apple trees, producing fruit as large as bowling balls. Shaken by an earthquake, the meteor is engulfed by giant waves. Tintin is saved in the nick of time by a lifeboat, after rescuing Snowy and salvaging a chunk of Phostlite. Science triumphs over finance, morality is upheld (though whisky gets the last word).

Never had a Tintin adventure begun in so apocalyptic a manner; the competition takes place in an atmosphere of anguish and stress. At every turn there is falsehood, fakery, and traps. Hergé's escapism seems firmly anchored in the perceptions of the moment, a sort of battle between good Europeans (representing the Axis powers and neutral countries) and bad Americans. Published just as America was beginning to shift away from neutrality toward German-occupied Europe, the rivalry in the book was not so innocent.

Three weeks after the adventure began to appear in *Le Soir* the U.S. government authorized the defensive arming of its merchant ships entering the war zones. In December, after the surprise attack against the American fleet in Pearl Harbor, first Japan, then Germany and Italy declared war against the United States. It is clear in Hergé's portrayal of them that the Americans are not the heroes, and they lose. There is a remarkable correlation between Hergé's strip and *Le Soir*'s editorials.

Nonetheless the story cannot be reduced to one dimension. Some interpret it as illustrating the conflict between science and religion; others believe it is an escapist fantasy. Madness is a recurrent theme, exemplified by the presence of spiders. Spiders pursue our hero from beginning to end, appearing when least expected, sowing fear and behaving like agents of ill omen. Certainly the words "crazy" and "insane" appear in other adventures, but with the spiders insanity enters the texture of the narrative. There is an unreality in the whole adventure.[39] Even Hergé had to admit that outside his comic strip the ship would have sunk.[40]

There is indeed a distinct lack of scientific accuracy in the narrative, which is surprising coming from someone as maniacally dedicated to detail as Hergé. Neither a comet nor an asteroid could generate the intense heat depicted at the beginning of the story. Only a white dwarf star could have that effect. But had such a star entered the solar system there would be nobody left to see it, as it would have destroyed everything. Moreover a comet falling to earth would not float on the surface of the sea but plunge down, causing a tsunami of unimaginable magnitude.[41] Clearly Hergé was following his imagination and conscience.

The character of the banker Blumenstein, the incarnation of evil, proves that he was also following the prejudices of his time. Of this anti-Semitic caricature Hergé would later say, "That was the style then." Between October 1941, when the series started, and its conclusion in May 1942, a number of regulations were passed forbidding the Jews of Belgium from leaving the country and threatening them with being interned in work (all

Belgians were subject to forced labor). Six days after the end of the serial, wearing the yellow star became mandatory.[42]

At the moment Hergé was creating Blumenstein, the collaborationist press was pointing out that the Liberal politician Camille Gutt, minister of finance of the Belgian government-in-exile, was in reality Gutt*stein*. And *Le Soir*, in its issue of March 4, 1941, started "investigating" the Jewish influence on European culture, publishing four articles under the heading "The Jews and Us." The conclusions willy-nilly denounced their appearance, tenacity, cunning, and the harm they had visited on Belgium. "Our anti-Semitism is racial in nature," it concluded.[43]

In his article written for this issue, "Jews in Contemporary Literature," *Le Soir*'s literary critic, Paul de Man, asserted that "a solution of the Jewish problem" would be "the creation of a colony isolated from Europe." Such a colony would have no "negative consequences for the literary life of the West," which "would lose, in all, a few personalities of mediocre value and would continue, as in the past, to develop according to its great evolutionary laws."[44]

Whether in the political commentary, or the cultural columns, or the hugely popular comic strips, there was a similar tone to the "stolen" *Le Soir* throughout.

Between 1940 and 1943 de Man wrote more than two hundred articles for *Le Soir* and also wrote for the German-sponsored Flemish-language paper *Het Vlaamsche Land*. It should be noted that of these, only two were overtly anti-Semitic. His last article for *Le Soir* was published in November 1942. Two days after the liberation of Antwerp in September 1944 he was denounced as a collaborator. Although brought before a military tribunal, he was released in May 1945 for lack of evidence.

After the war he invested in an art book publishing house, Éditions Hermes, which soon went bankrupt. In 1947 de Man fled Antwerp to evade his creditors, leaving behind his wife, Anaïde Baraghian, and their three sons. They soon emigrated to Argentina, where her family had settled after the war.

Once in the United States de Man secured a position teaching French at Bard College, where he met a student who became his second wife and started a new family. He continued his studies, earning a Ph.D. in French literature from Harvard, thus beginning a long and illustrious career, becoming a professor of comparative literature at Yale and the leading light of what became known as the Yale School. He died in 1983, but his wartime writing remains a subject of great controversy.

In 1942 paper continued to be rigidly rationed, and finding a supply was a major problem. Hergé's friend Paul Jamin tapped all his relations and gained access to a mysterious person (never named in the correspondence as a measure of precaution) who granted Casterman a large quantity of paper at a cost lower than black market prices.[45] In the spring the press received a shipment of ten tons.

As the book neared publication, Hergé hesitated between two titles: *The Shooting Star* and *The Mysterious Comet*. Neither was really satisfactory, but Casterman had nothing better to suggest. They preferred the first title but balked at placing a gold star in the *o* of *étoile,* as Hergé had wanted. The idea was dropped for technical reasons and because it would not have worked with foreign translations. Also, what would people have said at the image of a gold star on his cover? No one had even thought about that.

On March 5, 1942, Radio-Brussels presented a short interview with Hergé. The bilingual broadcast was now in French and German; it was not under German influence, it was under German control. The news gave minute details of the Allied troops' retreat on the island of Java and the Bolshevik losses on the eastern front, a precise summary of the British bombing of Paris, and a report on the death of the Duke of Aoste that deeply moved Il Duce. Finally it announced the opening of an exhibition of German books at the Palais des Beaux-Arts of Brussels.

People tuned in because they wanted to hear Tintin, but what came across was Hergé's shyness and natural reserve. His laconic answers seemed to unnerve his interviewer, the journalist André Colard, who asked questions about his lack of formal training and his method of working. Hergé spoke not as an illustrator, but as a film director.

"I consider my stories as films. Thus, no narration, no descriptions: I give all the importance to the picture. But my films are 100 percent talkies, with sound effects, the dialogue coming directly from the mouths of the characters."

"Yes, in fact you use all the film techniques—close-ups, panning, overhead perspectives, etc."

"I even have subtitles, but I rarely use them except sometimes to indicate the passage of time: for example, 'eight days later' or 'meanwhile.' As in films, time is the most difficult thing to represent."

"Since we're talking in movie terms, tell us about your script."

"I usually take a general theme, a canvas, on which I embroider a story. . . . I jot down ideas one after the other as they come to me. I accumulate gags, discoveries as I think of them. Everything is noted directly in my drawings and very often reworked until I obtain the best result."

"Then comes the cutting and editing."

"Absolutely. Actually, it comes down to making the story fit into the framework of the weekly or daily publication, as is the case."

"What exactly are the problems you encounter?"

"First, creating a connection with the drawings of the previous day. Then making sure that 'something happens.' Last, ending with a scene that anticipates the next day's drawings."

"Leaving the reader in suspense."

"Naturally! If the reader guessed everything that followed he would lose all interest. That's why you have to find the right balance between the comic and dramatic elements."

At the end of the interview Hergé praised his friend Jam, calling him the only great caricaturist in Belgium. Then he mentioned two pro-German newspapers that published his comic strip and said, memorably and perhaps unconsciously, that they had "enabled" him to "collaborate."[46]

Featured on the cover of the popular magazine *Voilà*, Hergé was an illustrator much in demand under the occupation. But even he was not spared censorship. Lieutenant Karowsky and Captain Karduc, names right out of a comic strip, were the censors from the Propaganda Abteilung who made sure that *Le Soir* toed the line.

And Casterman, already anticipating the risks they ran, urged Hergé to play it safe, such as by attenuating the anti-Japanese spirit of *The Blue Lotus*. The censors pointed out that the airplane in *King Ottokar's Scepter* was a Heinkel, the manufacturer of much of the Luftwaffe's air fleet and many of the bombers used in the Battle of Britain.[47] Hergé didn't have to be told twice. He immediately asked his editors to change the name on the

airplane cabin. "If it's too late," he added, "too bad! Heinkel will continue to benefit from this free publicity."[48]

Still, Hergé wanted to avoid problems at all costs. It wasn't the time to make waves. *Junior*, one of the best weeklies, featuring among others Tarzan and Charlie Chan since 1936, had to stop publication. So too *Le Journal de Mickey*, which was restricted to arbitrary publication dates, because the Huns in "Prince Valiant" were not to the censors' taste. As *The Crab with the Golden Claws* was starting publication in *Coeurs Vaillants* in France, Hergé agreed to let the separatists from Brittany, favored by the Occupation Authorities, start serial publication of *Tintin in the Land of the Soviets* in *O Lo Lê*, their new periodical for young people.[49]

By spring 1942, with new color-offset printing technology installed at the Casterman plant in Tournai, Hergé tried to focus solely on Tintin and Snowy. He turned down every offer that took him away from his characters. Solicited on every side to merchandise his characters in puzzles, games, coloring books, and so on, he asked Casterman to handle it, thinking it logical to concentrate his creative and commercial business in the same hands.[50] Casterman, however, did not want to expand from bookstores into the stationery stores, so Hergé turned to an agent named Bernard Thiéry. The terms were that Thiéry would negotiate all contracts for him, with exclusive right to represent him in Belgium as well as in foreign countries over reproduction of the images of Tintin and Snowy. On receiving the contract Hergé was shocked by the commissions Thiéry claimed—40 percent of all earnings—but agreed on the condition that this would apply only to existing work and not to any new illustrations Hergé created. Soon Hergé was reproaching his agent for not making an effort to pursue stationery, postcards, and wallpaper potential. Positive or negative, he wanted to see results.[51] He grew suspicious about Thiéry but let matters stand rather than risk a confrontation, which would just waste his time.

Hergé was simply overwhelmed with work. Between the daily serial in *Le Soir* and preparing the Casterman editions, as well as the reissuing of his previous works, he was completely exhausted. After he visited the newly installed offset presses at Tournai, he realized that he alone could not oversee the whole process of reformatting his earlier works, coloring and reediting them to fit the sixty-two-page limit. So much had to be redrawn. Doing it all himself would mean resigning from *Le Soir*, which he did not want to contemplate.

He had been considering putting together a sort of studio, which would help him produce books adapted to the new format and ready to go to

press. He would no longer be the sole creator of every aspect of the book, the unique illustrator and scriptwriter of his stories and everything involving them. On the other hand, taking on assistants seemed inevitable and inescapable, given the growth of demand. Nonetheless he was determined that nothing would cast doubt that the adventures of Tintin and Snowy were his and his alone.

Hergé began to search for backup illustrators. This wasn't merely a matter of finding part-time assistants. Whoever he hired needed time to assimilate the work.[52] In mid-March he hired on a trial basis a young illustrator named Alice Devos, at the salary of 1,200 francs a month (current equivalent, $340). The trial period must have been a success, because her salary was quickly increased to 1,500 francs (current equivalent, $431).[53] But in Hergé's eyes she was only a skilled worker, whereas he really needed a heavyweight. He had someone in mind but doubted whether that person would even consider such an offer.

A year earlier at the Royal Theatre in Brussels Hergé had attended a play, *Tintin in India, or the Mystery of the Blue Diamond,* a detective drama for children in three acts he had written with Jacques Van Melkebeke. It was an exotic piece of entertainment that made no great impression in the theater world. The audience loved seeing their hero on paper materialize on stage. Hergé was pleased but had been exhausted by the effort of overseeing every detail of the production. He even had a clause inserted in the contract with the director of the theater that nothing could be done without his approval, "so that the dramatizations of Tintin would maintain the atmosphere of the books."[54]

After the performance Van Melkebeke introduced Hergé to Edgar P. Jacobs, who invited them up to his studio across from the offices of *Le Soir* on the Rue Royal. Jacobs was an imposing figure with a sonorous voice, but a clownish quality (he was clumsy) made him seem like a comic book character. He never took himself too seriously. Nonetheless he had a keen sense for drama and a penchant for the theatrical. History and drawing were hobbies compared to his love of music, opera in particular.

On a glacially cold evening in February 1942 Hergé invited Jacobs to dinner at his house in the Boistford neighborhood of Brussels. Jacobs wondered what was up, because their mutual friend, Van Melkebeke, had not been invited. He soon found out. Hergé did not want any witnesses to his proposal to Jacobs, which was that he become his primary collaborator. He was prepared to take him on full time and pay him accordingly. But he needed an answer before he could speak to Casterman about the

arrangement.[55] Jacobs didn't turn him down, but neither could he accept the offer on the spot. He had just launched a comic strip and wanted to complete the project before starting work with Hergé. It meant a delay of several months at least.

ONLY ONCE DID TINTIN APPEAR in his professional capacity as a reporter outside of the comic strip in *Le Soir*. A solitary drawing has him calling his assignment editor and asking for a month's leave. "I need time to prepare for my departure to search for *Red Rackham's Treasure*," he explains.

Hergé had in effect started a new adventure. It opens with a news item about the sudden surge of crimes in Brussels, caused by an organized ring of pickpockets. The Thom(p)sons are on the case, but while strolling through the Old Market home of Brussels' antique shops and secondhand dealers, their wallets are stolen. Tintin for his part finds an old model ship he likes and purchases it. Two collectors immediately try to buy it away from him, but Tintin is determined to keep it. He wants to give it to Captain Haddock as a present. On returning home Tintin shows it to the Captain, who is stunned to discover its similarity to the *Unicorn*, a ship pictured in a painting of his ancestor, Sir Francis Haddock, who had served under Charles II and was famous for his drinking and cursing.

Later thieves break into Tintin's empty apartment, ransack it, and steal the ship. On his return Tintin by chance finds what the thieves were really looking for: a mysterious message that has fallen out of the ship's mast, where it had been hidden. Along with indecipherable signs, he can make out the following lines: "Three brothers united. Three unicorns sailing in company under the noonday sun will speak of the South. For 'tis from the light that light will dawn. And then shine forth."

Captain Haddock meanwhile finds and reads his ancestor's journals. He identifies completely with Sir Francis as he narrates in vivid detail his exciting journey. Setting sail from Barbado in the West Indies to Europe with a cargo of rum, his ship was attacked and boarded by pirates. Captain Francis Haddock was taken prisoner by the pirate chieftain Red Rackham, who boastfully showed him his hoard of diamonds taken from the Spanish and promised him a slow death. Captain Haddock managed to free himself, setting fire to the kegs of gunpowder in the hold before making his escape. Reaching an island where he was befriended by the natives, he remained there until a passing ship picked him up and he returned to his home, Marlinspike Hall. On the last page of his journal he included a will, leaving three models of the *Unicorn*, one for each of his three sons. In the main

mast of each was hidden a piece of parchment. Bringing together the three pieces would reveal the location of Red Rackham's treasure.

Searching for the missing pieces of the map, Tintin and Captain Haddock narrowly escape attempts on their lives, until the young reporter's luck runs out and he's kidnapped by the Bird brothers, antique dealers and current owners of Marlinspike Hall, who imprison him in the basement and try to make him reveal the whereabouts of the pieces of the map. Tintin escapes and warns the Captain, and they manage to catch one of the brothers. Finally they come into possession of all three pieces of the map. Examining it under a bright light, they discover the exact location of the *Unicorn*. What happens next is another story. As for the wallets, they were not stolen by a gang of pickpockets but by a kleptomaniac, a collector of wallets—a detail right out of Hitchcock.

The tale was clearly influenced by Robert Louis Stevenson's *Treasure Island* in spirit if not in detail and seemed to cater to a need for escapism. In 1942 the comic strips in *Le Soir* were avidly read in prisons and camps.

The ship was not entirely a figment of Hergé's imagination. After making an initial sketch, Hergé consulted his friend Gérard Liger-Belair, secretary of the Federation of Catholic Scouts, who was the son of a former naval officer and owned a shop in Brussels specializing in model ships. In Liger-Belair's subsequent research in archives and libraries he came across not just one, but three *Unicorn*s: a British frigate, a Dutch merchant ship, and a French battleship. Intrigued by the battleship, he discovered in a work of the period titled *Architectura Navalis* detailed drawings of ships that included a third-class battleship with fifty-six cannon in the navy of Louis XIV, dating from around 1690. The figure of the unicorn on the prow was borrowed from a British frigate.[56] Hergé first made a pencil sketch of the plan prepared by Liger-Belair, on the scale of 1/100, then built a scale model. He was so taken with the ship that it inspired the title for his book, *The Secret of the Unicorn*.[57] The original *Unicorn* in Admiral de Tourville's squadron sank in the Battle of La Hougue, the decisive naval battle between the English and the French during the Nine Years' War.

This new adventure marked a new development in Hergé's work, a flight from the topical to epics of pirate adventures set in distant horizons, with shipwrecks and buried treasures. In the character of Sir Francis Haddock, captured in all his glory in an ancestral portrait, we might make out a more intimate specter: that of Hergé's own mysterious, aristocratic

ancestor. He seems to have incorporated his family secret into his work and, consciously or not, may have been trying to exorcise his own demons.

OTHER DEMONS WERE AFOOT: at this time the Germans began taking action on their long-held plans. In autumn 1942 the streets of Paris and Brussels resounded with the terrible confusion of the great roundups. It became clear what all the regulations during the previous two years had been leading up to: the legal isolation of the Jews from the rest of the population. Their only purpose was to make ready for a solution of "the Jewish problem," which had only recently become "the final solution." The Belgian police turned them over to the Nazi police, a matter between colleagues, so to speak. They were being sent "there"; no one really wanted to know where "there" was. The Belgians found this terribly unjust, but nevertheless they did nothing. This was the key to the Belgian paradox: a hostility to persecution without any particular sympathy for Jews. But the sight of uniformed agents tearing children from the arms of their mothers was the last straw, and some Belgians organized associations to help, often at the risk of their own lives.[58] This of course was very far from the position expressed by *Le Soir* early in the first year of the occupation: "The transfer out of the West of all the Jews who are still found there is the only solution to eradicate from the body of Europe the foreign element that threatens its moral and physical health."[59]

Working at a newspaper, Hergé had access to all the news, and he received privileged information from his well-placed friends. Thus in October he could warn his editors of what was going to happen during the rest of the year, including the closing of certain industries to free up the supply of workers to meet the increased German demands for forced labor.[60]

His friend and editor in chief, Raymond De Becker, had switched to the fascist Rex Party, conferring on Léon Degrelle and his party a degree of respectability they had previously lacked. At a rally at the Sports Palace of Brussels, De Becker gave a speech announcing his allegiance to the ideals of Rex. In an editorial entitled "Marching toward Unity" and published the next day on the front page of *Le Soir*, he repeated the arguments of the Rexists, now without reservation or hindrance.[61] The editorial proclaimed the Rex Party not only the one party but the only hope of a strong Belgian nation and a German Europe. He declared war on "the political clergy, nonconformists, the idle and the swing voters, without forgetting those

parasites, the 130,000 customers of cafés."[62] Years later Hergé argued that
the editorial team at Le Soir had in no way been Rexist and that De Becker
himself was a committed anti-Rexist. "As for me, I have never been an
adherent of Rexism, for which I have always had an aversion."[63]

Hergé's memory is selective here, condensing or eliding events that did
not fit his sense of the past, especially when his closest friends were
involved. On the evening of January 17, 1943, the idyll of collaboration
came to an abrupt end at a new rally at the Sports Palace. This time Léon
Degrelle, just returned from Berlin, was the speaker. He launched into a
radical speech that made official his recent collusion with Himmler and, in
consequence, that of the Rex Party with the SS. In his exhortation he
asserted Wallonia's German roots and dreamed out loud about making
Belgium a part of the German Empire, abandoning the principles of a
united Belgian state. The Walloons who had been seduced by his ideas and
dynamism now turned their backs on him. De Becker immediately sent a
letter to Degrelle, breaking off any association, refusing even the thought
of the annexation of Belgium to the German Empire or of any German-
Walloon pact that excluded the Flemish or in any way diminished the
primacy of the monarchy.[64]

Was Hergé as innocent as Tintin? It seems doubtful. In the two dailies
where he worked, Hergé managed each time to thrive. Although about
thirty members of the Le Soir staff were sent into forced labor in Germany,
he knew that he would never be bothered. When the air-raid sirens sounded
and everyone rushed to the basements, he was among those who stayed
behind. It was as if he felt protected.[65]

Hergé and Germaine continued to pay regular visits to Father Wallez in
the Abbey of Aulne, where he did more than simply devote himself exclu-
sively to the restoration of the monastery. In favor of the integration of his
country into the new order of Europe, he gave a lecture titled "The Positives
and Negatives of the Walloons."[66] He was immediately reprimanded by the
bishop of Tournai, who reminded him of his obligation to remain silent.[67]

Though Father Wallez's attempt to return to public life failed, Hergé
still saw nothing wrong with his ideas; in his eyes the priest remained
beyond reproach. During a visit to the abbey he made the acquaintance
of a German officer named Burckas, stationed in Mons. They had a
friendly conversation in which Hergé became unusually chatty and expan-
sive, answering questions without hesitation. The next day he had an
autographed copy of The Secret of the Unicorn delivered to Burckas.
Shortly thereafter his editor at Casterman told him that they had received

a particularly inquisitorial visit from Mr. Kreift of the Occupational Authorities, accompanied by an officer named Burckas, who seemed awfully well informed.[68] Hergé was astounded, and it was not feigned. He had encountered the officer in the home of Father Wallez, and thus he had assumed there could be no danger.

In February 1943 the news spread that the Germans had lost the battle of Stalingrad. The surrender of the army commanded by Marshal von Paulus was as important strategically as symbolically. *Le Soir* began daily publication of the new adventures of Tintin and Snowy. The story would be told over seven months and in 183 comic strips. The previous story had ended a month earlier, and after a month of suspense *The Secret of the Unicorn* had a sequel.

HAVING SUCCEEDED IN PINPOINTING the location of Red Rackham's treasure, Captain Haddock and Tintin make haste to retrieve it. After a press announcement of their planned expedition, they are assailed by imposters with improbable genealogies who demand their rightful part of the future loot. The Captain sends them all packing, all except that is for one man, a scientist named Cuthbert Calculus. Professor Calculus has all the characteristics of an absent-minded professor; it's impossible to tell whether he's a genius or a lunatic. His clothing is archaic, his air of distraction a source of infinite gags; so too his deafness. All of this makes him a charming if exhausting character but also irresistible. Unlike the others, he is not motivated by greed. He simply functions on a different wavelength from everyone else. Though opposites, Captain Haddock, who is always talking, is inseparable from Professor Calculus, who is stone deaf.

The figure of the absent-minded professor—distracted, clumsy, gentle, disconnected from any reality other than scientific—is so universal that it would be inaccurate to point to any one source, such as the scientist in "Katzenjammer Kids." Two others might be Hergé's own father, Alexis Remi, always chivalrous, and Charlie Chaplin, the man who wipes his feet on the doormat before leaving the house in *How to Make Movies* (1919).

For the description of Professor Calculus, Hergé was inspired by the Swiss physicist Auguste Piccard, who invented the balloon with an air-tight basket to ascend into the stratosphere (except that he was as tall as Professor Calculus is short).[69] The supreme irony of history is that Professor Picard tested his bathyscaphe, the first self-contained diving craft, five years after Professor Calculus sent his mini-submarine down to investigate the wreckage of the *Unicorn*.

Our heroes set sail from a port on the Atlantic aboard the trawler *Sirius*. They are soon joined by the detectives Thom(p)son, who have learned that the antique dealer Bird has escaped from prison, so they invite themselves at the last minute to protect the Captain. Unbeknown to them, Professor Calculus is a stowaway, hiding in a lifeboat. He has brought with him his latest invention, a mini-submarine in the shape of a shark.

After many adventures Tintin, using the submarine, discovers the location of the sunken *Unicorn*. He brings up a gold cross and a bottle of rum. After much searching they also bring up an old chest containing fragments of parchment with enigmatic signs on them. The Professor manages to piece them together, and they decipher the message. The key to solving the mystery is to be found neither at the bottom of the ocean nor on the desert island where Sir Francis Haddock had found refuge, but back home. Using the money paid by the government for the patent on his submarine, Calculus enables Captain Haddock to buy back his ancestral home, Marlinspike Hall.

The Secret of the Unicorn and *Red Rackham's Treasure* reveal Hergé at a new level in his art. These adventures are among the most popular in the series because they are the visual continuation of a literary universe that stretches from Jules Verne to Pierre Benoit, passing by Robert Louis Stevenson and Joseph Conrad. By completing Tintin's family with Professor Calculus and giving them Marlinspike Hall as their home port, Hergé has settled them. (Interestingly he moved his characters into a communal residence at the same time that he himself purchased a property near Brussels, in Céroux-Mousty.) This does not prevent them from traveling, but it does give them a home to which to return.[70] It is, by the way, a stately British estate, but the façade and interior are inspired by Chateau de Cheverny in the Loir-et-Cher.[71]

But neither Marlinspike Hall nor the introduction of Professor Calculus is enough to confer on *The Secret of the Unicorn* and *Red Rackham's Treasure* the status of "key" works. They signal a break as Hergé turned from the political sphere to a more private and familial drama, in which humor is central.[72]

Professor Calculus embodies the gentle madness and subtle humor in comic strips. The delirious professor never understands anything, except when Tintin is in danger; then he is capable of a normal conversation.[73] Around him everyone tries to follow what he means and not lose the flow of the story. The gags are assured and unforced and not only situational but linguistic. Hergé gives himself over to it all, joyfully. Calculus: "Say,

Captain, was that a fish, that large animal that just jumped out of the water over there?" Haddock: "No, that was a grand piano."

The success of *Red Rackham's Treasure* was not a foregone conclusion. Hergé knew this better than anyone. Privately he admitted that he was proud to have accomplished so much with a plot that he himself thought "excessively thin."[74]

ON SEPTEMBER 3, 1943, Raymond De Becker called a special meeting of the editorial staff. Mussolini had been arrested and Italy had just surrendered. De Becker wanted to address his colleagues' concerns about the possibility of Germany's being defeated. In a long speech he harkened back to the Belgian surrender of 1940: "My friends, the fundamental psychology of the Germans has remained the same despite National-Socialism. It's characterized by undoubted good will, but also by being extremely out of touch with reality, stemming from their inability to grasp the psychological nature of other people."

Some wondered whether the time hadn't come to change sides. De Becker warned that this sort of thing, done too suddenly, risked the breakup of everything. He recognized that they had to evolve but argued, "We must remain at our post to defend the interests of Belgium and the West as much as the Germans will permit us to do so. We are politically committed to a course we must defend. The political unity of Belgium is not possible at this time but our moral solidarity is indispensable. That is why we must be very reserved in relation to everything about German propaganda. We are not a German propaganda agency, but a Belgian institution collaborating with the Germans, and that is the directive I have always given you."

De Becker warned his staff to be wary of the brand of German domination advocated by Rex, which favored German-English reconciliation and called for European unity.[75] He still dreamed of making the aims of Belgian Nationalism mesh with the interests of the German Embassy. It was a balancing act between realpolitik and utopianism.

A month after his speech De Becker was removed from office by his former supporters. The Propaganda Abteilung had him placed under surveillance and house arrest and then transported to a hotel in Austria. His job was offered to the writer-journalist Robert Poulet, a World War I hero, author of the best-selling novel *Handji* (1931). However, Poulet was scandalized when he saw a portrait of King Léopold III hanging on the wall next to that of Hitler at a festival celebrating the Walloon Guards.

Collaboration had its limits. "I realize everything that is due to the great European hope, and I would be the last to refuse recognition of the genius of the German Chancellor, or the importance of his services to the continental community. But there is a question of patriotic tact."[76] He turned down the Propaganda Office's offer in order to devote himself to his own writing.

The day after the publication of the conclusion of *Red Rackham's Treasure* Hergé was absorbed with the dilemma of the next adventure of Tintin. He was under pressure to produce it but saw no way of doing that. He was therefore being forced to do what he had not done since his work had become a success: illustrate someone else's story. The project came out of a casual conversation with his colleague and friend Paul Kinnet in a café on the Rue Royale. Kinnet, a writer of detective stories, asked if he could use the Thom(p)sons in one of his stories. "Lend them to me and in a day or two I will give you the first part of my story already broken down into pages, and all you have to do is illustrate them," he assured Hergé, adding that this would relieve him of having to write a scenario, thus giving him time to focus on his drawings.[77]

The experiment would last only a month, running to some forty comic strips, but Hergé was glad he had not killed off the Thom(p)sons, an option he had considered before the war.

Just before the downfall of De Becker, Hergé had been asked by another collaborationist paper, *L'Avenir*, to join their staff. He refused regretfully, remaining loyal to *Le Soir*. Then he was asked to create another Tintin-like illustrated series, which he refused out of hand.[78] He was being very prudent. He was preparing to start publishing *The Shooting Star* as a daily comic strip in the Flemish-language collaborationist paper *Het Laatste Nieuws*, but Charles Lesne warned him to postpone it: "I wonder . . . if it would not be more advisable for you to wait for the end of the war before you start publishing your illustrations in newspapers. It won't be long before the end of hostilities, and once the war is over there could be reactions which, although unjustified, would be extremely unfortunate. Have you thought about the consequences?"[79]

Lesne was looking ahead. Listening to the BBC like the majority of his compatriots, he knew that nine months earlier in London the Belgian government-in-exile had written a document outlining the legal and political basis for eventually dealing with collaborators. The legal decree was not notable for its flexibility. It would punish all those who helped the enemy, especially those engaged in propaganda.

Hergé knew of this decree but acted as if the threat were negligible. Whether from self-deception or denial, he also revealed the arrogance of those beginning to face a reckoning. Some believed his reply to his editor expressed this state of mind, which some would consider suicidal:

Now is the time to appear in the greatest number of newspapers possible, even if some of these papers are destined to disappear or change direction after the war. In any case I will have reached the largest public. It would be an excellent plan considering that when it's all over, American comic books will reappear on the scene backed by the propaganda of animated films. The reactions that you fear are entirely possible, I'd say most probable. There are unmistakable signs of it. But I'm already listed among "traitors" for having published my illustrations in *Le Soir*, for which I will be hanged or executed (they have not decided on this point). The worst that can happen to me is that having been shot or hanged for my collaboration with *Le Soir*, I will be executed again, or rehung, for my collaboration with *Laatste Nieuws* and reshot, and rehung, for my collaboration with *L'Afemeen Nieuws* in which "Quick and Flupke" have appeared since September 1940. The most horrible is being hung or shot for the first time. After that, it seems you get used to it. Whatever happens, I am the only one condemned. But on the other hand, think of the wonderful publicity this will give the books.[80]

On November 9, 1943, as readers of *Le Soir* stopped at newsstands to pick up their favorite newspaper on their way home, they discovered a radical change in tone. It was impertinent, funny, and insolent and, for once, very well informed. It seemed abnormally "de-Nazified," and for a very good reason: it was a fake *Le Soir*. For several hours the whole country shook with laughter. Militants of the Front for Belgian Independence had thrown fifty thousand copies of their "rag" back in the Germans' faces, launching a "southern satire with Anglo-Saxon bluff."[81] For a moment at least, Belgium had found again its sense of humor, laughing at Raymond De Becker and his collaborationist cohort in the press. Forged *Soir* versus stolen *Soir*. The editorial staff at *Le Soir* read it avidly, laughing feebly if laughing at all. It is not known how Hergé reacted to it.

In 1943 the censorship crackdown on the press became increasingly severe. In Paris *Coeurs Vaillants* was raided by the Gestapo, who shut its offices on the Rue de Fleurus and sent two chaplains to Fresne Prison for three months. The only charge they could come up with was that the paper

was promoting Scouting, which was forbidden.[82] The magazine *Spirou* ceased publication when Dupuis, the editor, refused the Propaganda Abteilung's demand that they place a German on its governing board.

Still, some of the most famous illustrators worked with the remaining collaborationist newspapers. In exchange for a guaranteed number of subscriptions by the Ministry of the Colonies, and with subsidies from the Ministry of Information, Alain Saint-Ogan placed his "Benjamin" comic strips at the service of Vichy propagandists who wanted to address young readers directly.[83] André Daix published his "Professor Nimbus" in the popular Parisian daily *Le Matin*. People had a laugh reading Henry Coson's pamphlet "The Judeo-Masons' Hold on the Press for Children," a violent diatribe against those accused of Americanizing all the adolescents of France. As Coson couldn't overlook the fact that the popular Daix had been publishing his illustrations in *Le Journal de Mickey,* he simply said that Daix had been shamefully exploited.[84] In Hollywood Donald Duck won the first and only Oscar of his career for his role in the satirical anti-Nazi film *Der Führer's Face*, a part of Walt Disney's war effort.

Most terrible was the fate of the illustrator Adelbert, proving that one detail could lead to dire consequences. In the October 1943 *Ric et Rac* issue, he published a casual drawing of a dinner party in which a guest is shown with his hand caught in the sugar bowl. By a coincidence this picture, called "The metaphor of the sugar bowl," had been used as anti-Nazi propaganda when Germans seized the city of Danzig. Worse was the fact that the guest had a mustache and his hair was plastered on his forehead. The directors of the paper pleaded Adelbert's cause, reminding the censors that his work had been favored by the Vichy Ministry of Information. Nothing could be done. *Ric et Rac* was shut down. Aldebert was hunted down, arrested, and deported to Buchenwald, then sent on to Mauthausen.[85]

Neither Hergé's name nor his books were on the list of works withdrawn from circulation, a list that included Jeanne Cappe's *Blue Fairy Tales* and every issue of the children's weeklies *L'Album de Lisette* and *L'Album de Pierrot*.[86] Hergé had already definitively moved away from politics and turned to escapism. To be entertaining above all else corresponded with the strategy of propaganda at the time. It may have been the reason he turned down a German firm's offer to publish *Tintin in the Land of the Soviets*.[87]

Tintin's adventures seeming oblivious to the events shaking Europe worked in Hergé's favor with the authorities in charge of allocating paper to the printing industry and who therefore controlled the lifeblood of authors

and editors. Hergé's friend J. Van Weyenbergh, acting as intermediary, assured him that if he emphasized the cultural aspects of his books, his request would be received more favorably. "It's important to stress the need to give young people works that are healthy, instructive and moral," he believed. Whenever Casterman sent in a request to the Censorship Office for authorization to reprint (generally ten thousand copies in French and an equal number of copies in Flemish for each title), the outcome was never certain. But they were never refused. No Tintin book was ever banned for the duration of the occupation. Sometimes officials from the Propaganda Office complained or raised their concerns (such as about *Tintin in America*).[88] But they never bothered Hergé himself, and he in turn was able to reassure his editors that he embodied "All that is harmless."[89]

On the whole he was right. Only two volumes posed a problem. *Tintin in America* received clearance to be printed, though just to be sure, Hergé had censored himself. In a plate in the next-to-last page he removed an American flag flying in full color; he was afraid it would leap out at the censors.[90] And Louis Casterman was called in and soundly reprimanded for *The Black Island* being "too British," particularly Tintin's kilt on the cover and the bobbies on the last page. The firm was placed under punitive sanction: no new authorizations for three months. Fortunately it had nothing scheduled during that time.

Later Hergé would claim that neither volume could be printed during the occupation,[91] trying to suggest that they were banned. The fact was that the Propaganda Office delayed the reprintings because of the scarcity of paper. But even that did not prevent *Tintin in America* and *The Black Island* from being readily available during the entirety of the war, according to his editor.[92]

Edgar P. Jacobs came onboard at the right moment. Hergé was swamped. Some claimed that Jacobs was hypersensitive and suspicious. But his qualities outweighed any faults, particularly his meticulous workmanship. "He taught me much," wrote Hergé. "He demanded so much of himself, and what honesty! He was an illustrator who never cheated."[93] What he appreciated most about Jacobs was his talent as a colorist, his sense of composition, and his feeling for dramatic intensity. In Hergé's eyes, he was more valuable for his drawings than for his narrative sense.

Jacobs in turn admired Hergé's exceptional ability to draw characters in motion. He pushed Hergé to pay more attention to the background: "Put real marquees on your movie houses," he advised. Jacobs's cars were recognizable. Those of Hergé were more comic-book-like, similar to those of

Walt Disney, lacking the maniacal precision of those by Jacobs. It's not that Hergé didn't know how to draw cars; rather, drawing them with precision seemed unimportant to him. He made his planes capable of flight and his ships navigable, but did not reproduce them down to every detail. With the arrival of Jacobs, these images became more precise.

Similarly Jacobs made Hergé temper the character of Captain Haddock. Daily contact with his colleague inspired Hergé to stress Haddock's plain-spoken honesty and self-pity.[94]

Jacobs's main job was to recast previous work. The oldest volumes had to be adapted to new parameters and condensed to sixty-two pages. They also had to be colored and the material enriched, taking advantage of the chance to correct any mistakes in both the pictures and the text. Sometimes it was a question of style, making something more precise, or sometimes simplifying something that in retrospect appeared exaggerated.

In the process of recasting and modernizing *Tintin in the Congo*, for example, the bubble in which Tintin says, "Let's get that beast!" becomes "What a great hunting trophy it will make!" The book would gain in the quality of its writing what it lost in comic bluntness. Hergé undertook to transform Tintin's adventures into a unified work. He furtively introduces the Thom(p)sons on the platform of the train station from which Tintin departs for the Dark Continent. To endow his hero with more universal appeal, he reworked the chronology even at the risk of being anachronistic and also minimized Tintin's Belgianness. Thus the journey of a Belgian to the Congo becomes that of a European to Africa. His lesson to the "native children"—"My dear friends, I am going to speak to you today about your Fatherland: Belgium!"—becomes a lesson in arithmetic: "Two plus two equals what?"[95]

The two illustrators complemented each other; they had become a team. Next they turned to the recasting of *Cigars of the Pharaoh*, the coloring of *The Blue Lotus,* and the Balkanization of the background and costumes of *King Ottokar's Scepter*. Jacobs was officially employed by Hergé starting on January 1, 1944. He was hired at a salary of 4,500 francs a month (current equivalent, $1,235). Hergé was planning for the future. He asked for six months' notice should Jacobs want to stop working with him. On the other hand he promised that within a year he would examine the possibility of Jacobs's receiving royalties on their work.[96]

WITH JACOBS WORKING BESIDE HIM, Hergé could breathe at last and was able to send his hero in quest of new adventures. The new serial began on

December 16, 1943, opening with a technique he would henceforth always use, consisting of a news clipping that sums up the problem and establishes the setting. The picture consists of news type with no illustration: "Sanders-Hardiman Expedition returns! The seven members of the Sanders-Hardiman Ethnographic Expedition landed in Liverpool after a fruitful two-year trip through Peru and Bolivia, deep into unknown territory. They discovered several Inca tombs, one of which contained a mummy still wearing a 'borla' or royal crown of solid gold. Funerary inscriptions established without a doubt that the tomb belonged to the Inca ruler Rascar Capac." Tintin is reading this on the train to Marlinspike, where he rejoins Captain Haddock, the majordomo Nestor, and Professor Calculus. Only the Thom(p)sons are missing, though they will soon appear. To make things even more familiar, Hergé introduces other characters from previous books. General Alcazar from *The Broken Ear* will turn up at the local music hall, and Bianca Castafiore, the Milanese Nightingale from *King Ottokar's Scepter,* also makes an appearance.

Recalling the tragic fate of the archaeologist who opened an Egyptian tomb, Tintin becomes intrigued when strange things begin to occur. One by one the members of the Ethnographic Expedition are struck down by sleepiness, caused not by a disease but by something more mysterious. Fragments of a crystal phial are found next to each sleeping victim. Tintin tries to warn them but arrives too late every time, except in the case of Professor Tarragon, who keeps the famous mummy of Rascar Capac in a glass case in the middle of his office. A lightning storm occurs during Tintin's visit, and all of a sudden a ball of fire comes down the chimney and flies around the room, levitating Professor Calculus in his chair before smashing the glass case protecting Rascar Capac. When the ball of fire disappears, so too has the mummy. The prophecy has come true; Rascar Capac will have his revenge. That night, sleeping at Professor Tarragon's house, both Tintin and Captain Haddock have the same dream: the ghost of the mummy laughs at them and breaks a crystal phial next to their beds. Unfortunately it's Professor Tarragon who is the victim of the sleeping sickness. Rascar Capac's jewels have disappeared, and so has Professor Calculus. Following the trail of the kidnappers, they find that they have set sail on a cargo ship for Peru. Tintin and Captain Haddock, in hot pursuit, hop on a plane for South America to arrive there before the criminals.

Hergé had developed a knack for diptychs; once again the conclusion is open-ended, leading to the next adventure. *The Seven Crystal Balls* achieves a more complete integration of narrative and illustrations. By having

characters from previous books return, Hergé adopted the literary tradition of the French nineteenth-century cycles of novels, as in the works of Balzac, Zola, and Jules Romains. His books now begin to form a coherent body of work, an oeuvre.

"LORD, LIBERATE US from our Protectors, and protect us from our Liberators!"[97] Hergé recalled that this was his prayer during an enforced bed rest caused by a bout of influenza in mid-June 1944. The Allies had landed in Normandy two weeks before. The liberation of Europe had begun.

In a Europe in convulsion for the second time in four years, Hergé was most concerned that his working papers were in order, as he still had to obtain a card as a regular working member of *Het Laatste Nieuws*.[98]

On June 1 King Léopold III was arrested by the Germans; he and the royal princes were removed from the Laeken Palace and transferred across the Rhine to a castle not far from Dresden. In Brussels the mood at the office of *Le Soir* was changing from hour to hour. The more hopeful and jubilant the workers and printers, the more morose the staff in the editorial offices. The spats between Hergé and the printer Henri Lemaire stopped altogether, as the typesetters observed that the newspaper's star illustrator had become preoccupied.[99]

In Tournai Louis Casterman, having borne the responsibility of being burgermeister of his town during the whole period of occupation, was determined to flood the market with the collected Tintin books as soon as the country was liberated. He was prepared to follow up with a major publicity campaign.[100] He was feeling positive about the future, planning to promote the work of his major author.

The fact is that for certain writers and artists, the occupation was a golden age, as shown by the abundance and quality of work produced during this period. (This is a paradox that some have trouble accepting, yet French cinema has never been as brilliant as it was in the 1940s.)

While the fate of Europe hung in the balance, illustrated comic strips continued to provide an amazing reflection of the times. On the one hand, Auguste Liquois, in a short-lived collaborationist periodical called *Le Mérinos,* published the comic strip "Zoubinette," in which the resistance fighters were depicted as truants, thugs, and killers without scruples. On the other hand, in the Auvergne region of France, Marijac, a prisoner who escaped from Germany, created *Le Corbeau déchaîné* (The Unleashed Crow), a satirical periodical in which he devoted a comic strip to the glory

of comrades in battle under the title "The Three Musketeers of Resistance." Between these two extremes appeared *La Bête est morte!* (The Beast Is Dead), by Victor Dancette and Jacques Zimmerman, illustrated by E. F. Calvo, which transposed the medieval *Roman de Renart* to World War II. All the protagonists are animals: wolves (German, with Hitler as the leader of the pack), a polecat (Goebbels), a hyena (Mussolini), polar bears (Stalin and the Russians), bulldogs (Churchill and the English), buffaloes (the Americans), rabbits and squirrels (the French), without forgetting the great majestic stork (de Gaulle).[101]

At the moment Paris was being liberated, Hergé was with Father Wallez at the Abbey of Aulne, where he spent several days. This internal exile of meditation and prayer was indispensable to him every time he went through a critical phase, a chance to take stock of himself and listen to the priest's advice.

Le Soir published the 152nd plate of *The Seven Crystal Balls* in the September 2–3, 1944, edition. Hergé's previous works had contained at least another twenty comic strips, but this one would stay unfinished, the fate of Professor Calculus remaining in suspense. So too Hergé's fate. He was thirty-seven years old, and his life was to be changed irrevocably in ways for which he was unprepared and which would prove painful. The fact was that Hergé was among those who had done well during the occupation.

part ii: solitude

7.

The Plight of the *Inciviques*
1944–1946

THE DAY BRUSSELS REGAINED its liberty, Hergé lost his. On Sunday, September 3, 1944, while Lieutenant General Adair's Armored Division of the Welsh Guards drove the Germans from the city, Hergé was arrested in his home at 17 Avenue Delleur in Boistfort.

The self-appointed representatives of the law were not after Hergé but a certain Georges Remi, and from the evidence it seems that the relationship between the two was unsuspected. Hergé didn't know whether he should be glad about this. The celebrations taking place throughout the capital only made it more confusing. The moment the First Belgian Brigade under Colonel Piron entered the city, no one knew who was doing what or by what authority. There were several days of tension and confusion.

Denunciation followed accusation, just as during the occupation but without the instigation of a foreign power. This was a matter among Belgians. The British soldiers often couldn't hide their disgust at witnessing this settling of old scores.

The members of the resistance who showed up at Hergé's home had read the last issue of *L'Insoumis* (The Undefeated), a bulletin of information for fighting enemy Belgians. It contained a sheet called "Gallery of Traitors" subtitled "From the Lair of *The Ersatz-Soir*," and it provided photographs, names, addresses, and curriculum vitae. For anyone hesitant about administering justice, there was a brief note of encouragement: "Dear readers, look at these faces! Vice is written on these faces. All commentary is unnecessary; these people's crimes are known. The punishment that we will exact from them is merciless."[1]

Of the forty journalists denounced, Hergé is the only one listed twice. The first listing, as "Hergé," includes his photo, address, and some biographical details: "According to our information was a Rexist, but could not confirm." The second listing, "Georges Remi," has no photograph but includes this commentary: "Impossible to obtain any information on this individual. Everything indicates that he must be closely watched." They had not made the connection between the two. Georges Remi would be arrested four times: by State Security, by the Judiciary Police, by the Belgian National Movement, and by the Front for Independence. Each time he was set free.

On September 11 he was arrested at home and driven to the courthouse, where he was questioned.[2] Then he was given a chance to appreciate the damp straw of a cell, an experience he would never forget. In Saint-Gilles Prison he ran across Paul Herten, the editor of *Cassandre*, in a cell with a dozen other detainees. They had much to discuss, and Herten told him that he faced a sentence of ten years for doing nothing.[3] Hergé was set free the next day; Herten was sentenced not to ten years as he had feared but to face the firing squad.

Five days after the liberation of Brussels the Allied Command placed a notice on the front page of all the newly reorganized newspapers: "All members of the editorial staff of a newspaper during the Occupation are now forbidden to practice their profession."[4] They were blacklisted. It was one thing to be forbidden to work, another to be targeted by the press. As one of the better known members of the press, Hergé was naturally one of the most often targeted.

After liberation the weekly paper *La Patrie* (The Fatherland), in its very first issue, carried a crudely drawn comic strip titled "The Adventures of Tintin in the Land of the Nazis." A sample of the dialogue:

TINTIN: Captain, free at last! Hergé had to sneak off!
HADDOCK: Hergé is a landlubber, a bachi-bouzouk, a bogey. Me,
 I've always been an anglophile....
TINTIN: Me, I've always liked cowboys!
SNOWY: Me, he never succeeded in turning me into a German
 shepherd![5]

In the next episode Tintin leads a division to discover the secret to manufacturing the V2 rocket before the Germans can use it. This time the comic strip is titled "In the manner of Mr. Hergé, who is indisposed due to the Liberation."[6]

In the third issue Tintin, at the head of a division, requisitions a Messerschmitt and parachutes into the Nazi general headquarters. The last plate is supposedly censored by the military authorities. In place of an illustration one reads, "The documents seized yesterday by the I.S. (Intelligence Service) from a member of the fifth column prove that the Germans who counted on Mr. Hergé to establish the formula for the V2 rocket are waiting for the end of this story to learn the formula."[7]

Hergé put up with it as best he could. During these September days he seemed stunned by events, more pained than revolted. For the moment he reacted as a spectator; he believed there was nothing for which he had to reproach himself. As a result not for a moment did he ever consider leaving his home, his city, or his country. He never even considered that he might be brought up for trial. But his pride had been deflated: "The optimists were wrong, wrong not to be more optimistic. The pessimists—I admit to being one of them—are also wrong, much to their shame. Everything happened with lightning speed, and for the second time, our country has been miraculously preserved. Two miracles [Belgium survived the battles of the occupation and the liberation] in four years, that's a great deal, more than I ever could have dared to hope for. I was wrong. So much the better!"[8]

Hergé had reduced four years of conflict between collaborators and resistors to a mere quarrel between optimists and pessimists. By the start of winter 1944 the government and the judicial system, not to mention the political world and public opinion, saw matters in a different light.

With each passing day Hergé discovered more about his country; he was nauseated by the spectacle of revenge, the evening-up of scores, denunciations and opportunism, jealousy, resentment, cowardice, and vanity—the same elements that caused such destruction during the occupation, except that he had been able to close his eyes to it then. Now he was the target of those seeking justice, for whom hatred of traitors was a sacred duty. He was less afraid of capital punishment than of moral and social censure. He was haunted not by the specter of imminent death but by the threat of becoming an *incivique* (noncitizen). This eighteenth-century French adjective had fallen out of usage until the First World War brought it back. The postliberation political purges gave it such a new lease on life in Belgium that historians of the Second World War believed it was a Belgian term. Military courts condemned thirty thousand Belgians on minor charges and approximately twenty-five thousand more on criminal charges, of which fifty-five hundred received either capital punishment or life imprisonment.[9]

When it drew up the legal basis of the purges in London in 1942, the Belgian government-in-exile did not bother with fine distinctions between the venal profiteers and the dedicated fascists, informers, and propaganda agents. After liberation politicians used these regulations as the basis for eliminating the extreme right, which had opposed them during the thirties and had delivered them up to the Germans.

As a result almost all Belgians were presumed *inciviques* until they produced proof to the contrary. That proof consisted of a "certificate of good citizenship." Without specific regulations governing the obtaining of these certificates, there were increasing numbers of abuses. Favoritism, collusion, and trafficking influence delivered certificates to true *inciviques* while less well-connected, innocent people were left to suffer under the ban. The government was divided over the requirements for the certificate. The Catholic Party wanted to do away with it altogether. They argued that the abuses and their unpredictable effects on people's lives made it analogous to the requirements for Jews during the occupation: "At every turn you needed a document to prove that you were not Jewish, and now you need a document to prove that you're a 'good citizen.'"[10] The opposition was equally adamant, wanting the certificate incorporated into the civil code.[11] Not until July 1947 was a compromise achieved by the Ministry of the Interior, one that combined the certificate of good citizenship with the traditional certificate of good character.[12]

One evening there was a rumor of a large, important patriotic rally taking place in Boistfort. The goal was to punish traitors. The judicial system seemed to be working too slowly, and some had decided to take justice into their own hands.

The doorbell rang at the Remi house after dinner. They opened the door and found not a delegation from a mob, but Edgar Jacobs. He acted as if he were coming home after running errands, placing his umbrella in the hallway stand, and making himself comfortable in the drawing room. Only on leaving at the end of the evening did he admit that he had come with the aim of protecting Hergé.

In the first months of 1945 Remi was forbidden from working in any capacity whatsoever with the press. However, Hergé could continue working with Casterman on recasting his earlier works into the new sixty-two-page color format. At the same time he was the subject of a judicial inquiry into his work with the German-sponsored "stolen" newspapers, *Le Soir*, *Het Laatste Nieuws*, and *Het Algemeen Nieuws*. His case was assigned to a deputy public prosecutor, Monsieur Vinçotte, who was well disposed

toward Hergé. "In principle," Vinçotte wrote at the end of the investigation, "I am inclined to close the case. I believe it would bring ridicule on the judicial system to go after an inoffensive children's book author and illustrator. On the other hand," Vinçotte added, "Hergé worked for *Le Soir* during the war, and his illustrations are what made people buy the newspaper. I will be forced to investigate literary critics and sports columnists whose personal writings, however, are not in question. But it could be said that Hergé as well as these columnists contributed to the newspaper's appeal and thereby helped increase its circulation."[13]

Having submitted his report, Vinçotte waited for an expert's decision as to whether to prosecute. Bitter and feeling defeated, Hergé had become fatalistic. He would let matters take their course.

One day in October 1945 three men came to see him. Raymond Leblanc—short, broad-shouldered, a snappy dresser—was a decorated soldier and one of the few Belgians who did not need a certificate of good citizenship. He was a young officer who had served in a prestigious unit of the Ardennes Light Infantry and written a book titled *Dés pipés* (Loaded Dice). Written in diary form in a sober and powerful style, it related the profound resentment of those who believed they had been deceived while doing their duty for their country. Belgium's capitulation had been abruptly settled in merely eighteen days, which made them wonder if the dice hadn't been loaded. Leblanc became a customs officer in the Ministry of Finance and was a member of the clandestine National Royalist Movement, an organization that wanted to counter the influence of the Communist resistance.[14] Along with André Sinave, a fellow resistance fighter, and Albert Debaty, a former journalist, Leblanc formed a publishing house that as yet had produced only a collection of romance novels and *Ciné-sélection*, a magazine reviewing new films. After liberation, with the supply of printing paper still scarce, they decided to launch a weekly for children. Sinave said they should approach Hergé.[15]

Leblanc was enthusiastic because of his childhood admiration for Hergé. His parents had been subscribers to *Le Vingtième Siècle*, where he had read "Tintin in the Land of the Soviets" in its original version and remembered it fondly.[16]

Hergé's *incivique* standing didn't seem to dampen their spirits. His past no longer presented an obstacle. They remembered that his brother, Paul Remi, had made several attempts to escape while a prisoner in Germany in order to reach England and rejoin the Belgian unit commanded by Jean-Baptiste Piron. When the stolen *Le Soir* came up, these new friends

preferred to remember how, when their fellow members of the underground had been imprisoned deep in Saint-Gilles by the Germans, they had waited for the paper to read Hergé's daily comic, which was like a breath of fresh air.

As for Hergé, the project immediately interested him. He realized, for starters, that working with former resistance fighters would help reintegrate him into society, and this overruled whatever reservations he might have felt about going into business with such young unknowns, lacking connections with the press or financial support.

The first meeting took place in Hergé's home and subsequent ones in their office at 55 Rue du Lombard. Their discussions were courteous and free of business specifics because they were all eager to reach an agreement. He could not publish without them, and they needed him. Leblanc took on the daunting task of obtaining clearance papers for Hergé. Debaty took charge of circulation. Hergé's role was artistic director, which would enable him to supervise the whole publication. He would be given exclusive control over the double-page spread featuring the new adventures of Tintin and Snowy. The number of pages of the weekly was set at twelve. Leblanc had found a backer, Georges Lallemand, a former resistance fighter, now working as a film producer.

Hergé was enthusiastic, though he still had some reservations about whether the project would come about, given his political situation. "That's my problem," answered Leblanc. "I have my resources. All I want is a contract."[17] For weeks Leblanc had been making inquiries and understood that there were two camps: those who replied, "That collaborator? Never!" and those who said more calmly, "There's an Hergé file; we have to study the case."[18]

Pierre Ugeux, a friend from the resistance, went before the Committee for Attribution, which controlled the paper supply. When he mentioned Hergé at a public forum, the tension in the room rose noticeably. Even though Ugeux was wearing the uniform of a paratrooper, someone from the crowd took the platform and questioned his motives. "We can't allot paper to a newspaper that collaborated! And are you a former member of the resistance?"

"Yes."

"Where?"

"In London. You?"

"I was also there."

"I was in a military unit. And you?"

"In the ministry."[19]

No further discussion on that score. Ugeux argued that it would be impossible to ban every newspaper published during the occupation. He got his allotment of paper.

His next stop was the office of his brother, William Ugeux, one of the leaders of the Belgian resistance and now in charge of censorship and of certificates of good citizenship. He had been the official delegate to London for the Belgian resistance movement starting in 1941 and was subsequently promoted to director of the secret service of the Belgian government-in-exile. On returning to Brussels he became head of the National Information Service as a member of the cabinet of Prime Minister Hubert Pierlot. He was in a position to help Hergé in several capacities.

First, in London he had participated in drafting the legislation for purging the press, which he believed was too severe. In this position he was at the heart of a network of information and was one of the best-informed men of the capital during this troubled time, when no one was sure who did what to whom in the recent past.

Second, as a former executive of *Le Vingtième Siècle,* he had known Hergé. In his opinion in 1945 Hergé was "a perfect example of the link between the basic Scout spirit and the elementary mentality of the Rexists: looking to the chief, remaining in line, wanting the uniform. He was a blunderer rather than a traitor."[20]

Other than the recommendations of his brother, William Ugeux heard from Leblanc and Louis Casterman, who had no interest in the case other than general concern about his star author. Sales of Tintin books had gone from 34,000 copies through 1939 to 324,000 between 1940 and 1945.[21]

Everyone waited for Vinçotte to decide whether to prosecute. Pierre Ugeux, who had known Vinçotte in London, called several times to overcome his reluctance to drop the charges. Vinçotte's investigation proved that Hergé's income went from 55,000 francs (current equivalent, $17,393) in 1941 to 78,000 francs (current equivalent, $21,980)in 1944. But there was nothing on him politically: he did not belong to a party or movement, and there were no compromising articles. Ugeux urged indulgence. He believed that *Le Soir's* collaboration had been relatively moderate. Hergé was merely "an illustrator whose livelihood was making drawings for children in the newspaper."[22]

The final decision on Hergé rested with Walter Jean Ganshof van der Meersch, general auditor to the Military Tribunal, known as "Jupiter" because he terrified everyone. Those who were not intimidated hated him

because he had cursed King Léopold III, a true example of lèse-majesté. In the satirical "false" *Soir* of 1943 he had inserted in the advertisement section, "I buy gallows, pillories, guillotines. Write Ganshof van der Meersch, London." Van der Meersch was in charge of purging the judiciary.

One evening he received a visit from William Ugeux, whom he knew from London. Ugeux's conscience was troubling him. Of all the unbearable appeals that came to him every day, the worst was one that came from a mother of two children. She was the widow of the journalist Victor Meulenijzer, an old friend of Hergé, executed by a firing squad for his activities in the Rexist press. "You did nothing to stop it!" she screamed at him. "You killed him!" Ugeux had been staggered by this. Since then he had saved seven or eight journalists from execution, commuting their sentences to hard labor in the Congo. For that reason he had come to ask his friend van der Meersch for permission to consult the Hergé dossier. He wanted his conscience to be clear. Everyone talked about the dossier, but no one had seen it.

The dossier was lying on the dining room table, and Ugeux immediately buried himself in it. The case against Hergé was that he had associated with collaborators, had been on friendly terms with the people of *Brüsseler Zeitung,* and had worked enthusiastically for the "stolen" press. There were also letters of denunciation. In going through the file, Ugeux realized that a number of professional journalists and editors would have been only too glad to see Hergé hanged. He could also see the insatiable desire for vengeance on the part of journalists who had "broken their pens" (refused to write) when their country was invaded. They were bitter now because nothing had been done for them.

"Nothing serious" was his conclusion on closing the dossier.[23] "A great deal of noise about nothing, in fact." He was convinced enough to make a final effort to have the case closed. Later William Ugeux would write in his capacity as president of the Committee of Chiefs of the Resistance Groups, "I am aware that during the Liberation, Hergé could be reproached for having his drawings used in the 'stolen' *Le Soir.* After making an investigation I can testify that Hergé had no direct or personal responsibility for the publication of his comic strips by the editors."[24]

On December 22, 1945, the dossier labeled "Georges Remi, a.k.a. Hergé" was reclassified as "closed." Justifying his decision in a letter to the minister of justice, Ganshof van der Meersch explained, "Concerning those who worked for a newspaper that was collaborating with the enemy ... this principle [of condemning collaborators] must be applied judiciously, with

measure and consideration. In regard to the particularly inoffensive character of the drawings published by Remi, bringing him before a war tribunal would be inappropriate and risky."[25]

The backers of *Tintin* magazine were not yet prepared to declare a triumph. Through the efforts of the Ugeux brothers and Raymond Leblanc, the royal prosecutor, Raymond Charles, another former member of the government-in-exile, examined the Hergé dossier and, after consulting with members of the resistance, gave a favorable verdict. The certificate was almost in their hands when an unexpected telephone call from the office of the prime minister threw the whole matter into question. They began all over again, knocking on doors, waiting for meetings, pleading their case, until finally matters were settled, this time definitively.[26] In May 1946 the attorney general delivered the certificate of good citizenship to Georges Remi, a.k.a. Hergé.

This good news was tempered by the fact that Hergé had just lost his mother at age sixty. She had been hospitalized, having never recovered from the traumatic shock of receiving the false news that her son Paul had died in a German prison camp. She suffered from a condition that dissociated visual from emotional recognition. When Paul returned after the war, she refused to believe he was really her son and thought him an imposter. Hergé had always felt that they had never really known one another.

The following month the police commissioner of Watermael-Boistfort delivered the first part of the certificate, which granted Hergé the right to recover his driver's license. In the fall this was followed by the second part, which permitted him to seek employment. In both cases the commissioner had to declare, "To my knowledge Georges Remi never failed his duties as a citizen during the course of enemy occupation."[27] For his part, Hergé was interested only in recovering his passport, which had been confiscated.[28] Finally his reputation had been cleared. His country held no grudge against him for his actions during the occupation.

But he held a grudge against his country. Even if in public he glossed over events or talked about them with the irony befitting an illustrator of comic strips, in private he could not disguise feeling profoundly shaken. The pain comes through in his letters and conversations. He was as appalled by the atmosphere of a witch hunt as he had been when being treated as an *incivique*. Later, when asked what was the most important event in his life, he would answer, "The war." Then he would correct himself: "The aftermath of the war." Specifically he would explain, "I mean the repression and the hatred.... It was an experience of absolute intolerance. It was horrible,

horrible!"[29] In his memory this period would remain stamped with a terrifying injustice. He convinced himself that half of Belgium had been thrown into prison then.[30] Like all those who were purged after the war, he gave little thought to the horrors of the war or to what some Belgians had endured during the occupation. He never found the words to denounce the raids, the arrests, imprisonment, torture, and deportations.

He never grasped what he was being accused of. When the illustrator Pierre Ickx, a childhood friend who had been hunted by the Gestapo for a whole year, told him that he "was on the other side," Hergé replied, "I have to say I don't understand. As for me, I belong on the side of those who work at their profession with the greatest conscientiousness possible, and I honor all the victims of the war, whichever side they are on."[31]

His reply revealed the way his mind worked, putting all the warring parties on the same level, including the civilians. In this spirit he would rewrite the fate of the two teenagers who had played the role of Tintin—one on his return from the Congo, the other returning from the Soviet Union. According to Hergé, the first became a great resistance leader and the other a collaborator who fought on the eastern front in the Walloon Division. Henry den Doncker did indeed fight in British uniform; Lucien Pepermans, on the other hand, claimed that for the whole duration of the war he remained steadfastly neutral, taking no side.[32]

Equating both sides was Hergé's way of attenuating the damages caused by the faction for which he worked. After liberation he often called the censorship office "our Propaganda Abeitlung nationale,"[33] as if they were comparable. In the end Hergé never renounced his attitude. In one sense he was an example of faithfulness to men and to the ideals of his youth. Despite the difference in standing, he would have agreed with his friend Robert Poulet, the fascist: "I was not a collaborator. I was a journalist during the period of the German Occupation of Belgium. I never collaborated with the Germans, I wrote for my country, for the people of my country, to support the nation, Christian values, and the royal dynasty."[34]

On June 5, 1945, his brother, Paul, returned from Germany, after having spent five years in a prison camp. They must have spoken about the camps, as well as other subjects, more secret because more criminal. Hergé gave the impression of never having learned, nor remembered, anything about the Final Solution. Much later, during the filming of a documentary on his life, Hergé confided to a producer off-camera, "It's true that there are certain drawings I am not proud of. But believe me, if I had know the nature of the persecution, and the Final Solution, I would not have

done them. I did not know. Or, like so many others, perhaps I made sure that I did not know."[35]

Hergé would not relax his attitude, even to his close colleague Jacques Martin, who had spent two years doing forced labor as an engineer with Messerschmitt in Augsburg. Martin told him about the death camps he had seen during his stay in Germany ("The walking dead, the unbearable smell ...") and what the guards told him when he asked them ("These are common law prisoners!"). Hergé was incredulous. "You are not remembering correctly, it made an impression, you mistook what you saw.... And, first of all, how do you know they were Jews? They were surely common law criminals."

Martin spent an evening trying but failing to convince him that he had seen a death camp. Hergé challenged everything. It wasn't from lack of interest; he did not want to know. In the future the two men would avoid any mention of the war.[36]

During these trying times Hergé gave himself over to his reading: Simenon, Balzac, Félicien Marceau. He returned again and again to two men, Norbert Wallez and Henri de Montherlant. They had helped him face the onslaught. He would never forget Father Wallez's total indifference to the articles that savaged him: "If a fly farts in my direction, what do I care?" he told his young friend, who was in such pain to see him made ridiculous.[37] In his essay "Letter of a Father to His Son," the author de Montherlant would give invaluable advice: "Arrange for times of disgrace; alternate them with periods when you are respected. When you realize that they have the same taste, you will have taken a major step toward a healthy view of things."[38]

Among Hergé's friends were no liberals, no Socialists, no Communists. However numerous and active, they were nowhere around Hergé. Except for his new relationships, formed around *Tintin* magazine, he had no real friends. The ones he'd had had been condemned or declared *inciviques*.

The subject of guilt was never mentioned around Hergé, nor were doubts about the king. The Belgian Parliament had appointed Prince Charles regent, but to Hergé the regent was the regent, and the king was Léopold III. Despite his esteem for Prince Charles, with whom he was on cordial terms, Hergé was among those who hoped the king's exile would soon end. Questioning whether the king had been right to sign the surrender and choose to remain in occupied Belgium was pure lèse-majesté.

Hergé remained as faithful to his friends as he was to Léopold III. He defended them tooth and claw. Whatever the facts, he always managed to

find extenuating circumstances for those defeated by the liberation. Years later, recalling the aftermath of the war, Robert Poulet would say that Hergé was generous toward the *inciviques*, those who were banned and disgraced but whose integrity he believed in.[39] Hergé's generosity toward them was greater than people would believe. He helped not only his friends, and friends of friends, but also individuals whom he did not even know. His reputation as the Samaritan of collaborators in distress spread beyond the borders.

It was a matter of keeping faith, even if it forced him to become radicalized, as was the case with Maurice Bardèche, the untiring propagandist of French neofascism since the end of the war, and his intellectual brother-in-law, Robert Brasillach. Hergé sent word to Bardèche: "What proof can I give of the spontaneous feeling of friendship I feel for all those people linked to the memory of Robert Brasillach? Do your children have all the Tintin books? If they are missing any, I would send them with pleasure."[40]

For months Hergé had been anticipating with impatience June 3, 1946, the date on which the trial of the stolen *Le Soir* opened. He had been de facto personally rehabilitated, having received his certificate, but he considered this tribunal the last stop on his stations of the cross, even if he did not figure among the twenty-eight individuals charged. He wanted to be present in the room to show his solidarity with those condemned, his friends. The trial was the last stage of his tribulations, and afterward the page would be turned at last.

The presiding judge was a former director of the old *Vingtième Siècle*, and the assistant prosecutor was Vinçotte, who had been in charge of investigating Hergé's case. Hergé felt he was on familiar ground. The accusation of the military prosecutor was damning: "The press played a major role in encouraging Belgians to volunteer in the ranks of the German army. Today the collaborationist journalists want to minimize the effects of their actions. The great error of *Le Soir* was helping people believe that they could collaborate with Germany without harming their country."[41] In vain the defendants protested their good faith and their sincerity.

The prosecutor was asking for life imprisonment for Raymond De Becker rather than the death penalty, which he reserved for "the intellectual leaders of the collaboration, such as Colin and Poulet." For the newspaper's administration the prosecutor wanted sentences of ten to twenty years. For the drama critic Georges Marlier he wanted ten years. And for Paul Kinnet, to whom Hergé had lent his characters the Thom(p)sons, ten years.

De Becker took the stand to plead his case:

I admit that I committed an error in thinking I could collaborate with
the Third Reich.... I was wrong and I don't ask for your indulgence.
I led a number of my colleagues with me, but I believed that I was
serving a great ideal.... It was an illusion to think I could influence
Germany and National-Socialism, but the politics of collaboration was
a necessity; we were disgusted with democracy, and we feared commu-
nism. We were wrong not to have seen the violence of fascism. I was
wrong to let myself be impressed by their will to power.[42]

There is no record of Hergé's reaction to this speech. It would be inter-
esting to know if he also took responsibility. In any case he feared less the
men on trial than their lawyers. The defense was liable to bring him up to
better defend their clients. The unexpected blow came from Paul Struye, a
member of the resistance and a founder of the clandestine wartime publi-
cation *Libre Belgique*, who was defending one of Hergé's friends, Julien de
Proft. His line of reasoning was simple: "My client was only a journalism
employee, he never signed anything." When the presiding judge referred to
his high salary of 10,000 francs a month (current equivalent, $2,810), the
defense didn't just remind the court that his client worked fourteen hours
a day: "The illustrator Hergé received more than 10,000 francs a month,
and he is not brought to trial even though he collaborated in making a
success of the 'stolen' *Le Soir*." Mr. Struye had broken an unspoken pact
that bound the former colleagues of *Le Soir*: not to make trouble for those
among them who had managed to escape the storm of the purges.

Three days later an article on the front page of the new *Le Soir* seemed
indirectly to regret the absence of Hergé among the accused. Not just
because he was Hergé but because they all had shared responsibility. No
one was exempt, especially the illustrators: "With illustrations the secondary
collaborators help attract the readers who tend to read the propaganda.
The collaboration of these talents should be brought to trial for their
complicity. It's hard to understand why the prosecutor has not pursued all
those scribblers who served the enemy."[43] The writer concluded with the
worrisome question of important cases that had not been followed up or
had been closed. Few knew that behind the scenes some important
members of the resistance had joined together to get Hergé cleared of
the vindictive reprisals of the purges in order to launch a publication in
partnership with him.

There was an official reason. Between two hearings a lawyer asked, "But why haven't you also arrested Hergé?" Vinçotte answered, "I would have appeared utterly ridiculous!"[44]

This would become the standard explanation, repeated endlessly. At the beginning of his investigation Gaston Duval, a lawyer with youthful ties to Hergé, stopped the assistant prosecutor in the hallway of the courthouse: "You cannot arrest Hergé, the father of Tintin! You will have the youth of Belgium up in arms against you!"[45] Hergé was saved by Tintin. His character had come to his rescue. For his fans it would be the height of absurdity to bring Hergé to trial as an *incivique* when Tintin was the paragon of civic virtue.

Nonetheless the prosecutor could easily have brought to trial the citizen Georges Remi, illustrator of the stolen *Le Soir*, without appearing ridiculous. After all, the young Jean Vermeire had been the children's illustrator for the periodical *Le Pays reél* (The True Country) before being enlisted by De Becker to work for the Rex publications. No one laughed at his trial. The heavy sentences imposed on sports writers and music critics for treason made no one smile either.

On July 24, two months after the beginning of the trial, the judge pronounced the verdicts. Six received the death sentence, among them Raymond De Becker; one was sentenced to life imprisonment, five sentenced to twenty years, two to fifteen years. The Rossel family, original proprietors of *Le Soir*, received the symbolic one franc piece in compensation for the appropriation of their property. The Belgian state received 12 million francs (current equivalent, approximately $3 million) in damages with interest. The sentencing stated that all those who collaborated with the publishing or the laying out of the newspaper served enemy policy and were thus the tools of the Propaganda Abteilung.[46] A year later De Becker's sentence was commuted to life imprisonment.

AT THE END OF SUMMER 1946 the launch of the first issue of *Tintin* was upon them. Hergé was able to show a mock-up of the magazine to Raymond Leblanc. He was enthusiastic. Hergé credited his "dear friend" Jacques Van Melkebeke, who would be the editor in chief.

The two men spoke without going into details; the pressure was on. They had to plan the publicity campaign, notify the press about the launch, and go over details with the printer. A few days later Leblanc received a telephone call from Pierre Ugeux: "Is it true that you have a certain Van Melkebeke on your team?" Leblanc said it was.

"You have one hour to get rid of him. The police are on the way. And don't breathe a word that he ever worked on *Tintin* magazine."

As forewarned, a police commissioner arrived and searched for Van Melkebeke.[47] This caused the first breach between Leblanc, who was scandalized, and Hergé. When Van Melkebeke was arrested and sent to prison, Hergé had to distance himself from him. A friend of Leblanc's was installed as the editor in chief. Nonetheless they continued to give Van Melkebeke work on the side, hiring him to make drawings and scenarios. The brilliant Van Melkebeke became the anonymous galley slave of the magazine.

Hergé never seemed to learn from his experiences. When the publication needed someone to start the Flemish edition, Hergé recommended a young man he said was irreproachable. From an outside source, Leblanc learned that he was the son of a condemned collaborator of the former Flemish Nationalist Party. Later, when the magazine was going full tilt, it was suggested that they run short stories from time to time. Hergé introduced one by an anonymous author. That he cashed his checks under his wife's maiden name eventually came to Leblanc's attention. The author in question was the convicted and condemned collaborator Robert Poulet.[48]

8.

The Dark Years
1946–1950

THERE WERE NOW TWO TINTINS. The first was born on January 10, 1929; the second came into the world on September 26, 1946. Hergé and his colleagues mobilized a great deal of energy and influence to launch *Tintin* magazine, but initially there was no crowd to welcome their efforts. Only those who had invested in the magazine followed its progress. According to the founding charter, those who provided the capital—and therefore reaped the benefits—were the executive director, Raymond Leblanc (50 percent), the managing director, Georges Lallemand (40 percent), and the artistic director, Hergé (10 percent). The first served as the editor of the magazine, the second was its treasurer, and the third was its soul.

Hergé hadn't recruited a team, but a group of associates. He believed Edgar Jacobs and Jacques Van Melkebeke the most talented. Still, he needed more than two people to produce his magazine. They brought in Jacques Laudy, an illustrator and writer lured away from *Bravo!* Everything seemed ideal at first, but eventually relations between Hergé and Laudy began to deteriorate. Laudy felt that he and Hergé were not on the same wavelength, because he, Laudy, considered himself an artist above all. He was prompt and meticulous about deadlines, but the practical details of publishing left him indifferent. Laudy couldn't care less that a comic strip was read from left to right. He also refused to recognize the fact that narrative dictated the illustration.[1]

A few months earlier this band of "four musketeers" had been joined by a fifth, Paul Cuvelier. One day Cuvelier came in and handed his sketchbooks to Hergé. One contained sketches of the American jeeps he had seen

during the liberation, as well as some studies of horses. Hergé was deeply impressed. And he was overwhelmed by the next sketchbook, which illustrated the story of Corentin Feldoë, a young eighteenth-century orphan who stowed away on a ship that was outward bound. "You came to me seeking advice," Hergé told Cuvelier, "and instead I should be asking you!"[2]

Cuvelier wanted to be Raphaël or nothing. Hergé encouraged him to be himself. He first turned Cuvelier's hand to illustration by integrating him into the staff of *Tintin* magazine. Hergé quickly realized that the Achilles' heel of this artist of such impressive qualities and talent was that he was too much of a perfectionist, always setting the bar too high. His profound dissatisfaction prevented him finding expression for his creative powers.[3] Hergé believed Cuvelier's intelligence and sensibility made him "self-conscious and critical." He told him, "This hinders you from being yourself and from being guided solely by your instincts." Cuvelier worked with Hergé on his comic strips, but he dreamed of another life.[4]

ON THE EVE OF THE PUBLICATION of *Tintin*, the market for children's magazines was fairly saturated. In Belgium *Spirou* had reappeared after the liberation, featuring a series involving a lone cowboy named "Lucky Luke" and another about a U.S. Air Force hero, "Buck Danny." Both would be hugely popular and influential. The magazine had a pronounced moral tone, even if it accommodated diverse sensibilities: the Dupuis, the owners, were solidly Catholic; Jean Doisy, the editor in chief, was a well-known and outspoken Communist; the illustrator, Jijé, was pro-American. Doisy knew enough to keep his views out of *Spirou*, as the Dupuis family insisted that the magazine adhere to a "Christian line."[5]

Children's magazines were in the process of transformation. No fewer than thirty-three periodicals competed for the market in France alone, for example. Among the major publications from before the war, *Coeurs Vaillants* now paid for its Pétain sympathies during the occupation by being investigated and condemned. Father Courtois was forbidden from ever publishing any magazine again. He turned over his interest to Father Pihan, making him legally responsible.[6] After two years of penance his publication was granted the right to reappear in spring 1946.

While *Coeurs Vaillants* was absent from the scene, two competitors tried to take over its readership. *Coq Hardi* (The Fearless Rooster) was conceived and published in Clermont-Ferrand by Hergé's friend the illustrator Marijac, with the backing of the National Liberation Movement.

Marijac's work was published in its pages along with the adventures of Colonel X, information officer of the Free French, which he signed with the pseudonym Jacques François. *Coq Hardi* also favored the works of Alain de Saint-Ogan, the old Pétainist, who continued to publish his series "Zig et Puce" in *France-Soir* while trying to launch another series with a young editor named François Mitterrand.[7]

The second competitor was created a year earlier by the Communists, under the name *Valliant*, which was not a coincidence. It was heavily influenced by the American press, yet boasted that it was "100% French!" No more revolutionary than *Spirou* or *Tintin*, it was as Boy Scout as the other two, but in a Stalinist mode, not Catholic. The heroes fought gangsters, pornography, and anyone who led children's souls astray.[8]

THE FIRST ISSUE OF *TINTIN* MAGAZINE appeared on the newsstands on Thursday, September 26, 1946. It was easily identifiable, its logo consisting of the silhouette of the young reporter and his dog saluting the reader. The cover was a drawing of the Temple of the Sun, from the new serial. The table of contents: *The Extraordinary Odyssey of Corentin Feldoë* by Paul Cuvelier; extracts from *The War of the Worlds* by H. G. Wells, and from *Zadig* by Voltaire, illustrated by Jacobs; the new adventures of Tintin and Snowy in *Prisoners of the Sun*; *The Legend of the Four Aymon Brothers* by Jacques Laudy; *The Secret of the Swordfish*, which was the first episode of Blake and Mortimer, the new heroes of E. P. Jacobs; the history of the navy as narrated by Captain Haddock, alternating with that of aviation by Major Wing.

Success was immediate and stunning: sixty thousand copies sold out in three days. Eighty thousand copies were printed of the third issue. The publication was unanimously praised, except for Voltaire's *Zadig*. They had tried to soften the tone and had to censor the story, changing the word "eunuch," for example, to "chamberlain" in order not to offend anyone.

Voltaire was on the Index of Forbidden Books of the Catholic institutions in Belgium, and Catholic organizations subscribed to as many as five thousand to ten thousand copies of the magazine. For the moment, and indeed for several years to come, *Tintin* was under their patronage.[9]

The success pleased them, though they knew a storm was gathering. Hergé had enemies, and they had been lying in wait.

The *Quotidien* (The Daily) set the tone for future hostilities in its announcement of the forthcoming publication of *Tintin* in an editorial titled "Chronicles of *Incivisme*." "Mr. Hergé was not condemned by the

tribunal for having collaborated with the 'stolen' *Le Soir* ... for it was judged that his stories had nothing offensive in them. Nevertheless, he helped De Becker's paper profit by his artistic collaboration, and he profited by it as well."[10] The editorial wondered how Hergé got away with it.

In *Drapeau rouge* (Red Flag), the editorial writer Fernand Demany was even more direct. Stating his regret that all politically compromised journalists had not been banned by law from practicing their profession, he used the news about the first issue of *Tintin* to denounce its creator. "No doubt this announcement is not sensational, but it will awaken painful memories among those who knew the 'stolen' *Le Soir* to which Hergé brought the support of his undeniable talent. Tintin and Snowy opportunistically placed themselves under the banner of 'The New Order,' and their adventures brought to Hitlerian ideology adolescent readers already disoriented by the war, the black market, and the unspeakable practices that the Nazis introduced to our society."[11]

The revamped *Le Soir* was less direct, as the editorial board had passed a rule never to mention the name of Hergé in its pages. The writers began by noting that it was regrettable that ordinary people had been hounded by the police prior to receiving the certificate of good citizenship. "By contrast there are notorious cases of *incivique* individuals who have obtained the certificate," they pursued, "which they should never have received with such disconcerting ease. Thus an illustrator who made the fortune of a 'stolen' newspaper has just obtained his certificate without opposition from the military board, and is going to publish a new weekly."[12]

La Cité nouvelle (The New City) rounded out these attacks without naming Hergé but nonetheless making abundantly clear whom they were denouncing: "An *incivique* and a traitor, this individual served the policies of the enemy for substantial remuneration, and can just pick up his pencil and commercially relaunch his little 'Hitlerjungend' brigade. Must the children of those who were executed and of political prisoners teach common decency to someone who openly exploited the innocent entertainment of children for the benefit of the enemy? Mr. Tintin and your 'Hitlerjungend,' your boss has his place in a cell in Saint-Gilles."[13]

Once the attacks eased, Hergé felt relieved but also deeply wounded. He would never forget this vitriol. It overshadowed the insouciance that gave his artwork such spontaneity and was the source of its charm. For the first time he felt little love for his country, because in his eyes it had stopped being lovable.

THE SUCCESS OF *TINTIN* MAGAZINE continued, surpassing the most optimistic predictions. It also gave an enormous boost to the sale of the Tintin books. But Hergé had come to the decision never again to engage Tintin politically. The days of *In the Land of the Soviets* and *King Ottokar's Scepter* were over.

Like everyone within the orbit of Raymond Leblanc, Karel Van Milleghem, the editor in chief of the Dutch-language edition of the magazine, published under the name of *Kuifje*, was enlisted to contribute a slogan. It was out of the question not to have one for *Tintin* magazine for the newsstands. *Vaillant* had "Young Patriot" until May 1945, when with great fanfare it metamorphosed into "The Most Interesting Newspaper!"

Having a slogan had been the rule during the period between the two wars. It seemed as if every possible slogan had been used. "The Newspaper for Boys" became "The Newspaper for Young People" (*Pierrot*). Others included "For the Valiant Heart Nothing Is Impossible" (*Coeurs Vaillants*), "The Greatest French Newspaper for the Young and the Whole Family" (*Benjamin*), "The Magazine for Young Readers" (*Le Journal de Mickey*), "The Magazine for the Young of All Ages" (*Robinson*), "The Great Adventure Magazine for Young Readers"(*Hurrah!*), "The Magazine for Young and Old" (*L'Intrépide*), "For the Whole Family" (*L'Épatant*), "The Newspaper of Good Cheer" (*Spirou*). Perhaps the most memorable was "*Heroïc* relaxes adults, entertains the young, and energizes the old" (*Heroïc Albums*), which made you think it was advertising a medicine.

As for *Tintin* magazine, Karel Van Milleghem finally came up with: "The Newspaper for the Young from Seven to Seventy-Seven."[14] In 1936 Marcel Dehaye, a friend of Hergé, had published a children's book entitled *A Book for Children from Six to Sixty Years Old.*[15]

Hergé buried himself in his work. The magazine gave him something vital that had been lacking for the past two years. Of course it had its drawbacks; having to deliver a two-page spread on a weekly basis was an exhausting task. He was also forced to create two versions: seventy-five spreads for the magazine and sixty-two individual pages for the future book. Same story, different versions. There was no way around it.

Hergé picked up *Prisoners of the Sun*, the sequel to *The Seven Crystal Balls*, where he had left off on September 3, 1944, in *Le Soir*. His challenge was not so much in the graphics as in the story. If he continued the action where it had stopped, some readers would not be able to follow. If he started again at zero, others would complain. He decided on a compromise: he would sum up the previous episodes in a long prefatory press clipping in which he reiterated the essentials of *The Seven Crystal Balls*.

Tintin, Snowy, and Captain Haddock fly to Callao (Peru) in the hopes of finding the traces of Professor Calculus, who has disappeared mysteriously. The professor had committed a sacrilege by wearing the sacred bracelet of the Incas, and the supreme punishment seems his fate. To rescue him, his friends embark on a tumultuous journey through the mountains, following their young guide, Zorrino.

As with all his previous tales, Hergé researched his subject meticulously. He was constantly afraid of getting the details of a local costume wrong. For descriptions of the towns and funerary inscriptions, he consulted Charles Wiener's monumental *Peru and Bolivia* (1880). The work was a gold mine for an illustrator. With eleven hundred engravings, twenty-seven maps, and eighteen city plans, it was both a travelogue and an ethnographic notebook, and it included a survey of an archaeological mission to the region conducted by the author himself. It documented everything: ceramics, frescoes, roads, instruments, even the latches on the doors of the houses. The work was all the more useful because the author had had the intelligence to be as interested in contemporary life in the region as in its ancient past.

For the costumes, houses, and landscapes, Hergé used for reference *The Incas: Empire Builders of the Andes* and *In the Realm of the Sons of the Sun*, a series of articles published in 1938 issues of *National Geographic* magazine.[16] Some of the ones devoted to pre-Columbian civilizations and the Mayans were illustrated by a certain "H. M. Herget." It seemed an astonishing coincidence. To evoke scenes of spell-casting, the ceremonies involving sun worshipping, and religious rituals, he used the 1929 novel *The Bride of the Sun* by Gaston Leroux, author of *Phantom of the Opera*. Some people said that Hergé copied the novel, others that he transcended it, just as LaFontaine had Aesop's fables.

Another influence even more important to the development of *Prisoners of the Sun* was Edgar Jacobs. Working with him inspired Hergé. The two illustrators carried on a Ping-Pong match of gags and ideas. It was Jacobs who thought of the seven crystal balls and the car separating from the train while it careened on its way, finally plunging into the water. If one was detail-oriented, the other was even more so.

They were a great professional team and also great friends, but temperamentally opposite. Jacobs developed his story lines methodically and with infinite concern for their verisimilitude, whereas Hergé was more ironic, susceptible to digressions, and in the end essentially detached from the contents. One developed the narrative line by convergence, the other by divergence. Jacobs assigned the greatest possible importance to the

commentary; Hergé wanted it reduced to a minimum. The first was heir to the great tradition of the popular novel; the second created his own world. Jacobs's imagination seemed to feed on darkness, Hergé's on the light of day. One adored murkiness and mystery, the other, light, clarity, and humor. Their contradictions and antagonisms proved enriching and fruitful, though it came at a certain price.

In September 1944, eight months after they had begun working together, Hergé offered Jacobs a 10 percent royalty for the works on which they had collaborated, including all the illustrations for the informational articles that appeared in *Tintin* magazine before they were reprinted individually as color chromo pictures. These could be collected to form a pictorial encyclopedia on various subjects, such as boats and airplanes. The exception was the comic strip of Tintin and Snowy. Hergé reserved for himself the responsibility for drawing all the characters, as well as 55 percent of the royalties and the copyright to all of the works. Jacobs drew the backgrounds and received 45 percent of the royalties.

Their collaboration was never on an equal footing because at the time Hergé was already Hergé, but Edgar P. Jacobs had not yet made his name. The year that Hergé was professionally banned and public opinion had turned against him, he tried to break the boycott by inventing new comic strips with Jacobs. Together they came up with three prototypes under the pseudonym "Olav": a Western, an adventure in the Great North, and a detective story set in Shanghai. Their agent, Bernard Thiéry, claimed to have no luck in trying to place them in various newspapers. This attempt was in addition to their ongoing work of recasting the old Tintin books.[17]

Hergé asked Jacobs to commit to full time. He had become indispensable. Jacobs requested a few days to think it over. The work schedule he had devised gave him time for his own work. Finally he accepted, but on one condition: he wanted to be the cosigner of the Tintin books with Hergé. Now it was Hergé's turn to ask for time to think it over. Eight days later, using Casterman's opposition as an excuse, he announced with profound regret that he couldn't agree to the condition.

In fact Hergé would never have agreed. He would never have shared authorship of his works even if he and Jacobs divided the execution of them. It was an irreconcilable conflict. On the one hand an illustrator with the beginning of a reputation who no longer wanted to be the right-hand man nor to work in the shadow of his boss.[18] On the other, an illustrator with an established reputation who did not want to have his name shadowed on the cover of his own books and his own magazine.

Their differences started with the weekly publication of *The Secret of the Swordfish*, the first episode featuring Blake and Mortimer, Jacobs's new heroes. Jacobs's success was immediate, which did not please Hergé. The team working around them could do nothing to avoid the rupture. They knew Hergé's work habits and the demands of the new magazine and worried seeing him push himself day after day. But neither did they think that Jacobs was in the wrong. Was he going to spend the rest of his life working anonymously on books signed by Hergé? The increasing numbers of enthusiastic readers of *The Secret of the Swordfish* could not understand why Jacobs would work behind the scenes, drawing backdrops and decorative chromos of ships, airplanes, and trains under the signature of Hergé. One day in May 1947 Hergé and Jacobs decided on a friendly separation. But there remained between them barely suppressed bitterness.

A month after their separation on June 19, 1947, *Tintin* magazine abruptly stopped publication of *Prisoners of the Sun*, right at the moment when Captain Haddock has taken a dramatic fall. Readers were puzzled. Hergé never skipped an issue. He had always said that to justify the name of the magazine there had to be at least two pages of Tintin in every issue. He would be damned rather than fail to submit the spread by the deadline. In the past this had occurred only twice, once when the German army entered Brussels, and then when it departed. This time, instead of Tintin and Snowy, two of his other characters appeared. The editors published an embarrassed notice:

> Our friend Hergé needed a rest. Please do not worry; he is in good health. But by expending all his energy to meet his deadline of two pages of *Prisoners of the Sun* our friend exhausted himself. He will be back very shortly, God willing. He is developing the further adventures of Tintin and his brave companions. We are taking advantage of this short intermission to publish, as many of you have requested, the new adventures of *Quick and Flupke*. We are sure that they will entertain you.

In reality Hergé had suffered a breakdown. He vanished without leaving an address. It was a flight into the unknown, a real escapade—that of a man who had come to the end of his rope.

WHEN HERGÉ RESUMED THE STORY of *Prisoners of the Sun* for the launching of *Tintin* magazine, his second plate showed Captain Haddock worried, mulling over dark thoughts, sunk in the depths of his easy chair in

Marlinspike Hall. The Captain was as depressed as his creator, but not for the same reasons. One was tormented by the disappearance of his friend Professor Calculus, the other didn't know what to do with himself. At the start of the year the journalist Dominique de Wespin paid Hergé a visit on her return from China, as she had promised. In 1939 she had left a man full of projects and ideas. Seven years later she returned to find him anxious, tortured, devoured by regrets and remorse. His work was his refuge, the act of drawing his salvation. His confused conversation was so unlike him that it only confirmed her worst fears. "There are too many selves inside me," he confessed to her. "The one with desires, the one who wants to work … I can't ever be myself with all these selves living inside me."[19]

He hadn't stopped working since 1929; now he was paying the price. He was so overcommitted that he couldn't meet his deadlines, and he had always made it a point of honor to meet them. He had resorted to delegating work among his colleagues. When asked to illustrate a life of Saint Louis Marie de Monfort, an eloquent preacher who ministered to the poor and sick, Hergé recommended Pierre Ickx and Joseph Gillain (Jijé).

The three doctors he consulted came to the same diagnosis: overwork. At the time Doctors Ley, Daumerie, and Lambert felt it was premature to say it was depression. However, that might well be the next stage if he did not agree to a period of rest. The day they convinced him that by his obstinate refusal to take a rest he was placing *Tintin* in serious jeopardy and would not be able to draw again until he regained his peace of mind, Hergé dropped everything.

He needed to leave, and his first impulse was to return to the places where he had found solace as a youth. He made his way toward the region of the Abbey of Notre-Dame-de-Scourmont, near the French border, run by the Trappist monks of Chimay. It was more a place of meditation than of prayer. Sometimes accompanied by his old friend Marcel Dehaye, who used to sign his letters to the "stolen" *Le Soir* as Jean de la Lune, he spent hours walking and speaking with the monks, notably Father Gall. When not teaching his classes on theology or preparing his sermons, this extraordinary figure would lose himself in the most erudite research on the lives of the American Indians. He had even been adopted by the Sioux tribe, which of course thrilled the author of *Tintin in America*. They even ventured into the forest to smoke a pipe of peace.

Hergé would also lose himself in conversations with Brother Baudouin, whose spirituality captivated him. These conversations were not merely social exchanges but life savers. The monks addressed an absolute need he

had always felt, but never as intensely as in these times of distress. Reading *The Prayer* by Alexis Carrel still moved him, but it was no longer enough. He was looking for something outside of himself, not through a specific religion but through an act of humility. His contact with the monks renewed him, but not to the point of wishing to become one of them.

This retreat brought him the beginnings of serenity. Formerly when he isolated himself among people of faith, he waited for a voice to speak to him. He waited for the apparition of an angel. He understood now that these things had to come from within him, and what he needed was faith to feel them.

He did not have faith. He would love to have had it, but it was impossible. Despite being drawn to the mystical, he could not imagine for a moment that he could leave this world. All he needed was a prolonged stay in a monastery to realize to what extent he felt a stranger to it.[20]

WHEN HE RETURNED TO BRUSSELS Hergé was confronted with the same problems as before. His retreat had resolved nothing. On the contrary, he felt his problems more acutely because his senses had been sharpened.

He left for another retreat that was less spiritual, in Switzerland, a small house near the village of Gland on Lake Geneva, with a little boat docked in front. It was the second home of the Fornaras family. Charlie was a printer, and his wife, Lise, was a seamstress with Borel; both worked in Geneva. When Hergé arrived, they had no idea who he was, but this simple and sincere couple quickly became real friends. When he left them at the end of two weeks he only wanted to return, to spend more days canoeing, napping, and taking photographs of the people of the community. He wanted to eat ice cream at Beck's and visit the wineries and restaurants. Yet the postcard Switzerland, the country he would return to regularly during his periods of depression, also had a darker side. His friends were steady country people who drank absinthe and who during the war had snuck across the lake to traffic in refugees fleeing the Nazis.

In Brussels *Tintin* continued to publish *Quick and Flupke* but assured readers that *Prisoners of the Sun* would soon resume: "The new and thrilling adventures of Tintin and his friends will be even more exciting." And indeed a month later appeared the headline "Tintin is finally back." The story picked up exactly where it had stopped, as if nothing had happened.

But by the fall Hergé was again feeling anxious. To lighten his workload and to give him time to renew his energies, he agreed to his colleagues'

suggestion that the third strip on the page be replaced with long historical texts under the heading "Who Were the Incas?" His doctors and those close to him began to understand that his condition was due not only to the accumulated pressure of work; there was another element to it. When his friend Marijac came to Brussels to celebrate with Hergé the parallel successes of their magazines, *Coq Hardi* and *Tintin*, he found himself face to face with a man who was disillusioned and sunk in melancholy.[21]

Hergé had difficulty accepting the fact that he would always be considered *incivique*. Public opinion (like the public itself) reserved the right to make up its own mind. Because his case had been closed (hastily, some people said), this continued to fuel doubt about him. Some who felt cheated by the liberation became obsessed about individuals they considered suspect. The problem was so widespread that Dr. De Craene, an eminent psychiatrist and a professor at the Free University of Brussels, made it the subject of a study: Can people deemed *inciviques* change the public's perceptions of them? He believed that it was possible, and urged *inciviques* not to give up hope. However, it would be a slow evolution and required long and patient effort, he concluded.[22]

Three years after liberation Hergé was convinced that he was the subject of a defamation campaign. He identified the instigator as Jeanne Cappe, a writer of juvenile books and an old acquaintance from when they had both worked together at *Le Vingtième Siècle*, and he decided to confront her. He sent her a registered letter demanding a public apology and threatening a lawsuit. He was determined to put an end to these attacks and the whole atmosphere of anonymous suspicion.[23]

Yet when things seemed to calm somewhat, the most insignificant event could cause the attacks to flare up again. Hergé had reached an agreement with the newspaper *Le Phare* (The Lighthouse). Hardly a year old, it was Royalist in its sympathies and regularly denounced the abuses of the political purges. The director, Pierre Fontaine, the former owner of the weekly *Le Rouge et le Noir* (The Red and the Black), was a polemicist who had fought through the occupation and remained a nonconformist spirit although a fervent Royalist.[24] Hergé agreed to publish the comic strip "Quick and Flupke" in the September and October 1947 issues.

There was an immediate reaction. In the Chamber of Deputies the Communist deputy Fernand Demany denounced the publication during a long diatribe against reclassification of the *inciviques*. "Do you know that Hergé is now collaborating with *Le Phare*," he harangued his colleagues, "this illustrator who was a propagandist for the New Order, who made

propaganda drawings aimed at children above all?"[25] Demany also denounced Minister of Justice Paul Struye, who as a lawyer had defended Julien de Proft in the trial against the "stolen" *Le Soir* and who had charged Hergé as part of his strategy. But he was now among those who stood up and defended Hergé, who was grateful and sent him an autographed volume of *Tintin*. Demany and others would continue to remind Struye that there was no such thing as amnesty and that he set a dangerous precedent with his unconsidered defense and exculpation of Hergé.

Demany's diatribe deeply wounded Hergé, who was still not aware of the full extent of the problem. Raymond Leblanc kept from him the details of his efforts in Paris to find a publisher who would launch *Tintin* in France. The project was vitally important strategically to regain his public in the enormous francophone market beyond Belgium. Leblanc never mentioned that he met with editors from a dozen publishers, among the most important Fleurus and Gautier-Languereau, and they all reacted the same way: "Publish Hergé? Not a chance."

Then he happened upon the directors of a small, dynamic publishing firm named Le Lombard, which also had a sufficient stock of paper and the authorization to publish.[26]

Éditions du Lombard, in partnership with a publisher named Georges Dargaud, launched the French edition of *Tintin* in October 1948. The contents were the same as that of the Brussels edition, but Lombard retained the right to adapt the layout, the editorials, the letters to the editor, and the publicity for its own readership. The cover for the first issue featured the hero Colonel Leclerc during the Battle of Fezzan in North Africa. Sales were slow at first because it went head to head with *Coeurs Vaillants* on the newsstands, but success did eventually come. Dargaud, who later published the Asterix comic book series, ignored rumors about Hergé and published his works until 1975. (Dargaud died in 1990.)

Though now regaining an international market, Hergé ended 1948 feeling profoundly isolated and disgusted with what had become of his country. He was thinking seriously of living in exile. Only Germaine and Louis Casterman were aware of this. These plans were wrapped in such absolute secrecy that even after his death most people were unaware of them.

Now forty, Hergé felt that in order to emerge from the postwar morass, he had to cross the Atlantic. He could have chosen France, as had his colleagues Félicien Marceau and Jean Libert, or found asylum in Spain, as

had Léon Degrelle and Paul Werrie. However, Hergé's choice was Argentina. Perhaps his depressive condition had pushed him to become even more perversely radical, but it seems almost impossible to understand his desire to become an expatriate in a land that was condemned for welcoming collaborators and former Nazis. At the end of the 1940s they came in the thousands to settle in Chaco and Tierra del Fuego, with a preference for Buenos Aires, Cordoba, Rosario, and Mendoza. War criminals were more numerous in Argentina than *inciviques* were in Belgium. And yet there Hergé saw his future.

Once his decision was made, his resolve seemed unshakable. At the end of January 1948 he requested a meeting with the Argentinean consul in Antwerp because it would be more discreet than meeting in Brussels.[27] While awaiting the results of his official application, Hergé wanted to learn about the situation of the press and the publishing industry in Argentina. He met with Nestor Orsi, press attaché to the Argentine Legation in Brussels.[28] By April his plans were taking shape. Louis Casterman was one of the few people in his confidence. Hergé promised him that he would not leave Europe without putting the final touches to *The Seven Crystal Balls* and *Prisoners of the Sun*. Once he was settled "over there" he fully intended to continue sending Casterman his drawings. He solicited from Casterman the two official documents required by the Argentineans for him to obtain a visa, one a professional reference and the other a character reference. Professionally he asked to be listed as "an illustrator of humor, author of numerous illustrated books for juvenile readers." For the second category he let his editor choose his words.[29] He was not disappointed: Casterman wrote, "As the owner and director of the publishing firm of Casterman, I have maintained business relations for over twenty years with Mr. Remi, who is an author and illustrator of great talent, and whose works, in terms of their form and contents, are morally irreproachable, justifying the great interest in them by the general public. In every way, I have been in a position to testify to his perfectly honorable character."[30]

At the same time Hergé made direct contact with Belgian friends and acquaintances living in Buenos Aires. In long letters to them he complained about the situation in "this sad country," and he referred to the purification campaign as the "great turmoil." His decision to settle in Argentina was "definitive and without second thoughts." Although Casterman remained the publisher of his books in all the editions, foreign and domestic, he used an agent named John Raynolds Heilbuth, a businessman residing in the capital, to be his representative in his negotiations in Argentina. Juan Peron

had come to power as president a year before, and the atmosphere was unsettled. Hergé urged Heilbuth to take the lead. He wanted an introduction to the minister of education to propose the creation of a magazine for young readers on the order of *Tintin*. This was a far-fetched plan, but also the surest means of obtaining visas for himself, his wife, and his mother-in-law. He was so impatient to leave behind "poor failing old Europe."[31]

While waiting he did everything possible to advance his plans. After seeing an amateur film animated with marionettes and more or less based on *The Crab with the Golden Claws*, Hergé contacted Walt Disney himself. He was inspired by the idea of an animated film produced by the Disney Studios. His characters were well-known in five countries in Europe—Belgium, France, Switzerland, Portugal, and Sweden—and together they formed a sizable market. He sent Disney seven of his twelve books, carefully selected according to their subjects: *The Blue Lotus, The Broken Ear, The Black Island, King Ottokar's Scepter, The Crab with the Golden Claws, The Secret of the Unicorn,* and *Red Rackham's Treasure.* "I know—and you will see for yourself on reading these books—that Tintin's adventures and those of his friends take place on a realistic plane, while your characters in general evolve—delightfully so—in a fantasy or poetic world. I believe that from this difference we can draw great advantage. But your experience in this realm is such that I won't insist any further, and I place myself entirely in your hands."

Two months later the head of public relations of the Disney Studios sent a letter declining his proposal. Their production schedule was booked four years in advance, and at any rate the Disney Company had at its disposal an infinite number of properties in reserve. As if to dissipate any misunderstanding, and to eliminate any shred of hope, he returned Hergé's books to him.[32]

While Hergé was waiting to prepare for his departure for Argentina, his workload was accumulating. He could not finish *Prisoners of the Sun* on his own and took on Jacques Van Melkebeke, the young Guy Dessicy, and his friend Frans Jageneau to help. They gathered at Hergé's Avenue Delleur home to work on the backgrounds, the perspectives, and the interior of the prison.[33] Even this wasn't enough. Hergé was also at a loss for inspiration. He called on Bernard Heuvelmans, a friend from the "stolen" *Le Soir*, who had worked with him on *The Shooting Star*, and asked for help with the plot.[34]

Heuvelmans came up with a final scenario, of which Hergé used only a portion, and furnished him with ready-made visual gags. Over dinner they

agreed on 250 francs (current equivalent, $53) per gag used. In 1947 Hergé deposited 23,000 Belgian francs (current equivalent, $4,890) into Heuvelmans's account and 20,000 (current equivalent, $3,930) the following year for "collaboration on a script."[35]

Nonetheless he still couldn't manage to complete the work that needed to be done, even when he finished the coloring for *Prisoners of the Sun*. He had to redraw *Cigars of the Pharaoh* from beginning to end, reformat other volumes, and complete some other projects—alphabets, folders, vignettes, and coloring books—all the while continuing the adventures of Tintin. He was thinking of giving up. He even thought of a face-saving last-minute solution: not to renew the contract with *Tintin* magazine. When that expired he might attack his backlog of work.[36]

Then one day Hergé vanished again. Even his most loyal defenders at the magazine became seriously worried, as much about his well-being as for the future of their publication. Leblanc was ignorant of where he might be, and he reacted as a newsman as well as an editor. He became convinced that the efficient functioning of such a large-scale company could no longer rest on the shoulders of someone so unstable and unreliable. His admiration for Hergé's creative ability was undimmed, but he could no longer rely on him. He had to invent excuses to mitigate the effect of his absence while waiting for a better solution. Otherwise the magazine was headed for disaster.[37]

For reasons never quite clear, Hergé had decided against going to Argentina. One reason he had wanted to move to South America was to be near Robert Poulet, who for the previous three years had been on death row, awaiting clemency, which finally came in October. The time between the commutation of his death sentence and his release from prison and exile would be a minimum of three additional years. Thus instead of going to the Pampas, Hergé returned to the shores of Lake Geneva.

This time the disappearance lasted six weeks. Hergé was accompanied by a woman twenty years younger than he, married and a relative of one of the illustrators at *Tintin*. There had been several other affairs in the past, passing interludes, nothing more. Those who knew considered them the usual midlife crisis of forty-year-olds trying to prove themselves, a metaphor for middle age. Hergé also had never taken these incidents very seriously. This time, however, he confessed to Germaine that he loved this woman "madly, completely, with [his] whole being." Despite this admission, the affair went nowhere.

His neighbors on Lake Geneva believed that his being constantly under scrutiny in Brussels had made him more anxious. Hergé agreed that he never

felt better or more at peace with himself than at the home of the Fornaras family on the lake. He did no drawing but wrote long letters to Edgar Jacobs, his old colleague, who was himself depressed and seemed the only person who could understand his pain.[38] The letters provided an inventory of symptoms: nerves stretched to the breaking point, insomnia, extreme fatigue. He complained that his head felt heavy. He could feel his face becoming wrinkled, the nape of his neck growing rigid, and an animal burrowing into the base of his spine. "Depressed" and "neurotic" were terms he used about himself, but ordinarily he just used the vernacular, "I am dead."

Having consulted doctors, he turned to healers. First there was the homeopathic priest in a village near Annecy, consulted by government ministers on the verge of a breakdown. Hergé was disappointed in him and sought certified homeopathic healers. They had no remedy for anxiety.

Hergé could no longer read, except cheap thrillers that did not require his sustained attention. He dreaded solitude as much as socializing. He could bear only the company of old friends, notably Jacobs and Marcel Dehaye. Fishing, canoeing, swimming, and walking exhausted him, so he spent most of his time doing nothing. He slept with his eyes open, dwelling on the familiar specters: the stress of launching *Tintin* magazine on top of his responsibilities as an illustrator, the frantic pace of meeting deadlines and managing a team.

On the periphery of his work were personal problems, as with the agent he hired to handle his business interests during the war. He ended his association with Bernard Thiéry in 1947 through lawyers, with each side bitterly blaming the other. The last straw came when his dear friend Gérard Liger-Belair mentioned that Thiéry had just made him sign a contract that gave the agent 20 percent of the proceeds on each copy sold of the Liger-Belair plan of the *Unicorn*. Hergé was scandalized and ripped up the contract on the spot.[39] He felt betrayed by Thiéry, in whom he had placed his confidence.

Hergé could admit to Jacobs that there was a dark side to his character, which made him more vulnerable. During the years right after the liberation, many of his comrades had turned to him. To keep up their morale, especially the most downtrodden, such as Marcel Dehaye, he pretended to be serene and confident about the future. He fought pessimism with humor and irony. However, he felt exactly as they did, only he repressed all his feelings. "I was in a state, forcing myself to appear carefree and completely optimistic," he wrote Jacobs. "But in fact, old man, I was frightened."[40]

In both his private and his professional life, Hergé felt that he had been carrying the world on his shoulders for several years. The weight was crushing him morally and physically. Had his colleagues at Casterman or *Tintin* magazine in Brussels and Paris understood his state of mind, they would not have appealed to his sense of responsibility through the intercession of Jacobs or Germaine. "If you won't come back for me, then at least return for Tintin," Germaine wrote him in a note.[41] He was too drained to be persuaded by this sort of argument.

Yet he also missed Germaine, whom he used to call his "Hergée" in their younger days, and his work. These were the two axes of his life, indispensable to his equilibrium. Every time he tried to get away because he felt the need either to save face or to prove to himself that he was capable of the work, he suffered terribly. However, he had to face the reality: the liberation had shattered something in his relationship with Germaine. He thought only of moving forward, trying to take advantage of his increasing fame and rising sales. Germaine seemed overwhelmed by the new rhythm of life and her husband's ambitions. He was simply going too fast for her. The greater the distance between them, the more he showed a cynical, even cruel side, struggling to control sudden bursts of anger. He still believed that brief holidays could smooth matters over. They went to Paris, where he bought a ring for her, and also to Venice, Lugano, and Brittany. But it was like cauterizing a wooden leg.

One day in the summer of 1948 he discovered that a childhood friend, Jean Libert, was spending several weeks in Glion, located just above Montreux, along with his wife and five-year-old daughter. He was also there for reasons of health. Libert had worked for *Le Nouveau Journal* during the occupation. He had been acquitted in 1945, then, on appeal, sentenced to ten years in prison, and finally released after serving two and a half years. Hergé spent two days with him. They spoke for hours at "La Primavera," the family pension where they were staying.

Libert found his friend almost unrecognizable from the effects of his depression. He was above all an artist anguished at being unable to find inspiration and powerless to give life to his characters. Hergé even asked Libert to find writers and joke writers to help him produce his books. He was desperate. In contrast to Libert, who had recovered with an unshakable confidence in Providence, Hergé was convinced that he had failed in life. "I aspired to be a great painter," he kept repeating, looking off into the distance. Hergé was persuaded that all the great adventures were internal ones; he wanted to stop drawing in order to take up painting. His ability to take risks had atrophied.[42]

Unable to confide in anyone during the best of times, Hergé was even more secretive and closed off when he felt conflicted. The number of people with whom he could speak openly were few. He spoke to them only about his illness and his unhappiness, never about his work. The only exception is in a letter to his wife:

> Tintin has been for me the means to express myself, to project my desire
> for adventure and violence, the bravery and resourcefulness within me.
> That *was* within me. The need to express my vision of the modern
> world, so much ugliness, immorality: arms dealers, the great interna-
> tional corporations sacrificing the lives of men without a second thought.
> Standing against them, a hero without fear and without faults. It's not
> Tintin himself who interests me, it is his actions, his adventures them-
> selves. . . . Tintin would like to become a man. People have often
> commented ironically to me, "but he never grows up, your Tintin!" Alas,
> yes! He has matured without anyone noticing it. He has remained young
> in size, but he has grown up, matured to the point of wanting to go
> inside himself and to thus be able to contemplate the world![43]

Hergé had dragged Tintin into his depression, and it was Tintin who would save his creator. After all, hadn't he always triumphed over all dangers?

Hergé returned to Brussels filled with resolve. He bought a drawing table, a chair, and filing cabinets. All the original documentation for his books (drawings, photos, texts) was stored not in a bank vault but at home. Now he wanted them filed in order, not only to conserve them but to use them for reference.

That fall Hergé picked up the story of *The Land of Black Gold* after an eight-year hiatus. Contrary to what his faithful readers had feared, he had not abandoned the adventure, only suspended it. Learning from the tech- nical problems he had with *Prisoners of the Sun*, he changed his method of working. The weekly version and the book would be identical. He gave up the sacrosanct principle of the double-page spread that had justified the name of the magazine. So that readers would not feel cheated, he would still give them two pages of Hergé each week, one devoted to the adven- tures of Tintin, and the other to the exploits of Jo, Zette, and Jocko.

Resuming the story required some delicacy. Tintin's family had grown since 1940, and Hergé had to use sleight of hand to integrate Captain Haddock into a story at the fifty-sixth plate. It was plainly artificial but

worked because it was done with zest and humor. It was precisely because Haddock's intrusion defied all logic that it was successful. Hergé continued with other adjustments and changes: he reshuffled the sequence of several incidents and introduced Professor Calculus into the story and Marlin-spike Hall into the background décor, replacing the Thom(p)sons' convert-ible with an American army jeep stripped of its camouflage paint.

Several months after the relaunching of this series with all its fanfare, the comic strip suddenly came to an abrupt end. Hergé had disappeared yet again.

This time the magazine took the lead. It was not possible to invoke reasons of health again. They decided to reassure their readers by having each member of the Tintin family talk about the event. Readers were invited to do the same. They transformed the depression of their favorite illustrator into a parlor game.

Finally, in October 1949, after a year's absence, Hergé returned. He drew a self-portrait for the cover of the magazine: an author surrounded by his characters.

As the year came to an end Hergé appeared to have regained his equi-librium. But not everything was going smoothly, his marriage least of all. Father Wallez had worked hard to prevent Georges and Germaine from separating, acting as a go-between to keep them from breaking their vows. He wrote them long letters, and in one counseled Germaine, "Let him know how hurt you are, and that you are waiting, but leave it at that. The Good Lord will do the rest." When that proved insufficient, he recom-mended that they read the medieval monk Thomas à Kempis's spiritual guide *The Imitation of Christ* and follow its wisdom.

Paradoxically Georges had never felt such intense love for Germaine as during these dark years. He had rejected her when he thought there was no room for her in the confines of his self-imposed isolation. It was evident that they had not evolved in unison. But despite this he felt great love for his wife. The long letters he sent her from Switzerland in 1948–49 are heartbreaking in tone. When his depression had not paralyzed him, he professed his love on page after page in a closely written script of lucid prose. Germaine was wife, mistress, mother, best friend. Running out of adjectives to praise her, he recognized that she had given him everything. There was nothing for which he could reproach her. But he had the feeling that they had come to the end of their marriage.[44]

When he returned they took up their life together as before. It was a precarious balance, but they wanted to believe in it. Again Hergé sought

refuge in his work. He did not want to set up a separate office at Rue du Lombard, and so his team came to his home. The big issues were saved for the weekly editorial staff meetings.[45]

In a few years *Tintin* magazine had done remarkably well. The subscription base was more than sixty thousand in Belgium and fifty thousand in France. The success was due to the dynamic and enterprising spirit of Raymond Leblanc. Despite his problems, Hergé remained the artistic director of the publication, in name and in fact. He took his duties seriously, as demanding of his fellow workers as he was of himself, uncompromising about the quality of the drawings. He took it as a compliment when people called him stubborn and a nag. He never deviated from his standards, although he was sensitive to those he dealt with. This was Hergé's studio, not Walt Disney's. In California the star was Mickey, and not those who drew him. Most often their names were not even listed. They were members of a union and anonymous. However, in Belgium illustrators wanted to be recognized. Their signature was precious to them. If you changed their work, they became absolutely ill.

Hergé understood this, but it did not prevent him from telling his colleagues exactly what he thought, without being hostile or devious. In his relations with his colleagues the artistic director of *Tintin* magazine revealed himself to be as implacable as the author of the Tintin books while unfailingly courteous, urbane, and attentive.

He judged his colleagues according to their worth and without consideration for their age, their status, or their reputation. This was the experience of Pierre Ickx, his senior by eight years, a friend since they worked together on the supplement "Jeunesse" of *Le Vingtième Siècle*, when he took it upon himself to correct Hergé's sketch of an English rifle in one of his notebooks. He showed him how it should be, down to the smallest detail. The incident remained in Hergé's memory. One day the same Pierre Ickx submitted three drawings for Hergé's approval.

Hergé's judgment had the dry finality of a verdict. They all looked hastily put together. "The boat in relation to the horizon line reveals a mistake in perspective. The cacti: a simple glance at a Larousse dictionary would have shown you how it is done. As for the wave breaking on the beach, it looks like a stone wall covered with crème fraîche. An illustration for *Tintin* deserves as much care as any drawing that is 'pure art.' It's a question of integrity, don't you think?"[46]

The words were the worst insult that could be addressed to an illustrator worthy of the name. Even those he admired had to endure them, such as

the young Paul Cuvelier, for example. When something did not seem right in his last plates of the adventures of Corentin Feldoë, Hergé told him that they appeared thrown together at the last minute. He attributed this drop in quality to the young man's recent stay in Paris. Money, women, night life, bohemian life in Montmartre, the illusion of the easy life of Montparnasse. It was only work that produced art—only work.[47] To help Cuvelier, Hergé put him in contact with Father Gall at the Abbey of Scourmont so that they could work together on an illustrated history of Indian tribes.[48] He understood that Cuvelier's ambitions risked leading him into a dead end, which he wanted to avoid at all cost. That was also true of Hergé.

Those who had his confidence and abused it paid a heavy price, especially if they committed the abuse in the name of friendship. Eugène Van Nijverseel, known as Evany, his pal from *Le Petit Vingtième,* had a bitter experience. As head of the Tintin Studio he was responsible for producing all sorts of other uses for the illustrations. A prime example was the famous "Tintin coupon," to be reproduced in millions of copies as part of a promotional campaign. After Evany submitted a drawing, Hergé railed about the "dirty and crumpled rag."[49]

When Hergé called something botched, it reflected his philosophy of life. Nothing made him angrier than snobbery. It was more than a crime against intelligence, it revealed a lack of education and a contempt for others.

For Hergé it was a matter of principle. Only the editors of *Coeurs Vaillants* thought that it was about money. From the time they had started publishing him, they had never understood him. Father Courtois might have remembered that their first fights were over the casualness with which they modified the texts of his drawings without telling him. Although Hergé had been a beginner, he had banged his fists on the table. Twenty years later nothing had changed. Twice they had major disputes. The first time, Father Courtois took the liberty of editing some slides based on the adventures of Tintin without telling Hergé and selling the rights to a Parisian film company. Furious, Hergé decided that from then on he would speak only to Courtois's assistant, Father Pihan. He at least did not believe that everything was permitted him because he worked for God. The second time, they went even further. Their firm, Fleurus, published a pamphlet titled *Tintin and Snowy among the Toreadors,* signed Jean Roquette and "based on Hergé." They had simply taken his characters without his authorization. This was unacceptable. He took them to court, suing them for a million French francs (current equivalent, $23,305) in damages and interest.

He wanted to teach them how to behave, even if they started immediately trying to negotiate to avoid going to court.

These were all mere peccadilloes compared to the crisis he had to face concerning Raymond Leblanc. The three-way relationship among Hergé, Leblanc, and Casterman was highly complex. In the beginning the publisher from Tournai was in complete agreement about the publication of *Tintin* magazine. Hergé had always had the courtesy to keep them well informed about his business dealings. Casterman had the first right of refusal on his commercial projects, most of the time. It was by mutual agreement that Hergé became associated with Leblanc for the production of writing paper, decals, and toys derived from the world of Tintin.

The friendship between Hergé and Leblanc started fraying. The success of the magazine made Hergé want to be more closely involved with the business side of the venture. Furthermore he became concerned about the production of books signed by the magazine's illustrators that appeared a little too close to his style. The resemblance struck him more than once, and he started worrying that the confusion would spread.

The misunderstandings and mutual incomprehension reached such a pitch that Leblanc finally threatened to resign from *Tintin* to start a rival magazine. Hergé in turn threatened to turn control of the magazine over to Casterman. Lawyers were brought in to start negotiations, to avoid a break everyone feared would be irreparable. Fortunately their mutual respect managed to survive. Each took a step toward the other. From compromise to accommodation, they found common ground. The day the two partners realized that they could easily do without each other, they also realized that it was in their best interest to work together. They would continue their partnership, though on completely different terms.[50]

Before he became one of the most astute publishers of illustrated books, Leblanc was a newspaper man. He knew how to listen and make himself understood, and he could distinguish simple illustrators from authors. Organized and efficient, he knew how to command. But his conception of work did not mesh with Hergé's sudden and repeated absences. That would have been difficult enough to cope with had he been only the creator of double-page spreads. But Hergé was the magazine's artistic director.

Six months after the publication of the first issue, the editorial staff drew up a tally of the results and came to their initial conclusions. The magazine's format needed to be more tightly controlled. Too much space was given to improvised material that reflected last-minute panic to meet the deadline. The typographical errors, the clumsiness, the inversions, and

other bungling would not be tolerated. An effort had to be made to supply a drawing for most of the titles of the columns. In general the mock-up needed to be more attractive and stylish. And as for the contents, "the general philosophy would be inspired by orthodox Christian principles in the broadest sense. The magazine's guiding spirit should be instruction, education, and entertainment for young people."[51] The two men decided that every other Saturday, together with the editorial staff, they would examine the mock-ups of the next two issues.

Two years later, in 1949, something was still not right. Hergé felt it at the anniversary lunch at the Auberge du Chevalier. In the middle of the meal he turned to Leblanc, hoping he would make a little speech. Without explanation the director said that he didn't feel like it. But everyone, and Hergé most of all, knew that something was wrong.

Later that day he wrote a letter to Leblanc, addressing it to his home and not his office. Hergé had serious concerns about the slumping standards of the magazine. After all, it bore the name of his creation, and he did not want the name degraded, out of pride, of course, as well as business considerations. The equivalent of a patent of invention or a registered brand name, *Tintin* was his only asset.

With the latest issue before him as he composed the letter, he wrote Leblanc that he no longer recognized "his" publication. *Tintin* had become too serious and boring. A color photograph had replaced the traditional line drawing. A number of magazines, even the most prestigious American ones, had remained faithful to the tradition of line drawings. Hergé had always been vocal about his opposition to replacing drawings with photographs. Now he regularly had to face the fact that it had already been done.

Hergé didn't need to have the qualities that Leblanc had. He agreed that his domain was limited to illustrations. This included his understanding of children's psychology, which was alien to the rest of the magazine's management. He was the only one with twenty years' experience in this particular field.

In fact, through his many complaints—pointing out a mistake here, an omission there—he had one major reproach to make to his partner: hiring his friend André Frenez, a former lawyer, to replace Hergé's friend Jacques Van Melkebeke, who had been too compromised by his activities during the occupation. Frenez was "a cold functionary," even the magazine's "public enemy no. 1."

Hergé saw only one solution: that he take charge of editorial as well as artistic responsibilities. He wanted to control everything about the

publication other than administration, finance, and distribution. He would restructure the magazine into a two-headed organization. It was the only way of achieving his dream of what *Tintin* could be: the best illustrated magazine in the world.[52]

Leblanc replied by return mail and with equal frankness. They were in agreement on many subjects, both technical and artistic. As for the rest, he reminded Hergé that he could not effectively consult an art director when said art director vanished without warning and without leaving a forwarding address, and then reappeared when he felt like it, only to disappear again for a year's time a few months later. Had the editorial staff waited for his return, the magazine would have folded. Leblanc was upset and indignant but as firm and determined as the illustrator had been with him. He was not about to be pushed around.[53]

Some storms clear the air. Hergé answered Leblanc's letter with another, filling five detailed pages. But they had within them the seed of reconciliation. Their differences remained but now seemed less ominous and dramatic, and in fact quite reconcilable. Hergé made honorable amends on certain points, pleaded his case, and offered explanations. In brief, he was able to focus on what had motivated their partnership originally: the desire to make a great magazine.[54]

Only a year earlier Hergé had been making plans to drop everything and move to Argentina, there to found another *Tintin* magazine. He had taken great care to conceal this fact from Leblanc. The contradiction between his principles and his actions revealed that he believed he could permit himself much because much was owed him. He was famous. Georges Remi now believed himself to be Hergé.

part III: **recognition**

9.

Toward Fulfillment
1950–1958

THAT HE KNEW HOW TO BE GENEROUS is undeniable. Ingratitude was not in his character. He never abandoned a friend in adversity. Yet these virtues belonged to Georges Remi rather than to Hergé.

Having begun a new start in midlife, the illustrator maintained a curious balancing act: the more he delegated work, the more he drew all the attention to himself; the more he was surrounded by others, the more he wanted to present the image of the solitary artist. He insisted repeatedly that the adventures of Tintin were the work of a single author and not of a factory or a collective. Interviewers sometimes had to persist to get Hergé to recognize the contributions of others and to praise their work.

Given the vanity of artists there is perhaps nothing paradoxical about this. In Hergé's case, however, his self-involvement grew the moment his work became a truly group effort. No longer was Edgar Jacobs backing up Hergé, occasionally joined by temporary helpers. Now there was a team at his house working full time.

Either Hergé denied them rights, or he would praise them as if they were Benedictine monks working at their illuminated manuscripts. Whether disparaged or praised, they constituted the Hergé Studios.

The company was created on April 6, 1950, shortly after Belgium, always unsettled about the "royal issue," voted in a referendum in favor of the eventual return of Léopold III, who had been exiled to Pregny-Chambéry near Geneva, Switzerland. (It disturbed Hergé, a fervent royalist, of course, that the king led with a slight majority among the Flemish voters but not

among the Walloons.) Start-up capital amounted to 250,000 francs (current equivalent, $44,240). Hergé was naturally the principal shareholder and took the title of director. On the board of directors with him were his father, Alexis Remi, Germaine, his mother-in-law, Albertine, and old friends, such as his secretary, Marcel Dehaye; his artistic advisor, Maurice Lemmens; and the illustrator Guy Dessicy.

He had created Hergé Studios for several reasons. The most important was personal: to overcome his depressive state and insecurity, he needed to be part of an organizational structure. Being surrounded gave him reassurance. The second was technical: considering the scope of his production, he was forced to delegate some of the execution and even the conception to his colleagues. The last reason was purely financial: by incorporating himself, he could charge things to the company, and these things were becoming increasingly numerous.

Right from the start Hergé Studios created a false comparison to the Walt Disney Company. Disney was a visionary who had somehow succeeded in bringing talking animals to newspapers, books, and the screen. The illusion was such that the viewer forgot that Disney's characters were animals. He was also a pure businessman. Workers found lacking were pitilessly dismissed. So were those who revealed too much talent. There was no room either for the mediocre or the prima donna. Whether scriptwriters or illustrators, they knew that they were sentenced to forever be effaced by Disney, the brand name.[1]

Hergé adopted another plan. In his mind, his work was that of one man, even if carried out by many. He hadn't created the Studios to diminish his creativity but to expand it. He hoped to gain time to think about his work instead of always being concerned with producing it.

For Hergé, time did not matter, and his depression only confirmed this. It did not matter how many hours, days, or weeks his work demanded. Costs be damned. Material consideration should never outweigh quality. He had trouble drawing, for example, old telephones (because of the number of lines) and derby hats (because of the lack of distinguishing characteristics).[2] Therefore, he devoted to the drawing of these objects an amount of time disproportionate to their importance to the illustration.

What distinguished Hergé Studios from Walt Disney was not solely the differences in the personalities of the two founders. When it came to comic book art, the European mentality was distinctly more individualistic than the American. If you didn't sign your work, you didn't exist. Everyone had

heard of Mandrake the Magician, Superman, Spiderman, and Batman. But who outside an inner circle of fans and specialists knew the names of their creators?

FOR THE FIRST THREE YEARS the Studios remained small scale. In addition to Germaine, there were only three people working around Hergé: an illustrator, a colorist, and a secretary. The atmosphere was congenial. Hergé behaved less like an authoritarian than like the guy in charge, a subtle but important distinction. He still had not given up the idea of gradually bringing his colleagues at *Tintin* magazine to the Studios so he could exert more direct control over its artistic direction without setting foot there. Starting in 1953 Hergé Studios took on more people; there were now fifteen full-time employees working solely on his projects.

Hergé Studios had something of the atmosphere of a Benedictine abbey in its rigor and in the quiet determination with which the copyist-monks performed their labors. It was also a gathering place, an out-of-control classroom, and an English club, where every day at four o'clock honor was paid to the ritual of the cup of tea over which Hergé tested his ideas. Finally, it was a utopian commune that seemed to unite a diverse range of talents.

At the Studios, more than at the magazine, Hergé had all the latitude he needed to help those damaged by the liberation. Over the years would appear the discreet but continuing presence of individuals in a delicate position with the justice system. Jean Libert and Paul Jamin had not simply come knocking at Hergé's door on their release from prison. They were too prominent and did not want to awaken the suspicions of the vigilante committees and thus put their friend Hergé in an embarrassing situation.[3] Libert, under the name "Paul Kenny," would turn his hand to writing immensely popular detective novels around a character named Coplan. Jamin would become an illustrator for the weekly *Pan* under the pseudonym Alidor. Had they overcome their own scruples, it was likely that Hergé would have employed them somehow, just as he had the others: Jacques Van Melkebeke, Marcel Dehaye, and Evany.

Sometimes his assistance manifested itself in a less visible form, such as when he took on as a colorist the young widow of a member of the Walloon Legion (a Belgian brigade that fought alongside the Germans) mysteriously assassinated while out riding. Or lent large sums of money to Robert Poulet for a down payment on an apartment outside Paris, money that Poulet would conscientiously repay.

Had it been up to him he would also have hired Raymond De Becker, his former editor in chief. But Hergé was afraid that it would become a reason to apply Article 123 of the penal code against De Becker, who was of course forbidden from working for any newspaper, play, film, or broadcast. Hergé paid the fees of De Becker's lawyer, Guy Delfosse, who was helping him in his case against the Belgian state and in the European Court of Human Rights. He also lent De Becker money so he could find decent housing in Paris, where he struggled to earn a living. Through his recommendation, De Becker obtained a job as a sales inspector in Swiss bookshops, mainly to study distribution issues involving *Tintin* magazine.[4]

De Becker would continue to be haunted by poverty and would always have trouble keeping up with the times. He became increasingly spiritual and mystic, for a period writing a great deal for *Planète*, a journal of parapsychology and parascience. It was naturally to Hergé that he submitted the outline for *La Politique de "collaboration" en Belgique*, an essay of four hundred pages that he wanted Hergé to cowrite. Hergé hurriedly but politely declined.[5]

Another key person during this difficult postwar period officially became a member of the Hergé Studios in 1953 and would remain with it for twenty-one years as Hergé's secretary, replacing Marcel Dehaye, who became the editor in chief of the magazine. Everyone at the Studios called him "the Baron." Baudouin van den Branden de Reeth would play a major role when the *Tintin* phenomenon became international. Ten years younger than Hergé, he was a journalist who had begun his career with *L'Indépendance belge* before joining the staff of *Nouveau Journal* toward the end of 1942. Both were accused of having Nazi sympathies. For this, after liberation he was sentenced to three years in prison and a heavy fine, despite the fact that his brother Adrien was a major figure in the resistance. Van den Branden was a fervent Léopoldist with close ties to the royal family (hence his nickname). For four generations a member of his family had held a post in the Palace of Laeken.[6] This was naturally the sort of thing that would have deeply impressed Hergé.

Van den Branden was in charge of everything aside from drawing, specifically internal organization and public relations. He was the filter, the éminence grise. When fans and invitations became overwhelming, he acted as the screen, protecting the master from importuners of all sorts: journalists, collectors, publicity hounds. He helped Hergé by editing out the adverb that slowed the sentence, or fighting for a semicolon that modified

the pacing of the sentence. But one duty superseded everything: that of personal secretary in charge of correspondence.

With Hergé's increasing fame, the volume of his mail took on frightening proportions. He was one of those courteous men who not only acknowledged a letter but answered by return mail. Any deviation from this rule would have seemed an unbearable ethical failure on his part: "Not answering children's letters would be to betray their dreams."[7]

A new routine was established: every morning Hergé read all the letters and answered everyone with the humor and humility that were his trademark. Whenever he thought it necessary he assured young fans that Tintin—like Tom Thumb, Gulliver, and Ali Baba—really and truly existed, but only in books.

Hergé left to his secretary subjects that were too technical and required research. When he was traveling or ill or simply overwhelmed, he turned over all correspondence to van den Branden. But he didn't want this to be made public, and more than once corrected his secretary's more polished literary style. He preferred a more neutral tone, more spontaneous, less pure, a vocabulary of words in current usage among teenagers of all social classes. The letters on which Hergé prided himself became more and more surreal, reflecting the atmosphere in some of his books.

The letters ran the gamut. Frequently children addressed their letters to Mr. Casterman, as if he were the illustrator, and to Mr. Hergé as the publisher. Others, having heard about the "School of Brussels," asked Hergé for its address in order to apply. Not to mention all those who had matrimonial designs on Captain Haddock. And it was a national sport to find the most infinitesimal errors in his books. But there were also a huge number of correspondents who asked for advice on how to become an illustrator. To which Hergé invariably replied: Learn to see, make sketches from nature, study perspective and anatomy, learn spelling, and work, work, work!

A typical *Tintin* book contained an average of eighty-three thousand typographical characters, and Hergé was terrified of typographical errors. He felt it reflected sloppiness. He was always scrupulous about his usage and familiar with subtle issues of syntax. Whenever anyone questioned him about something, he was prepared with a defense, having consulted his authority, Joseph Hanse's *Dictionnaire des difficultés grammaticales et lexicologiques*. His obsession with language did not extend to foreign translations. How could it have? The exception, which was naturally understandable, was Dutch. After noticing grammatical errors in the

Flemish-language versions of *The Broken Ear, The Shooting Star,* and *The Crab with the Golden Claws,* he solicited the expertise of a professor at the Atheneum of Schaerbeek.

His main advice was to look and work. In other words, only by drawing can you become an illustrator. This was not a casual remark, but the most sincere expression of his faith in his art. It might appear simplistic or elementary. Nevertheless it reflected the intimate truth of an autodidact who could not believe what he had become.

Once you joined Hergé Studios it was to stay. Hergé could not bear anyone leaving. However, in the course of the years many did. Some were only passing through, and Hergé encouraged them to go when he thought their future lay elsewhere. Right from the start of Hergé Studios, two names would stand out: Bob De Moor and Jacques Martin. These two men would have an impact on Hergé, each in his own way, just as Jacobs had symbolized the early years.

In 1948 De Moor, a twenty-three-year-old from Antwerp, was introduced to Hergé when he timidly showed him the illustrations he had brought for *Tintin* magazine. The Flemish-language press could testify to his enormous productivity. De Moor could accomplish in half an hour what other illustrators would take a day to do. After having illustrated *The Lion of Flanders* in *Kuifje*, he moved to the French edition of *Tintin* magazine as illustrator, most notably of *Conrad the Bold* and *Cori the Sailor Boy*. One day on leaving an editorial meeting, Evany introduced him to Hergé, who was already a living legend for illustrators of his generation. Face to face with him, and to please him, De Moor reverted to Flemish and said, haltingly, "I know your work, it's really not bad at all."[8]

De Moor's professional skills were such that he made himself indispensable without trying. Hergé appreciated his kindness, generosity, and discretion. His specialty was drawing, and in the drawings, the backgrounds. Hergé considered him an extension of himself. Known for his technical talent, De Moor revealed a creative quality that raised his work well above mere reproduction. Down to the smallest detail in the décor of a vignette, De Moor did such a complete job that nothing remained to be done. In his way he was even more obsessive than Hergé; he even erased pencil marks on the back of plates. Both he and Hergé had the habit of rendering their own pencil drawings in ink, one with a pen, the other a paint brush. This modified the unified tone and the depth of the black. Without ever being slap-dash, De Moor could draw faster than his own shadow.

He could complete eight plates a week (each plate being a full page of final art, ready for the printing process). De Moor knew he had arrived when, comparing two identical drawings of locomotives with Tintin as the only figure, Hergé had to admit that he couldn't tell his drawing from that of De Moor.

Jacques Martin's contribution to Hergé Studios was altogether different because he was someone else altogether. Trained as an engineer, he came from an aviation family and was passionate about history and classical painting. His tastes were eclectic, ranging from comic books to high art. In his imagination Tintin stood alongside Titian. His passion for drawing was born at a precise moment: between the publication of *The Broken Ear* and *The Black Island*. After the war he worked with a number of publications before he gathered enough nerve to submit his drawings to *Tintin* magazine. Raymond Leblanc was embarrassed because he had to reject them, saying that the artistic director thought them too detailed and overworked; they sacrificed harmony for precision. Several years would pass before Hergé revised his judgment.

Hergé had admired the way Martin presented the action of *The Golden Sphinx* and started calling for his assistance in 1949. He had discerned in him not only a universe, an eye, and a skillful hand, but also an infallible documentary memory. He never hesitated to call on him, such as when he needed a drawing of a 1949 Buick. In return Jacques Martin borrowed Hergé's *National Geographic*s, looking for pictures of Carthage or of the Azore Islands archipelago, which he needed for *Alix*. They started working together on a regular basis when Martin was commissioned to draw the chromo illustration for the section "Voir et Savoir" (dealing with airplanes, locomotives, airports), very popular with young readers of the magazine. Hergé then invited him to lunch and asked him to work with him at the Studios. He had to ask twice, because six months later Martin still hadn't decided. He was not ready to sacrifice his independence, even to work with the man whose work had dazzled him in his youth, whose discipline, probity, and perfectionism had made such a lasting impression. When he finally accepted, it was on condition that Hergé, against his will, also hire Martin's two assistants. On January 1, 1954, Jacques Martin officially joined the team at Hergé Studios.[9]

Hergé considered Bob De Moor his closest assistant; Jacques Martin would become his most indispensable critic. Unlike his Flemish colleague, he lacked the temperament of a diplomat. When people said that he was one of the most difficult persons to deal with, they meant that he was one

of the few who told his superiors what he actually thought. The structure of a story was key, and if it didn't work, he said as much. If the story held together, the rest would follow. And if he was obsessed by perspective, it was partly due to Hergé's reactions to his early work. "You have all the right ideas," Hergé told him, "but still need to learn to draw."

Hergé would always be grateful to Martin for his honesty, even if he was as irritated by Martin's critical attitude as he was by the linguistic punctiliousness of van den Branden.[10] Anyone other than Martin would have been upset. Martin felt vindicated. He was flexible enough to take ribbing by the boss.

There was one thing on which they never agreed. Hergé wanted gags everywhere, in every comic strip. Martin believed that they took up too much room and wanted them to be used in moderation. He would explain, in vain, that his stories did not rely on the comic element but on suspense. Even their concept of the gag was different. Hergé's notion was less and less mechanical, more and more free form; Martin remained in the slapstick spirit of Max Sennett. Hergé indulged in situations that were more and more absurd; Martin preferred the car chase.

Once the lineup at the Studios was complete, the division of responsibilities occurred fairly naturally. To Bob De Moor fell the work of the background and décor, to Jacques Martin the plot and characters. But as soon as he received his first assignment, Martin realized that were he ever to become known it would not be thanks to Hergé. His job was to finish *The Valley of Cobras*, the final adventure of Jo, Zette, and Jocko, of which only the first twenty-five plates had been completed. They both worked on the story, but Martin did all the drawings. However, the publisher would not let him cosign the book with Hergé. Hergé also opposed it; he had, after all, paid Martin to do it.[11]

Martin and De Moor quickly were given the space necessary to devote to their own projects. But when they worked on projects for the Studios, it was as hired hands. Though he treated them as colleagues and friends rather than as employees, Hergé always distanced himself from them. The Studios was named for Hergé, not Tintin. When someone had the good fortune to become a member, he or she understood the terms.

It was about telling a story—nothing more, nothing less. If you wanted to make pictures, give up comic strips and show your work in a gallery. Hergé had been saying this for twenty-five years. He had an ideal conception of the comic strip and held to it. He could not conceive of

his profession in any other terms. His experience only reinforced his conviction.

A story began with an idea. He did not look for it because that was the best way of not finding it. It came naturally, out of the moment, the news, chance meetings, the circumstances of life. Hergé was a sponge; he absorbed everything he observed. Intense periods of receptivity sometimes alternated with long dry spells. Why? He did not want to know. He was afraid of discovering the inner mechanism that made them function. Or stagnate. He was schooled in the adventure novel, the detective story, and silent movies; he could not start without a thread. When he had it firmly in hand right from the start, then he could advance fearlessly into the maze of empty plates.

When he was pressed on the subject of the inspiration of his work, Hergé always maintained that nothing was premeditated. The artist was not an intellectual; he was intuitive. Everything was born of instinct. In his mind the line came directly from his unconscious, where it proliferated without losing the pace of an adventure. Among his imitators everything became too premeditated. Talented illustrators were able to imitate Hergé's hand and plagiarize his stories, but none other than he could ever reconstitute his touch.

Hergé believed that the comic strip artist was a kind of novelist with pictures, and consequently sui generis. The goal of this humble artisan in a subgenre was to entertain young people by offering and cultivating a type of morality. He would feel guilty if his work degenerated into violence or vulgarity, which he loathed. Yet for all that, he refused to see himself as a moralizer or an educator.

From his illustrators he expected a steady hand, confidence when confronting the blank page. Shadows and chiaroscuro were to be banished as worthless conventions. Hergé's aversion to shading and toning down the colors stemmed from the days when such techniques were prohibited by the poor-quality paper. It coincided with his tendency to focus on only the essentials, with just one goal: maximum comprehension. Hergé played the card of absolute clarity to the point of transparency. Clarity was the one great quality he granted the American comic strips of the 1930s.

He let himself daydream as he was drawing, but only within strict limits. His imagination was free but always under surveillance. Traditional in his storytelling techniques, Hergé was modern in his rejection of nostalgia. The legibility of the composition and the soundness of the graphics were

indispensable qualities of a naturally creative person, the results of a highly trained eye. Learning to draw was first about learning to see.

Hergé's Guide to Comic Book Composition

1. Find a story line sturdy enough to hold for the whole course of the adventure. A simple chase connecting gags is not enough.
2. Find a story that is believable enough to seem true. Jot it down on paper, in twenty lines, maximum.
3. Divide up the story, panel by panel, plate by plate. Each page has to conclude with an element of suspense.
4. Penciling-in stage: sketch the figures with a cursory background drawn with 9-cm (3.54-in) squares on Steinbach paper measuring 51 by 36 cm (20 by 14 in) in size, within a useful format of 40 by 29.5 cm (15.75 by 11.6 in), which is to say twice as large as a book page. Divide the sheet into four strips of 9.5 by 29.5 cm (3.74 by 11.6 in) each, separated by a blank space 6.5 cm (2.55 in) wide. (The blank areas were used as scrap paper, combining all the early versions. All sorts of notations were scribbled there: portraits, objects, landscapes, lists of names, addresses, and telephone numbers.)

When the characters are sketched, everyone takes turns posing, including Hergé himself. Everything is still open to debate. The plate is often criss-crossed with broad strokes of the eraser and things crossed out. It will only start looking "normal" when the action is set.

5. Final drawings are copied square by square to offer a better selection and reframed and placed on another white page, which will become the definitive plate. Touch-ups and final details are added. Copy is moved around. Hergé ceaselessly sought simplification. His objective: hide the scaffolding.
6. Coloring stage: focus on the costumes and the background décor, relying on a solid base of documentation. Exactitude is required, as the settings (desert, sea, moon, jungle) aren't static.
7. The inking stage is done on Schoeller-Parole paper, with a Gillott's Inqueduct G-2 pen (made in England) of stainless steel, which can be cleaned in water and has a small ink reservoir. (Hergé stocked up on these pens before the war. Thirty years later he still had a few. He used to sharpen them with a steel file to conserve them as long as possible.)

8. Photographed by the photo engraver, the black-and-white plate is transferred to transparent film accompanied by several proofs on blue-gray paper.

9. More coloring: the colors applied in flats do not take into account shadows or shading. Watercolor is used for delicate tints, Ecoline for bright colors, and, if necessary, gouache for opaque colors. (Hergé established standard guidelines. For example, there were to be two superimposed layers for Tintin's sweater to bring out the color's full intensity.)

10. Set out the dialogues on the typewriter to gauge the exact number of letters for each vignette, to calculate, with the help of a grid, their position in the dialogue balloons. Draw in the letters. Lettering is delicate because it poses numerous problems. (At these times they also had to consider the English translators, who had to change the French Milou into "Snowy," the only acceptable name in five letters that would not exceed the line when Tintin spoke to his dog.)

11. Last, add the graphics of sound effects, which consist essentially of "Crack!" "Bang!" "Bzzzz."

IN THE BEGINNING "Tintin" was a serial. As such it obeyed the fundamental law of the genre: using suspense to send the reader from one page to the next. Suspense marked a hiatus that increased the reader's expectation. Had Hergé been a musician, it would have been a pause. He could create suspense from the most improbable elements. For example, Tintin bursts into a cave where bandits are holed up. A trap. "Hands up!" But in the opposite corner a bandit is sleeping. He also yells, "Hands up!" Tintin is disarmed. They are going to kill him. A speech by the bandits recalling certain past incidents. Then one of the bandits asks to speak: he declares that he alone should have the honor of killing Tintin. They give him the Browning automatic. He walks toward Tintin, takes aim, then spins around, shouting, "Hands up!" Tintin had once saved the life of his brother.

All the elements (the panel, the page, the picture, etc.) are subordinate to the story. It's all about facilitating the narration, and, as always, clarity and legibility are the two fundamentals. The reader should be able to identify the characters and understand the action when opening the book to any page. There are no panels remaining purely for atmosphere once the

book is finished. No panel is extraneous. Ideally each one serves a double function: it picks up on the preceding panel and anticipates the panel that follows. To accomplish this Hergé sometimes had to make substantial cuts. When done successfully, the result is as intricate as lace. His colleagues understood this only when it came time to recast one of his earlier works. It was sometimes easier to start from zero rather than risk ruining the miniaturist character of his work.

His gags were the only narrative element that maintained their autonomy. They could be displaced without damaging the story, but there was one absolute condition: they had to obey an internal logic that corresponded to a rhythm in three parts: the set-up, the crescendo, and the fall. In his personal notes Hergé always marked them briefly in a telegraphic style, summing up the gag in a few words. Without realizing it, he had created a madcap inventory:

> Mistake due to darkness: saddles a cow instead of a horse, turns on the switch of the television instead of the lights, beats up his partner instead of the enemy.
>
> Policemen: they come to board the boat. The gangplank is sawed through. Plouf.
>
> Distracted scientist or policeman: Put a fishbowl on his head instead of his bowler hat.
>
> Detective takes Snowy's paw prints.

It's evident that he never outgrew Chaplin's influence. There are Hergé books lacking suspense, even without narrative, but never without gags. In his mind, the ideal reader was an attentive child who could laugh out loud from time to time. He never sought to place himself at the level of children; they had to raise themselves to his level.[12]

THE MOST TIME-CONSUMING of all tasks, and the reason Hergé eventually hired a dozen assistants, involved the recasting of his older books. In 1942 he was resigned to hiring help for technical reasons: reformatting, converting from black and white to color, reducing the number of pages, and so on. But after the war another reason emerged, one more connected to the spirit of his work. No longer was it merely a matter of correcting errors or changing the aesthetics, but of changing the work's whole orientation. Hergé was no longer merely adapting old works to a new format; he was reinventing them.

Modernizing *The Blue Lotus*, which he'd undertaken at the end of the war, had not completely altered the work. The changes were minor and mostly involved Edgar Jacobs's maniacal precision. Jacobs had searched obsessively for a way of obtaining a Chinese-looking red for the lacquered columns. With a little vermillion, a dash of ochre, he finally discovered it—in vain, it turned out, because the photo engraver and the printing process produced another shade. Hergé was helped by a translator-illustrator sent by Father Gosset, who had corrected the Chinese text in the narrative as well as on the posters, shop signs, walls, and storefronts in the background. Mainly Hergé worked at condensing his original black-and-white book, from 124 to 62 pages. He knew that readers would notice a difference in style and a thickening of his lines in the beginning, but he had resigned himself to redrawing the first four pages of the book.[13]

With most of the other early books Hergé had to go much further. He had profoundly reworked *King Ottokar's Scepter*, and the hand of Edgar Jacobs jumps out at you in the Balkanization of the background and the costumes. They had worked cheerfully together; proof of this can be found in the last scene at the ball in the palace, where the two colleagues and their friend Jacques Van Melkebeke are pictured standing next to a sumptuously dressed Germaine. Paul Remi, Ginette Van Melkebeke, and the painter Marcel Stobbaerts are also in the crowd.

Modernizing *Tintin in the Congo* and *Tintin in America* during and after the war, Hergé had to do more than condense them. He also wanted to make his hero more international, less Belgian. Tintin no longer teaches the history of the Walloons and the Flemish to the children in the jungle, but arithmetic instead. And when his life is in danger Tintin no longer cries, "Let's die like a true Belgian!" He also stops commending his soul to God.[14]

Once the Studios were fully staffed at the beginning of the 1950s, Hergé was looking forward to fine-tuning his early works. Correcting errors was the most obvious task, though he was also aware that a growing number of readers, especially the hardcore younger readers, delighted in searching them out. In *Prisoners of the Sun* the *Pachacamac*, like all boats more than 300 feet (100 meters) long, should have a nighttime light not only up front, but also in the rear. In *Cigars of the Pharaoh* Snowy appears on page 52 between Tintin and the maharajah, though he had been separated from his master on page 47 and last seen on page 50 at the end of a leash held by the Thom(p)sons searching for ... Tintin! Hergé suggested to Casterman that they hold a contest "with the goal of finding and notifying us when a

character is not where he should be. This without saying that it was done on purpose but also without denying it either."[15]

Some of the changes were not to correct errors as such, but to defuse awkward moments. For example, Casterman received complaints after the publication of *The Seven Crystal Balls* that the Indian with a skull for his head appearing on the title page frightened children. Hergé agreed that it had not been a felicitous choice and replaced it with a comic image of Haddock. Likewise a scene with snakes was eliminated from *Cigars of the Pharaoh*.

While Jacques Martin was redrawing all the airplanes, Hergé was erasing ambiguities from his characters. The Egyptologist Sophocles Sarcophagus, for example, joins the ranks of victims and becomes a good man, and Rastapopoulos's status as a villain is confirmed. Inside jokes and references were added. In the cover image of *Cigars of the Pharaoh* one of the mummies, resembling Edgar P. Jacobs, has the label "E. P. Jacobini." In the story the enigmatic Grossgrab is a reference to the German Egyptologist Grossgrabenstein, a character from *The Mystery of the Great Pyramid*, by a certain Edgar Jacobs.[16]

Sometimes the changes were less innocent. In 1946 Hergé agreed to Casterman's demands to alter the race of a mother and child, the porter at a hotel, and a gangster in *Tintin in America*. Simon and Schuster, his New York publisher, which was bringing out his second book, also wanted some race changes in *The Crab with the Golden Claws*. Hergé explained to a reader, "I have not replaced the blacks in *The Crab with the Golden Claws* with white people; they are now of an indeterminate race. You can immediately see that they are not from here, but exactly where they come from remains a mystery. What the American editor wanted was the following: No blacks. Neither good blacks nor bad blacks. Because blacks are neither good nor bad: they don't exist (as everyone knows, in the USA)."[17]

In the new version the black sailor onboard the *Karaboudjan* becomes white. In the same spirit Captain Haddock's insulting epithets follow the temper of the times and a new sensitivity. He no longer shouts, "Anthracites! Blackamoors!" but "Doryphore! Boob!" and the (curious) "Black Marketeers" becomes "Iconoclasts!" because the objects of his anger have been whitewashed. However, he continues to use the expletive "Licorice Juice!"

A more complicated problem to resolve was alcohol. It is true that *The Crab with the Golden Claws*, the first story in which Haddock becomes a presence, holds the record for the number of pictures with a direct

relationship to alcohol: 27 percent.[18] So as not to provoke the wrath of the national education lobbies and moralistic groups, both of which influenced American critics and editors, Hergé proposed to attenuate the text here and there. Afraid that he had not gone far enough, he eliminated all images of Haddock drinking straight from the bottle, filling in the blank spaces with "continuity texts."[19]

If it wasn't censorship, it looked like it. Hergé seemed to find it natural not to resist and made no secret of all his alterations: "The blacks have been whitened, and Captain Haddock has to refrain from guzzling his drink," he wrote a reader.[20] He resigned himself to puritanical American morals. However, the expurgated version was not confined to his overseas readers. Though his publishers claimed the demands originated with his New York editors, they seemed to agree with the changes and incorporated them.

But there were limits. Hergé himself was a connoisseur of all sorts of alcohol, and though Belgium had had a law against drunkenness on the books since 1919, Hergé never for a moment even considered the demand that the brave Captain undergo a detoxification cure. Haddock had indeed appeared to be an alcoholic when he first met Tintin, but he had evolved into a connoisseur of whisky.[21] His lapses were rather exotic: *pisco, spadj, aguardiente*. When a major cognac producer proposed that he replace whisky with cognac to stress the prestige of the European drink, Hergé agreed, as an exception. In the next adventure Haddock is offered a glass of cognac and drinks it to demonstrate his appreciation. But immediately afterward he returns to his preference for malt.[22]

GENERALLY CASTERMAN WAS IN FAVOR of updating the *Tintin* books, but they became alarmed by the scale of the reworking. At the end of 1956, for example, they urged Hergé to cut back on his ambitious reworking of *The Broken Ear*. It did not matter to them that he redrew a panel to change the language, but they balked when he proposed redrawing ten whole pages (out of sixty-two) to deepen the background, such as when Tintin goes up the River Badurayal to find the Arumbayas. They were most worried about the readers noticing a difference between Hergé's style in the 1930s and twenty years later, not to mention the technical issues raised by having to match the color schemes and the textures.[23] Casterman's sensitivities to readers' reactions were well founded. When Hergé made extensive changes in a book, his readers expressed their reactions even more virulently than his publishers did. They felt it was their right to complain because the books had had such an influence on their imaginative life.

Hergé had to face up to his critics, as was the case when he made significant changes in *The Shooting Star*, a work shaped by the events in 1941. The first change concerned the American expedition launched against their European rivals in a pitiless race to recover the precious mineral Phostlite. In the new version the team lost its American identity. New York, the headquarters of the "villains," was replaced by Sao Rico, the capital of an imaginary state. This team's flag is a black cross on a red ground instead of the Stars and Stripes.

His second revision concerned the depiction of Jews. Some have assumed that this was when Hergé erased the two panels showing Isaac and Salomon rejoicing at the coming of the end of the world because they would avoid their creditors. He had in fact removed them in 1942; they appeared in the serial but not in the original edition of the book. Hergé thought that the sequence was filler, which became superfluous in the finished work. But he did change the name of the most odious villain in the book. "Blumenstein" became embarrassing after the end of the war, less for Hergé than for his publishers. Casterman himself took the initiative, to forestall critics.[24]

Interestingly the second run of the book in its original version after the war did not cause the dreaded public outcry. A Parisian complained, and the author replied. One reader sent a long letter explaining that whereas before the war her family considered anti-Semitism merely asinine, she now considered it a crime. Hergé wrote her a detailed letter assuring her of his aversion to all forms of prejudice. He pointed out that his caricatures of British colonials, African sorcerers, and Japanese swindlers were no more racist than his portrait of Blumenstein was anti-Semitic. "The suffering of a people, of a race," he wrote, "did not automatically confer a certificate of virtue to certain isolated villains in the community (who usually escape the common fate)."[25] These were the only two reactions, which Hergé did not consider worrisome: "You can't call it a general outrage."[26]

Later, when asked about this subject in an interview, he replied, "*The Shooting Star* was composed before the Nazi atrocities and the death camps became known; otherwise you can be sure I would never have written this."[27]

Although Hergé was not happy about these changes and grumbled about his publisher's thin skin, he complied. He replaced "Blumenstein" with "Bohlwinkel," whose irony was clear only to those familiar with the Brussels dialect. "Bohlwinkel" was inspired by *bollewinkel*, a small candy store. Ironically one day he would receive a bitter complaint from a Mr. Bohlwinkel, a reader of Jewish origin, shocked that Hergé would use such a name for a character as unscrupulous and villainous as this.

Blumenstein would pursue Hergé to the end of his days and was the origin of a curious incident regarding the painter Pierre Alechinsky. Alechinsky was a native of Brussels who used to say that he was Belgian by "distraction" and French by adoption. Jewish on his father's side and Walloon on his mother's, he had been a devoted reader of *Tintin* in his youth. (He had read the stories as books in their black-and-white version, not in *Le Vingtième Siècle*.) He was fascinated by their expressive action and cinematic sequencing, which later influenced him as an artist. He saw Blumenstein in the wartime *Le Soir* as a young refugee.

When Hergé and Alechinsky met in 1969 and decided to exchange works, the painter inscribed in the margin of one of his large ink drawings, titled *Sources of Information,* "To Herger [making his name look Jewish], source of pictures, with admiration from Pierre Alechinsky, Jan. 4, 1969." When Hergé pointed out the error, Alechinsky replied, "I hope an eraser will do the trick, but so many family names end with an 'r': Bamberger, Blumberger, Braunberger...."

Alechinsky recounted this event in one of his books, and once he'd read it Hergé answered him immediately. "This being the case, you are a little too severe with me for this Blumenstein from the year 1940. I admit that I was wrong, but (and I hope that you will believe me) I was far from imagining that the Jewish stories that people told (and still tell today, like stories about people from Marseilles, or the Scotch, and, more recently, stories about the 'belches' [Belgians]) would lead to such horrors."[28] Again Hergé's equations seem willfully obtuse.

Although Hergé could not erase the past, he could play it safe. At the end of 1950 he completed a list of "corrections to be made in the *Tintin* books" and listed the details to be worked on: the curve of the mustaches of the Thom(p)sons, the color of a cap, the number of steps to the entrance of Marlinspike Hall. He underlined two changes. The first was to turn the blacks into whites in *The Crab with the Golden Claws*. The second was to change the shape of Mr. Bohlwinkel's nose in *The Shooting Star*.[29]

Henceforth when readers tried to catch him in an error by pointing out the contradictions among the different versions of his books, Hergé was ready for them. When the old accusations of colonialism, racism, and anti-Semitism cropped up, he had a prepared response: "I am not excusing myself, I am explaining."[30]

He felt that was all he needed to say. For commercial reasons he wanted to satisfy his publishers, but not to the point of being false to himself. He believed it was an honorable position, whatever his opinions and his past.

Others changed their stripes out of opportunism or weakness of character, but not Hergé. When he refused to rework *Tintin in the Land of the Soviets*, it was not out of fear of arousing the Kremlin's wrath; he was thinking of what it would do to the illustrations and the story.[31]

THE 1950S WERE A PERIOD of return to the moral order. That, at least, was the avowed policy of the authorities.

In the United States warning signs of censorship appeared in 1949, when the reporter Debbie Dean, the heroine of a hugely popular comic strip, was suddenly forced to say farewell. Her creator had let the word "drugs" appear in one of her speech bubbles. At the same time, a public opinion campaign led to the censoring in three states (Michigan, New York, and Massachusetts) of comic books that vindicated crimes. Launched by a psychiatrist named Frederic Wertham, who believed the comics were making violent crimes seem enticing, the campaign reached its apogee in 1954 with the publication of his book, *Seduction of the Innocent,* and the promulgation of the "Comics Code Authority." It was a charter of self-censorship of McCarthyite inspiration, and it had the same effect on the publishers of comic strips as the Hays Code had on film directors. Women had to be modestly dressed, their bodies should not be flaunted, government and religion deserved respect, the word "horror" must not appear in the title. Though it all seemed puritanically American, Europe was not far behind.

At the beginning of the fifties in France a meeting was called of all the members of the new Commission for the Surveillance and Control of Publications for Children and Adolescents. Among its members were representatives of several concerned ministries and agencies, youth groups, and family associations, as well as newspaper editors and even illustrators. They gathered to hear the inaugural speech given by the Keeper of the Seals, René Mayer, highlighting the importance of this new struggle:

> We have seen publications, supposedly "for children," offering them exaggeratedly dramatic adventures, whose generally unrealistic inventions, arbitrary or absurd, only serve as the pretext for upsetting episodes of human violence and fantastic deeds accomplished by brutal force. The legislators wanted to protect children from being exploited by people more concerned with their own self-interest and assuring their profits than in exercising a moral and salutary influence on young minds.[32]

This was the tone set by this assembly of diverse people, which owed its existence to an alliance between Communists and Catholic legislators. Since 1947, when the Communists proposed a law concerning children's publications and the Catholics seconded the motion immediately, an alliance of *Vaillant* and *Coeurs Vaillants* had been formed. This surprised only politicians ignorant of the world of comic strips, unaware that these two lobbies controlled this industry. At this stage it was only a question of guaranteeing the morality and patriotism of those in charge of children's publications. The worst was still to come. A campaign was forming in the press. A purely nationalist argument began to be aired, but the polemics went beyond the left or the right. The writer Jacques Perret was one of the few to denounce the muzzling of children's publications, which was simply a pretext for eliminating the American competition.

"If you have to censor everything that is idiotic and vile, let the censors start with the adult press, some of which outdo us by far!" wrote Perret, railing against the hypocrisy underlying this proposed law.[33] You did not have to be a genius to understand that behind the moralizing other factors were at work aside from wanting to protect young people: *Vaillant* was 100 percent French, *Coq Hardi* was 12 percent American, *Tarzan,* 50 percent American, *Donald* and *Zorro,* 100 percent American. Protectionism lay behind the debate.

The illustrators were naturally in favor of the projected law; it was in their interest, even if they were not proud of it. The exception was Alain Saint-Ogan: "The newspapers are flooded with American cartoons so that a person cannot earn a living in that profession."[34]

The struggle against violence, vulgarity, and pornography was only a screen for those frantic for protectionism in the face of foreign competition. They continued using the cultural excuse. To hear them you would believe that the genius of Descartes was menaced by the muscles of Tarzan.[35]

The law on "publications destined for young people" was finally voted on in July 1949. The Communists walked out because they refused to include a clause that would have reserved 75 percent of each publication for French illustrators. Certain articles of the law were constraining. Article 2, for example, stipulated that "said publications cannot include any illustrations, any stories, or chronicles, any categories, any insertions presenting in a favorable light acts of banditry, lies, theft, laziness, cowardice, hate, debauchery, all acts categorized as crimes or violations, or of a nature to demoralize childhood or youth."[36] Five years later the law was amended

with additional restrictions. The paragraph was completed with "or that inspire or entertain ethnic prejudices."

Hergé, already so sensitive to the currents of decolonization, was directly affected by this clause. The commission recommended that illustrators not characterize natives as cruel, treacherous, or foolish, and "in stories called 'colonial' should take extra care not to offend foreign readers, and encourage domestic readers to feel sympathy and solidarity for them."[37]

The new censors had three measures at their disposal: warning, indictment, and legal penalties. They had their offices in the Ministry of Justice. Their first target was *Tarzan* magazine. He was not deemed a suitable hero for the family: he was too naked, too lascivious, too wild. "Man must at least control the myths he shows children. We have good reasons to deem Tarzan, the Ape Man, suspect."[38] But Tarzan was not the only one caught in the machinations of the censors.

In Brussels everyone understood that this accursed law was conceived of as a weapon against American comics. However, the Belgians also had to suffer the consequences. The censors were openly supporting French interests against the foreign press, and *Spirou* and *Tintin* were naturally the first targeted. Commercially the risks were considerable: a Belgian publisher could lose the right to distribute the offending works in France. Morris and Goscinny were forced to tone down *Lucky Luke*, which was deemed too violent. Their lone cowboy had to temper his efforts to defeat the villains. The atmosphere in the industry became such that everyone began to self-censor.[39] Before publication publishers would show the plates to one of the censors for his opinion.[40]

Tintin magazine was not spared, but censors had more difficulty faulting it. The publishers had been extremely skillful. Hergé's hero had nothing to fear; he was virtuous, and his upright nature served as moral caution to other, less enlightened characters, such as Haddock. The most effective censor of Hergé's work was Hergé himself. He had learned to be prudent.

AFTER EXTENDING HIS CONTRACT with *Tintin* magazine in the beginning of the fifties, Hergé renewed it for a period of thirty years in 1953. His depression and his repeated episodes of absenteeism had shaken the morale of his team. Marcel Dehaye was one of the few who could get through to him. One day he asked Hergé either to leave or to help them accomplish their goals; Hergé had to decide one way or the other. "Is there anything more disappointing than seeing a master failing?" Dehaye wrote him.[41]

By 1953 Hergé had taken hold of himself, and the magazine was thriving. The Tintin coupon had really given a boost to sales. Beginning in 1950 the coupons could be found in three different designs in magazines, but also with a number of products, such as Victoria chocolates and Materne preserves. The idea was sheer genius. In the first year 200 million were printed. Needless to say this marketing tool spread the name and picture of Tintin, increasing the sales of books.

Hergé reached an understanding with Raymond Leblanc. The proof of this is an illustration he did for the magazine's seventh anniversary. It showed Haddock, rowing a boat named *Tintin* and tossed about by waves, calling out to the panicked Thom(p)sons, "Don't worry, landlubbers! There's no danger. It's Leblanc at the stern!"[42]

Hergé seemed much more involved with what was, after all, his magazine, yet his assumptions were still based on the flourishing trade of 1940. Now new magazines for young people were appearing all the time. First came *Mickey Magazine*, launched by Armand Bigle, Disney's man in Europe, in conjunction with the Belgian publisher Éditions du Pont-Levis, with a print run of one hundred thousand a week. The real danger was that it included not only comic strips from the Disney factory, but also stories and illustrations by well-known French illustrators. Shortly afterward Paul Winkler, back in Paris, revived *Le Journal de Mickey*, with equal success. In Belgium Hergé was most concerned by the competition from *Spirou*. It wasn't just a question of sales, which were comparable, and soon *Tintin* would surpass *Spirou* by fifteen thousand copies.

Since the appearance of the magazine and the opening of the Hergé Studios, people had been speaking of a "Brussels School," referring to those artists favoring what would be called a "clear line," following Hergé's example. His influence on young talents was such that the public called it a "hergémony." The idea of a school was a little farfetched. But as soon as creative people gather together, drawn by their affinities and with similar ideas, history is quick to label them as such. History, or rather, those who write it—journalists, professors, and others—feel reassured by such labels.

Tintin magazine was unquestionably imaginative. Hergé had gathered a constellation of talent that was the envy of everyone: Jacobs, Cuvelier, and Étienne Le Rallic in the beginning. Others joined them, authors of series that made a lasting impression (even if mostly obscure today): *Bob et Bobette, Alix Lefranc, Chlorophylle, Dan Cooper, The White Knight, Ric Hochet, Modeste et Pompon.*

With such a wealth of material in the content, it was difficult to understand the public's relative lack of interest. The overall circulation of illustrated works had been larger before the war. In drawing up an inventory of the symptoms and causes, Hergé marked the growing distance between the magazines and the public. The readership had matured, he believed, yet were being fed the same simple comic lines as the generation before. Yet he didn't agree with those who touted *Superman* and *Flash Gordon*, which were escapist to a fault and not above demagoguery. If concessions had to be made to modernity, they should involve technological progress and scientific discoveries.

Hergé was persuaded that this gap in communication became a problem the day the cultural level for adults was lowered to such an extent that it appealed to the more mature young people. The divide between publications for children and publications for their parents had gradually been eliminated, transforming the market. This was Hergé's analysis. Newspapers included more and more comic strips, which were shared by all members of the family. Even text-based periodicals (*Constellation* and *Reader's Digest*) covered the great new discoveries so expertly that they drew young readers away from publications designed expressly for them.

Hergé was inspired by the success of *Paris-Match. Tintin* too ought to follow the news: "It looks like it was made by and for people who lived outside of our time. Our magazine is up to its neck in fiction, in the unreal, in fairy tales old and new." He pointed to the illustrated stories with historical characters: *Cori the Sailor Boy, Hassan and Kadour, Till Eulenspiegel,* and others. Characters set in modern times were the exceptions: *Barelli* by Bob De Moor, *Blake and Mortimer* by Jacobs, and, of course, *Tintin.* As for novels and short stories, he believed those in *Coeurs Vaillants* were superior. Hergé was convinced that if the public wanted entertainment and escape, young people wanted something other than fiction, something "real, true, solid, and serious."

He was basing his opinion on the results of a survey of publishers of general literature, according to whom the best nonfiction about society would sell as well as Pierre Benoit's *L'Atlantide* (1919), a novel combining fantasy and adventure. Translated as *The Queen of Atlantis*, it was a worldwide best-seller in the period between the wars. A general evolution of ideas had to be taken into account. It was urgent that the magazine catch up. He did not believe they should take a survey of readers. For him the best proof was the success of Edgar Jacobs's *The Secret of the Swordfish* in the first few issues of the magazine. The heroes, Captain

Blake and Professor Mortimer, are working on a secret weapon to combat a Far Eastern empire that is taking over the world. It should have served as an example: "Jacobs used recent events and anticipated the future. His novel was both historical and a projection. It resonated profoundly with all readers (children, adults, soldiers). The subject was in the air."

To hear Hergé speak, or to read his writings, it would seem as if the magazine was sinking. Nothing of the sort. He simply didn't like what was going on at *Tintin*. He never really accepted the editor in chief, André Frenez, whom he always felt had usurped Jacques Van Melkebeke. Were it up to Hergé, everything would be redone. He criticized the feature on cars, saying it looked too much like a showroom. The editorials? Excellent, but old-fashioned. His major criticism he reserved for the illustrators in charge of the comic strips, however. With few exceptions, their graphic talent was infinitely superior to their storytelling abilities. And, after all, it was about telling a story in pictures. "Everywhere it's the triumph of mechanical action, always a tragic or comic situation, never a comedy or tragedy of feelings." More and more, their "puppets" were merely characters and less and less heroes.

Hergé was no longer asking his colleagues at the magazine to modernize, but he wanted to prevent *Tintin* from becoming fossilized. For the growing distance between reader and the magazine not to become unbridgeable, they needed to follow a map of reality, but not to the detriment of poetry, mystery, or magic.[43]

In his quest to save *Tintin* Hergé resorted to citing his own work, which had come to grips with actual events. He had only to make an inventory of his sources to prove the relevance and timeliness of the adventures of Tintin: the cold war, arms and drug trafficking, the Sino-Japanese War, the Anschluss and the Sudetenland, the conflict between the Arabs and the Jews. Hergé could not be dismissed for being passé. He wanted to be contemporary, but without demagoguery or smugness. For him, to be modern was to be ahead of events.[44]

In 1952 space travel was still in the realm of science fiction, which was not his genre. Hergé was fascinated by the speed of scientific progress, and nothing excited him as much as hearing of a new discovery or invention. This time Hergé sped ahead of progress and took Tintin to the moon. The word can be found in the titles of his next two volumes, *Destination Moon* and its sequel, *Explorers on the Moon*.

He began with a structure rather than with a clear story line. Using tried and true means throughout—gags, reversals of fortune, chase scenes—Hergé

intended to tell the epic story of Tintin's space odyssey with Snowy and Haddock. They are following Professor Calculus, who has always dreamed of reaching the moon using a rocket with atomic propulsion. Foreign spies attempt to disrupt the expedition, adding suspense to the technical preparations: manufacturing plutonium, readying the atomic fuel. Explanatory passages became rather dense, and Hergé seemed to sense this, as halfway through he expresses what the reader may be feeling through Captain Haddock. An engineer wonders, "What is going to happen to all the other neutrons?" "Yes, I was worried about them," the Captain replies with mock interest.[45] In fact the poetry and pace of the action, hallmarks of Hergé at his best, really come into play only once the rocket is launched.

Before plunging into this universe about which he knew nothing, Hergé collected an enormous amount of documentation, gathering scientific articles and space primers: *Astronautics* by Alexandre Ananoff, the first encyclopedia in French to popularize the latest discoveries in space technology; *Our Friend the Moon*, by Pierre Rousseau; *Between Earth and Sky*, by Auguste Piccard; and *Man among the Stars,* by Bernard Heuvelmans.[46] These works were as valuable for their scientific data, presented for the layman (the physics of the atmosphere, flight into the stratosphere, interplanetary and interstellar travel) as for their illustrations: pictures of craters, mountains, and lunar seas. He relied most heavily on two new books of popular science, *Humanity in the Face of Interplanetary Travel* by Albert Ducrocq, with its wealth of details about the problems of combustion and atomic energy, and *The Conquest of Space* by Willy Ley, filled with fascinating illustrations by Chesley Bonestell. Though he set it in outer space, Hergé wanted this adventure to be grounded.

From the start, a number of colleagues and friends helped him prepare. Rarely had such a diverse group been assembled for one of his books. After his episodes of depression, as we've seen, Hergé needed to be surrounded, reassured, and stimulated. He was paralyzed by the vision of coming to a sudden halt, dreading the consequences of his collapse, the confusion followed by flight, and everything that that entailed.

So that he would never be thwarted by technical problems, he gathered experts, including Louis Brouwet, chief of air traffic around Brussels. Hergé consulted him because he planned for the story to conclude with the return of the rocket, and he wanted the landing to seem plausible.[47] In the same spirit Hergé interviewed Max Hoyaux, head of the Center for Atomic Research in Charleroi. Hoyaux became actively involved, entering into the problems, suggesting that if there was ice on the moon they use

solar heat to thaw it, and pointing out situations that were scientifically doubtful, such as the oxygen supply being sufficient for two stowaways. Or the fact that Snowy regains consciousness before anyone else, although it was a known scientific fact that dogs withstood the pressures of accelera-tion less well than humans.[48]

Then came the illustrators, who formed a vital support system. Bob De Moor was of course the first among them, playing a pivotal role in completing some of the illustrations of *Destination Moon* and drawing the background. The famous red-and-white checkerboard rocket came entirely from his pencil.

Hergé had M. Van Noeyen construct a model of the pilot's control room in the rocket, based on Alexandre Ananoff's specifications and drawn from some of the illustrations in his book. Ananoff advised him to project on a circular screen the pictures of what would be visible from the rocket piloted by Professor Calculus.

None of this prevented Hergé from taking certain liberties, such as with the astronauts' helmets, which he made transparent so that his characters could be identified. Other liberties would make any scientist burst out laughing. A meteorite striking the moon would have been moving at such speed as to send projectiles flying like bullets, which none of the astronauts could have escaped or survived. Our hero, however, is barely thrown off balance. There is the picture of the asteroid Adonis, which Professor Calculus spots in his telescope and recognizes at first glance; no one had ever been able to identify it by sight.

One of the most appealing of Hergé's paradoxes was that his dedication to accuracy never overwhelmed his sense of play. He knew perfectly well the gravitational pull of the asteroid Adonis but could not resist the idea of sending Haddock orbiting around it.[49] Hergé always chose being true to the story over being factually exact. Launching the rocket at night may have been dreamlike, but it made no sense.[50]

Another of his entourage to play a major role was Bernard Heuvelmans, "Bib," a friend who had written the column "Scientific Humanism" for *Le Soir* during the occupation. A professor of zoological sciences, known as the "father of cryptozoology," he was a man who hesitated at nothing. Hergé liked him because he was a serious scientist but with a sense of humor, and as imaginative as a novelist. When Hergé was depressed he called on Bib to help him get through *Prisoners of the Sun*.

There was no contract drawn up now; among friends a handshake or a word was enough. Bib was eager to start and went directly to the source,

scientists who would eventually form NASA. He invented nothing; like Jules Verne he extrapolated from what was known, if theoretically.

When Bib and Jacques Van Melkebeke delivered the script, however, it had one fatal flaw: the text and the drawings were conceived in the manner of Hergé but seemed like a pastiche of his work.[51] Although the script was rejected, Bib continued on the team as the scientific advisor. Nothing remains of their original version of the book.

Hergé acknowledged his debt to Bib's 1944 book, *Man among the Stars*. The book's illustrations helped him visualize his story. At the beginning Hergé wanted his characters to benefit from all the latest discoveries. He asked his friend to gather information about atomic plants, security codes, controls, cyclotrons, and a hypothetical rocket capable of carrying seven people and one dog, including its interior design (cockpit design, navigational instruments, sleeping accommodations, helmets, emergency equipment, fuel reserves, and the propulsion engine). Afterward he never failed to credit Bib for all his "interplanetary documentation." But Hergé also owed to him certain visual gags: the games with gravity, the whisky turned into a bubble, and Haddock in orbit around the asteroid. Had Bib been an employee of the Studios, Hergé would have taken all the credit for everything. His colleagues were there to support him, not to outshine him. "I'm afraid I'm deeply ungrateful," Hergé once admitted. "I forget immediately and completely the person who gave me the idea in the first place. I instantly appropriate it for myself. It's not very nice, but that's the way it is."[52]

Unlike Van Melkebeke, who took the appropriation of his work badly, Heuvelmans never complained, though he knew Hergé owed him more than he would ever admit to: "In going through the two books we really had the impression that it was what we had originally done at the beginning. In broad outline, that was it."[53] Hergé always insisted that he never used Bib's scenario, just as Heuvelmans never relinquished his claim that the second volume's title, *Explorers on the Moon*, was his invention. He even made it the opening intrigue of the second volume.

On New Year's Eve 1953 *Tintin* magazine published the last plate of this lunar expedition, more than three years after the appearance of the first. Never had the publication of a series by Hergé been so chaotic. The idea for it had initially been raised in 1948, then dropped, then picked up again in 1950, delayed for six months, then dropped for two years, then finished in 1953.

Hergé's depression dogged him. Retreats, medicinal plants, and medications offered only temporary respite. He was in a shattered state.

His readers, who were unaware of these problems, wondered whether he was tired of carrying his hero after such a long time, and whether he didn't intend to kill him off, the way Conan Doyle did with Sherlock Holmes. To those who inquired he answered, hoping to allay their concern. "If you ask doctors, they will tell you that there is nothing that takes longer to cure than a nervous depression, or more exactly, cerebral anemia," he said in an interview. "It took twenty years to destroy me consciously, how do you expect me to recover in six months?"[54]

Again he sought refuge by fleeing to Lake Geneva and the wide open spaces with the vertiginous drops in the mountains. When he returned, so did his anguish. His team was his crutch. Too many people depended on him, both at the magazine and in the Studios, for them to allow him to self-destruct.

THE PUBLICATION OF THE TWO MOON BOOKS did not have the same impact as his two previous two-book adventures, the search for Captain Haddock and following in the footsteps of Professor Calculus. Those titles had played on a familiar register of secrets, treasure, mystery, and paranormal phenomena. He had taken a great risk on leaving the planet Earth. Had it not been for Hergé's pedagogical gifts, he could have lost his readers well before the moon landing.

As a sign of the times, the moment his serial began publication in *Tintin*, the Commission on Censorship met in Paris to deliver its first report. Apparently they wanted guidelines for depicting future scientific advances:

> This anticipation is valid precisely to the extent that it remains worthy of being called "scientific." Whereas Jules Verne anticipated the development of science by projecting actual progress, the imagination of writers of children's books absolves itself too often of any scientific consideration, and improvises according to the needs of the fantastical story without any concern for linking these to some sort of scientific category. It seems that a great show of caution is required in projecting the advances in science and to remain with science in its actual state to find all the authentic marvels rather than to exaggerate dangerously in the realm of pure fantasy.[55]

The only regret Hergé felt concerned a minor character in the story, the engineer Frank Wolff, assistant to Professor Calculus from the beginning

and guilty of double treachery: not only had he agreed to deliver the plans of the rocket to spies, but he had agreed to hide a stowaway from his fellow passengers. To make up for his misdeeds he confesses to Tintin and is forgiven. But when the oxygen reserves run out, he redeems himself by sacrificing his life for the others. The engineer Wolff is neither completely a villain nor one of the good guys. He is torn by inner conflict. His leap into space is the ultimate escape.

When this sequence first appeared in *Tintin*, the Catholic press did not react well to Wolff's suicide note: "Farewell and forgive me the wrong I have committed toward you."[56] It provoked heated discussions among priests. Though the word "suicide" was not written in bold letters, the idea was there. Casterman encouraged Hergé to rethink things. In the book version the engineer leaps into the void full of hope. "As for me," he says in his note, "perhaps a miracle will also enable me to escape. Forgive me the wrong I have committed toward you."[57]

Hergé himself had no hope. He didn't even have the energy to fight; he saved all his strength to complain to the publisher about the flaws he found on receiving the first few copies of *Explorers on the Moon*. The paper was too yellow and porous; he blamed the photo offset and the printing. He complained that in order to obtain a deep violet red he had tried everything, going from watercolor to gouache to mixing the two before settling for watercolor. All these efforts had been in vain; his work was destroyed. He kept praising the Éditions du Lombard for the sharpness of its coloring in publishing Jacques Martin's books and thought Jacobs's *The Mystery of the Great Pyramid* a model of printing.[58]

His unhappiness stemmed from the care with which he and his whole team at the Studios had shepherded the plates through publication. In adapting his narrative from the magazine into book form he had taken delight in introducing large drawings with a wealth of details. In the magazine their presence would have hampered the flow of the action. Still he felt he had not gotten his due. Whether because of all the interruptions in *Tintin* or the futuristic spirit of the story, the adventures left Hergé's readers bewildered.

Destination Moon and *Explorers on the Moon* nevertheless mark a stage in the development of Hergé's work. It was simply a matter of time before it would receive the recognition it deserved. In 1969, fifteen years after Tintin and his crew, Neil Armstrong became the first man to walk on the moon. Some seemed genuinely surprised that they didn't find footprints. Later, during a psychiatric and neurological convention, several notable

specialists would use *Destination Moon* to illustrate the symptoms of temporary amnesia, which in the story Dr. Calculus exhibits when he can't recognize Captain Haddock and his space suit loses all meaning. Since then, the condition has sometimes been called "the Calculus syndrome."[59] At the suggestion of Jean Meeus, an astronomer fascinated by Tintin and his world, a small planet previously known as "1652" was renamed "Hergé." It was discovered by the Observatory at Uccle in 1953, the same year as the publication of *Destination Moon*. An asteroid discovered in 1950 had already been named "Castafiore."[60]

AT THE END OF 1954 Hergé started publication of a new adventure, *The Calculus Affair*. For some Tintinologists, it represents the summit of Hergé's oeuvre.[61]

The opening panel starts with a "Rrring!" and the last one ends with a "Brrrom!" which prepares the reader for subsequent events. There are spies in the gardens of Marlinspike Hall, and a series of strange events results in the disappearance of Professor Calculus. Rarely had Hergé concentrated the action to such an extent. First a lead takes Tintin and company to Switzerland, and later to Borduria, an imaginary country, pursuing the production of a bomb infinitely more destructive than the atomic and hydrogen bombs, which would give mastery of the world to Marshal Plekszy-Gladz.

Needless to say, Professor Calculus knows of the plot and refuses to turn over the plans of his invention, because he does not want to create an engine of death. Finally his friends manage to rescue him and escape from their prison, and by commandeering a tank, flee the country, literally crashing through the border.

This time Hergé has both feet firmly planted in his own cold war world. The plot takes readers back to *King Ottokar's Scepter*, putting them in familiar territory. The illustrations and the scenario are vibrant and rich; the story thread holds from beginning to end. Jacques Martin's gags and sense of humor are present throughout. Hergé inserted himself as a reporter speaking to a local peasant in the crowd gathered at the gates of Marlinspike Hall. He portrays his friend Jacobs as Jacobini, an opera singer with Castafiore in *Faust*. He offers a wink and a nod to Walt Disney by naming the Italian scientist Topolino ("little mouse"), the Italian name of a character known to everyone as Mickey.

This playfulness extends to the cover of the book, which Hergé submitted to his editor in total disregard for the cost of production.

He was not satisfied with the drawing, which has Haddock and Tintin hiding a groggy Professor Calculus behind some boulders. He wanted to intensify the drama by placing it in the center of shattered glass. Real glass. He proposed having the shards cut out of a plastic or mica material and superimposed over the drawing in transparent relief, creating a dramatic illusion.[62] Needless to say, Casterman didn't go for this.

Hergé had scouted the locations in the manner of a film director. The shores of Lake Geneva in French-speaking Switzerland had become familiar to him over the years, of course. The Hotel Cornavin, built in 1933 near the train station of the same name in Geneva, would acquire an international reputation thanks to Hergé. For years it received letters addressed to Professor Calculus in room 122 on the second floor. There was no room 122, though eventually the owners decided to have a door with a plaque indicating room 122 made and placed against a wall.[63]

In general, researching the book was easy. The Bordurian language resembles its Syldavian cousin (aside from using the Latin alphabet instead of Cyrillic). Its spelling and syntax is Slavic. As for the vocabulary, it is a dialect spoken in Brussels sprinkled with slang words from across Europe.[64] The laboratory in which Professor Calculus makes his ultrasound experiments was based on plans for the construction of a laboratory in the Congo drawn up by Armand Delsemme, a professor of astrophysics. Hergé also obtained a copy of the American scientist Leslie E. Simon's 1947 book *German Research in World War II*, reproducing its cover in one scene and copying every detail exactly except for the swastika, which he eliminated. He had conceived of it as a story of the cold war, and not World War II. Marshal Plekszy-Gladz of Borduria is clearly a product of the two. His physical appearance, his authority, and his regime use elements borrowed from both Hitler (uniforms, insignias, even the salute "Amaïh, Plekszy-Gladz!") and Stalin (his mustache is promoted to a national emblem).[65] Just before 1956, the year of the Twentieth Congress of the Soviet Communist Party, the events in Poland, and a bloody rebellion in Hungary, only a few dared to point out the similarity between the crimes of Stalin and those of Hitler.

The Calculus Affair is, however, focused less on politics than on the moral dilemma confronting Professor Calculus as a scientist and the use of his inventions. Again Hergé was ahead of his time, because the cold war was not as yet a subject in popular culture. Not until 1966 would Alfred Hitchcock direct *Torn Curtain*, in which Paul Newman plays an American scientist trying to escape from East Germany.[66]

EIGHT MONTHS AFTER the last appearance of *The Calculus Affair* in *Tintin*, the magazine started publication of *The Red Sea Sharks*. It almost seemed as if Hergé had regained the pace and rhythm of his most creative period. However, no one was fooled: the support of the Hergé Studios, the imagination of Jacques Martin, and the energy of Bob De Moor were behind the effort. Hergé remained the catalyst, however. This time a chance article in a newspaper caught his eye. The reporter had investigated the mysterious disappearance of some pilgrims on their way to Mecca. They reappeared later, only to be sold off as slaves. Hergé immediately wrote a fifteen-page synopsis, then proceeded to make an initial storyboard outline, while his colleagues did their own versions. Pieced together from the different contributions, a story of sorts emerged.

It begins with the words "The End," projected on a screen. On leaving a movie theater, Tintin and Captain Haddock, by the greatest coincidence, run into General Alcazar, an old acquaintance from the times of *The Broken Ear* and *The Seven Crystal Balls*. He is in such a rush that he drops his wallet. It holds enough clues that they try to find him. Quickly the family gathers at Marlinspike Hall: the Thom(p)sons, Professor Calculus, old Nestor, and even Abdullah, the irritating boy from *Land of Black Gold*, whom the Emir Ben Kalish Ezab entrusts to the Captain, fearing an imminent coup d'état. Tintin quickly realizes that Alcazar is in Europe trying to buy arms for a war to overthrow his rival. When Tintin finds the general, he is conferring with Dawson, chief of the International Police from Shanghai in *The Blue Lotus*.

Tintin and Haddock jump on a plane for Khemed, where the revolution feared by the emir has overthrown the government. Dawson, now an arms dealer without nationality or scruples, tries to eliminate them and orders an attack that makes their plane crash. After numerous intrigues they manage to find the emir in his hiding place. The real reasons for the coup become evident and less than revolutionary. The cause was a conflict with the airline Arabair, which the emir had authorized to land in Wad ès Dà (from the Flemish for "What is that?" pronounced "Wad ès dà" in the Brussels accent), a city on the road to Mecca. The emir had threatened to reveal to the world that Arabair was trafficking in black Senegalese and Sudanese, who were sold off as slaves. Tintin and Haddock take a sailboat toward Mecca, which is attacked by war planes. The survivors escape on a raft and are rescued by the yacht of the Marquis of Gorgonzola, a multinational capitalist working in films as well as trafficking in arms, and the owner of Arabair. As it turns out, he is the slave trafficker and none other than Rastapopoulos, another

old acquaintance. One of his guests at the masked ball he is giving is Castafiore. Rastapopoulos manages to sideline our heroes by sending them on the SS *Ramon*, a cargo ship captained by Allan, from *The Crab with the Golden Claws* and *Cigars of the Pharaoh*. Abandoned on the ship, which has been set on fire, they succeed in releasing the prisoners from the hold and manage to make port so that the pilgrims can continue on their way to fulfill their religious duty—or, if they value their lives, to put ashore at the nearest harbor. The ship has to avoid the torpedoes from Rastapopoulos's gang. When they finally turn the tables on him, the villain manages his escape in a mini-submarine. Once back in their country, Tintin and Snowy expose the whole intrigue in the press and return to Marlinspike, only to find that their haven has been invaded by Jolyon Wagg, who first appeared to irritate Captain Haddock in *The Calculus Affair*. He is holding an automobile rally.

Hergé often said that by having characters return in his work, he was humbly imitating the great novelists, such as Balzac and Proust.[67] But with *The Red Sea Sharks* he gave himself over to it more wholeheartedly than ever. The book is a real reunion of friends and enemies, major and minor characters. Rarely had he convoked so many in one place. New readers unfamiliar with the Tintin cast of characters had to consult his earlier works. In this nineteenth book, the biography of Tintin can be seen to be emerging, like pieces of a mosaic being reconstituted.

Hergé seemed to have acquired a taste for travel after his recent expedition to Switzerland, reconnoitering the settings and locations of *The Calculus Affair*. Preparing for *The Red Sea Sharks* he was no longer satisfied by reading books. Now he wanted to travel to possible locations, place himself in the atmosphere, make sketches, and take photos. He had never traveled during all these years except through Tintin. At the age of forty-nine he finally decided to change that. With permission from the Department of Military Armament in Brussels, Hergé and Bob De Moor set sail in mid-August 1956 onboard the steamship SS *Reine Astrid* of the Thornton Line, bound for the Mediterranean.

Hergé now was in the habit of sending copies of his books to notables. When he learned from reading the papers that the novelist Françoise Sagan was reading *Tintin* during her convalescence from a car accident, he immediately rushed her a copy of *The Calculus Affair*.[68] Starting with *The Red Sea Sharks,* his public relations list became organized, since it was now as much a matter of marketing as an homage. A permanent list was drawn up,[69] with some receiving a deluxe copy with a printed dedication, others

a handwritten dedication, and still others a deluxe edition that was not numbered. The name of the recipient and the quality of the dedication ranged from "respectful recognition" to "best wishes" to "amicably yours" to the neutral "sincerely." As *Tintin* became famous, the list grew longer; some names were dropped, others passed through a purgatory before reappearing later. This list is an accurate indication of Hergé's social standing. The Royal Family of Belgium (Prince Alexander, Princess Marie-Christine) received the finest copies, now sought after by collectors. Copies were also sent to the following:

> His publishers (Raymond Leblanc, Georges Dargaud)
> His friends (Edgar Jacobs, Bernard Heuvelmans, Robert Poulet,
> Adelin Van Ypersele de Strihou, Father Gall)
> High-ranking Belgian political officials (Paul-Henri Spaak)
> Officers of the resistance (Jacques Chaban-Delmas)
> President of the National Assembly (Maurice Chevance-Bertin)
> Journalists who were also Tintinophiles (Oliver Todd)

Nor did he neglect those who had been asked to contribute to the research, such as Paul-Emile Victor, who was asked to procure the photo of a boat photographed through the periscope of a submarine, a delicate mission that took the polar explorer five years.[70]

Some felt that Hergé reached his peak with *The Red Sea Sharks*. Here was the culmination of his golden age, which had started more than twenty-two years earlier with *The Blue Lotus*. As always, Germaine's influence could be felt throughout the book; she stood by him as his wife during good and bad times over three decades. Her mark on the work is less in the technical details than in the moral dimension of the story. She was upright, rigorous, and demanding about all things, traits largely inherited from her long work with Father Wallez. This encouraged perfectionism in her husband, pushing him toward the heroic and his Boy Scout instincts, which had always remained a part of him. Her impact on his behavior, however, seems less profound, as Hergé would always be the first to concede.[71]

His readiness to acknowledge his indebtedness to Germaine may have been sincere, but it was also colored by guilt. In 1952, between two interims of crisis resulting from his depressive state, the Remi couple went through a terrible year. Speeding along the highway at the wheel of his Lancia, Georges Remi had a serious accident. He emerged unscathed, but Germaine was left with a limp for the rest of her life. In addition, their friend Father Wallez succumbed to cancer. Toward the end, to help him recover from the

effects of his imprisonment, the Remis took him into their home for three months. Georges, who stayed by his bedside as he lay dying, attended his funeral in his native village, one of only a few people present. He felt that he had lost a father.

IN 1957 HERGÉ TURNED FIFTY. To his readers, especially those of *The Red Sea Sharks*, he would always remain the same. However, he had changed. He went through another serious crisis of conscience, which threw him into paroxysms of depression. Few outside of his very close friends and colleagues at the Studios were aware of it. It was there, where he least expected it, that the roof fell in.

In June 1956 Fanny Vlamynck, a lovely young woman of twenty-one, was hired as a colorist. After a trial period she was assigned regular duties. She had expected to meet a serious old man and instead discovered a mature man, reserved but warm. She admired him instinctively, the man more than the artist. Like everyone else, she had read *Tintin* though had never been a devotee of comic books. They seemed to understand one another, and at the usual afternoon tea, when the little group at the Studios came together to relax and laugh, their glances crossed.

Five months after she was hired, just before the weekend preceding All Saints' Day, they found themselves alone in the elevator at the Hergé Studios. They kissed between the fifth floor and the lobby.[72] On leaving her in front of the door at 194 Avenue Louise, Hergé was no longer the same man. From now on there would be a before and an after in his life and, consequently, in his work.

WHENEVER A MAJOR EVENT occurred in Hergé's life, his immediate entourage at the Studios, and a little later those the magazine, were generally the first to learn of it, whether to their detriment or to their benefit. When he had his self-destructive impulses under control, Hergé would have countless projects on the boil, some of questionable merit.

By the fall of 1956 he had been thinking for some time about what he called "the Tintin problem" before putting all his ideas on paper, with Casterman as the intended recipient. That things were going well should have made Hergé optimistic, but he was persuaded that it was an urgent matter that he find new distribution outlets. In his eyes, time was working against him; he was afraid that his characters would become outmoded. There were young rivals everywhere you looked, more aggressive, modern

and dynamic. What did they have in common? A publisher called Le Lombard. If they succeeded it was because Lombard was aggressive. *Tintin*'s director, Raymond Leblanc, had won Hergé's admiration for his business acumen, and Hergé was the first to admit that wherever the *Tintin* books had appeared on the market ten years earlier—in Italy, Portugal, and Germany and in South America—they had done well. But now other illustrators such as Craenhals, Cuvelier, Macherot, and Willy Vandersteen reaped the benefits.

Hergé was therefore convinced that the moment had come to explore new outlets such as Spain and Scandinavia. He wanted a promotional campaign with publicity in all bookstores, book-signing ceremonies and press stories, and the distribution of books to hotels and vacation resorts where young people congregated.[73] He hoped that his publisher would see things his way. To the public at large, Georges Remi had ceased to exist; he had become Hergé. He had to maintain his image and protect his reputation, and anything that slowed the distribution of his work was a problem. The novelist Marguerite Duras wrote in the *France-Observateur,* "The *Tintin* books published by Casterman have gone around the world. You could say there is an international Tintin. Every child in the world has a Tintin culture before having their own, and they drink their Tintin milk like water from a fountain."[74] *Paris-Match* devoted several heavily illustrated pages to what it called "the Belgian who scared Walt Disney."[75]

Divided between two women, Germaine and Fanny, one whom he could not manage to leave, and the other whom he could not resolve to join, he was paying dearly for his indecision, which he attributed to his being a Gemini. His suffering made him acutely aware of everything.

HERGÉ KNEW NOTHING about Pol Vandromme when Vandromme's secretary transmitted his proposal to write a book about Hergé, citing his friendship with the playwright Félicien Marceau as a recommendation.[76] Pol Vandromme was an up-and-coming young writer, an editorial columnist and literary critic, age thirty-one, from Charleroi. He was of a satirical and polemical bent of mind and a pamphleteer. He had written major essays sympathetic to Pierre Drieu La Rochelle and Robert Brasillach, the two writers who symbolized Nazi collaboration.

There was no question of their working on it together, but Hergé assumed he had complete control. Vandromme submitted forty pages to him, and after reading them Hergé expressed certain reservations but never censored anything. Vandromme, he thought, was as perceptive as he was

admiring. It would be the first book written about him, and all the better for being written by a nonconformist who was skeptical and yet cared a great deal about the characters.

When the manuscript was delivered, *The World of Tintin* was less a biography than a monograph; the author had always conceived of it as an essay on the universe of Hergé's imagination. However, the publisher, Claude Gallimard, wanted Vandromme to add three chapters on the life of Hergé at the beginning of the work.

Vandromme was more convincing as an essayist than a biographer. In the first instance he wrote with a culture, an irony, and an irreverence that was refreshing. He showed the Thom(p)sons as more like Flaubert's Bouvard and Pécuchet than cops on the beat, and saw in Tintin more of the legendary Vidocq (a criminal turned policeman) than a Boy Scout. He likened Snowy to Sancho Panza and ranked Haddock among the great Shakespearean figures, Macbeth most notably.

As a biographer Vandromme was hamstrung. Hergé was not communicating at all. He would feel Hergé's eyes looking over his shoulder, especially when the Dark Years were the subject. "Hergé's life started imitating Tintin's only in the years after Liberation. Since then, it has been without any interest, and could be summed up as an anti-novel."[77] That was it.

Roger Nimier, an advisor to Gallimard, was in charge of commissioning authors to write prefaces to the classics of the Livre de Poche (paperback series). He wanted to write the preface to Vandromme's biography, which he saw as revolutionary. He wrote an essay titled "Tintin Makes His Entrance in Literature!" evoking a mad world of great authors to support his enthusiasm. Nimier compared *The Blue Lotus* to Malraux's *The Conquerors* and *Tintin in the Congo* to Hemingway's *The Green Hills of Africa. Tintin in America* was paired with Simenon's *Maigret at the Coroner*, and the influence of Alfred Hitchcock was everywhere. It was overwhelming; to be more succinct, "The world of Tintin is actually a universe."[78] *Tintin* was being offered a place next to the works in the catalogue of the *Nouvelle Revue Française*, the pantheon of letters.

Hergé feared, very simply, being made to look ridiculous. He could not see Tintin praised to the level of Zola's characters. He was embarrassed and asked that Nimier's preface not be used. Vandromme pushed, but Hergé refused to budge. If they kept in Nimier's preface, he would withdraw permission to use the illustrations that had been promised.

Even when the book was published—without the preface—in the series "L'Air du temps" by Gallimard, he remained dissatisfied. His complaints

went beyond what was reasonable. He was infuriated by the heading "Illustrations by Hergé" on the cover. He had given Vandromme permission to draw from his reserves of illustrations, and together they had made a selection of three facsimiles and two dozen small drawings. Hergé had even asked one of his assistants to make a montage of the heads of his characters for the cover. Nonetheless, he thought that calling this "Illustrations by Hergé" was an abuse of confidence and "false marketing." He insisted that the line be eliminated from all future editions of the book. He did not want it to look as if he had participated in any way with this panegyric of his work.[79]

Everything about Vandromme's book embarrassed him, but after his initial response, and after his bad mood had lifted, he was thrilled. In one way or another the appearance of *The World of Tintin* in bookstores was deeply gratifying. He enjoyed it all the more because it had not been his idea. He believed that he still had work to do before earning that kind of recognition. But now that it was out, the myth was in place.

10.

The Demon of Purity
1958–1960

TOWARD THE END OF THE FIFTIES there seemed no hiatus in Hergé's life, private or professional. For three years he had managed to have a life with Fanny without leaving Germaine. Neither was satisfied, and the situation became increasingly unbearable. "If she had been a great actress, or an artist, I wouldn't have objected. There would have been a certain flair to it. But a nobody, a little colorist from the Studios, no!" Germaine exclaimed to anyone would listen.[1]

She was frustrated and appalled. She had endured his dalliances, though they had hurt her deeply, but this time she felt stabbed in the back. He had told her immediately about Fanny and his burgeoning feelings of love for her, all the stronger because they were reciprocated. He preferred to be open about it, even if this pained her. In any event, she'd had her suspicions. She knew him better than anyone and could guess what was happening from the expression on his face, the way his shoulders slumped, the way he avoided looking at her. She also knew as no one else that his Achilles' heel was his powerful sense of guilt, the one trait that he retained from his Catholic education. To unsettle him she had only to touch this sore point.

The staff at the Studios did not need a picture to understand what was going on, realizing that it was a midlife crisis. Fanny's beauty, youth, and freshness were undeniable. Georges was untiring in his praise of her sense of humor, her good nature and thoughtfulness, and her way of smoothing things over. A quarter of a century younger than he, she was a classmate of the daughter of his old friend Paul Jamin.

Germaine represented the irretrievable past and Fanny the future. Germaine hadn't known how to handle her husband's success. Even some of their friends found them staid and preoccupied with petty conventions. Proud and reserved, driven by her sense of duty, she hadn't changed and adapted because, Georges felt, she stubbornly chose not to. Her perspective had remained locked on *Le Vingtième Siècle*. Their marriage seemed indestructible, past the point beyond which anything could be put into question. She had been lulled for years by that thought. But her sense of security was an illusion. When they were first married, she had been the one who was sociable and read books. She took him everywhere, opening his mind. He had admired her unreservedly. Over the years the roles were reversed; he went out and she stayed home. Since the end of the war they had gone in different directions. Little by little home life had been poisoned. They were both driven by ambitions, but not the same ones.

In the aftermath of Hergé's depression he had turned inward. In his retreats on the French border and on Lake Geneva he had engaged in intense meditation, having discovered Oriental philosophy. The religious texts affected him morally and philosophically rather than spiritually, toward Taoism and revelations foreign to the Judeo-Christian tradition. Fanny was a catalyst for him to change what Germaine and Father Wallez had inculcated in him. For three decades he had been rigid, buttoned up, and virtuous. All of a sudden he discovered different instincts: openness, tolerance, and sense of freedom.

He wasn't able to reconcile all these contradictory aspects of himself. He still adhered to a moral code, where a word once given is for life. To leave his wife would be to abandon her. To renounce their vows, twice blessed— once by the Church and again by Father Wallez—would be to deny his faith. It was sheer torture. Although he had become less and less of a practicing Catholic, he still did not have the strength to resolve his problem: to be free and also free of sin. He had to break his vows without feeling that he had betrayed his wife. His pride and self-esteem would always be in conflict with his vanity. He wanted to look at himself every morning in the mirror without shame.[2]

The crisis dragged on for months, and at first even his old friends were angry with him for the way he was treating Germaine. Some people were shocked and disappointed that the big brother they had admired for being so straightforward wasn't in the end. They might have altered their opinion had they known what Hergé wrote about Tintin to Olivier Todd, one of the first (and rare) journalists who understood his work: "Tintin's primary flaw

is no doubt that he is too virtuous: I, more than anyone else, have become irritated sometimes by his obstinate refusal to stray from the path of duty."[3]

In 1960, following three years of procrastination, the situation became untenable. A series of crises and exhausting scenes culminated in his slamming the door on his conjugal home and moving into a hotel in Brussels. To make his point he left both women. He was in a no man's land, the ideal place to pull himself together. At this point he was beyond self-recognition; he who abhorred violence surprised himself by ripping off the sleeve of a shirt, or shattering an ashtray. At first he thought of leaving definitively, then changed his mind and thought of making his double life official. This time it was Fanny who put his back against the wall. He had to choose. "If I continue this way there will be three unhappy people," he confided to one of his colleagues. "It's better if there is only one."[4] There would be only one—his wife. In 1960 Georges and Germaine separated, but it would take Georges an additional seventeen years to obtain a divorce. Throughout, Germaine clung to the hope that he would return. He did not abandon her, either materially or morally. Until the end of his life he would spend Mondays with her in what had been their home in Ceroux-Mousty.[5] Still, Hergé felt as if at last he had killed off the puppet in him and was now set free.

SINCE THE PUBLICATION of *The Red Sea Sharks* Hergé had been running in circles. He wasn't lacking in ideas or the desire to work; the problem was settling on a subject. He no longer hesitated about working on a scenario with others, even if his experiences were not entirely satisfactory. With his loyal and efficient assistants Jacques Martin and Greg Régnier, he set to work on a project titled *Tintin and the Thermozéro*. A story outline was drawn up, along with a few working sketches: a container of a deadly radioactive material is taken by mistake by someone Tintin would pursue, catching up with him just as the product is about to wreak its devastation. As the story would evolve, J. W. Howard, a British physicist defecting across the Iron Curtain, contacts the CIE (Central International Espionage agency), headquartered in Berlin, which would slip him through the border. The scientist is carrying atomic secrets plus a container of deadly radioactive material. On landing in Europe, to minimize the risk Howard gives the container to a German spy named Schülte, who, disguised as a salesman, takes it to Berlin.[6]

The problem was that it was all done in the style of Hergé. Every time he worked with others, the project became too calculated and elaborate.

Hergé had always needed to improvise, finding ways of keeping the material fresh. In fact he was only at ease with what was his. Working with the most talented colleagues in the world he still could never feel free from all restraints or inspired to create those strokes of genius balancing logic and the madcap.

Then in the last months of 1957 he read an article on American Indians, reviving his youthful passion. He found his thread: Tintin finds himself on a reservation trying to prevent unscrupulous businessmen from evicting the natives in order to drill for oil. He immediately wrote to his old friend Father Gall to ask for his advice on the project. The Cistercian monk was an expert on the Plains Indians, who had named him "Lakota Isnala." He sent Hergé five single-spaced typewritten pages filled with details and anecdotes about the geography of Little Rock and the Bureau of Indian Affairs, the Indians' hostility toward white people and the despoliation of their land by big corporations. He even wrote of how Indians had been on the front line when the Allies landed on the beaches of Normandy.[7]

Like the previous project, the story opens with an incident on the road to Marlinspike Hall. An accident, or is it an attempt on the life of a Sioux? At the hospital, in his delirium, the man mentions a peace pipe, a tomahawk, and a monastery. Going to the monastery and visiting an exhibit of Indian artifacts, Tintin discovers that the peace pipe has disappeared. It contained a precious official document proving the claims of the Indians to their hunting grounds. As all the other copies have vanished, it is the last thing to prevent their being forced from their land by an oil company. Hergé abandoned this project instinctively.

At the end of *The Red Sea Sharks* Hergé had drawn a sketch of a story about Nestor, the butler at Marlinspike Hall, being involved in a mysterious murder. Then he abruptly changed the subject: "General theme, very simple. But what? Tibetan wisdom—the Lama. Abominable Snowman. Why do they leave for Tibet: the yeti?"[8]

Hergé had always been fascinated by Tibet, and using it as a subject remained in a corner of his subconscious. A recent book by his friend Bernard Heuvelmans, *On the Trail of Unknown Animals*, had been a worldwide best-seller, popularizing cryptozoology, the study of legendary animals. Heuvelmans attacked the commonly held view of the yeti as an "abominable snowman." His yeti was neither hungry for human flesh nor a kidnapper, but a friendly and misunderstood giant.

Hergé plunged further into his research: Fosco Mariani's *Secret Tibet*; Heinrich Harrer's *Seven Years in Tibet*; *Tibet my Homeland* by Tsewang

Pemba, the first Tibetan doctor with a degree from a Western medical school; *Annapurna* by Maurice Herzog; *Nanda Devi, the Third French Expedition to the Himalayas,* by J. J. Languepin and L. Payan; and, naturally, the writing of the Tibetan explorer Alexandra David-Neel. Aside from their information, these works were invaluable for their maps and photographs, such as those in Herzog's book showing yeti footprints in the snow. Hergé went to the Belgian Alpine Society for more photographs and documentation. They sent him Richard Lannoy's work on India. On one page he found a photo that showed only the lower half of a New Delhi policeman, forcing him to write the author to ask for the original photo so he could see the entire uniform.[9]

Hergé's research led him back to where he began: with his friend Heuvelmans. Bib was the specialist most up to date on the subject; in 1959 he had received a letter from Nepal sent by Peter Byrne, head of the American Slick-Johnson expedition, which had set out to capture a yeti alive.[10] He appreciated Bib's erudition, his sense of humor, and his originality in his approach to science; he started with a character that was half-man and half-beast, which legend had turned into a monster but that turned out to be less frightening than pathetic. Right from the start Hergé had the idea of making Tintin come face to face with some beast.[11]

Heuvelmans's sketch of the abominable snowman convinced Hergé to make him a creature closer to humans than to animals (if only to absolve the young Hergé for having slaughtered so many animals in *Tintin in the Congo*).[12] After a number of false starts he proceeded to make an outline of his story. Once he felt he had the structure set, he started the drawings. The first plate of *Tintin in Tibet* came out in *Tintin* magazine on September 17, 1958.

The story opens with a vacation in the Alps, invigorating to the young reporter but not to Captain Haddock. Learning from the newspapers of an airplane accident in Nepal that has taken the life of eighteen people, Tintin has a nightmare: his friend Chang from *The Blue Lotus* is in danger; he is buried under snow; he is calling for help. In the morning Tintin receives a letter from Chang, announcing his imminent arrival. Our young reporter verifies from the passenger list that Chang had been on the plane. Tintin weeps, a rare occurrence; the last time had been in the final panel of *The Blue Lotus* onboard the steamship taking him back to Europe. Getting hold of himself, Tintin rejects fatalism, choosing to believe his dream is a premonition. Convinced that Chang is still alive, he books passage to India with Haddock.

In Katmandu the sherpas who found the wreckage try to dissuade them from pursuing their search, which they think is both dangerous and doomed to failure. Determined to go it alone, Tintin forges on with a small group, Haddock in the lead. During the ascent, dizzy and disoriented, Haddock and Snowy nearly lose their lives several times. Tintin discovers Chang's name written in a cave near where the wreckage is buried in the snow. He survived the crash. The expedition cannot even find Chang's remains, however, and is forced to return to base camp. As they are about to leave, Tintin spots a yellow scarf caught on a boulder. He continues his quest with Haddock, his guides and porters having fled. Only the sherpa Tharckey, in a fit of remorse, returns. During a stop in a lamasery nestled in the high mountains they find the trail of the yeti that he believes has taken Chang captive. Haddock, who does not believe any of this and wants to turn back, is forced once again to follow Tintin. In the end they discover Chang in a cave, guarded by a so-called abominable snowman, a sort of giant gorilla. He is about to attack the intruders when Tintin's camera flash frightens him off. They take Chang back with them, with the yeti sadly looking on from a distance. "Well, as for me, I hope people never find him," Chang tells his friends, "because they would treat him like an wild animal. But I can assure you, Tintin, that he acted toward me in such a way that I have often wondered if he wasn't a human being. Who knows?"

There are no savages. Tintin, who is goodness personified, made this journey to understand that man is the problem. Chang would also have made him conscious of that dark region of the soul where absolute evil comes in conflict with the spirit of brotherhood. The same evil has driven the abominable snowman to haunt the solitude of the mountains.

The sixty-third and last plate of the story appeared on November 25, 1959. In March, the Year of the Pig, a massive popular uprising against Chinese domination in Lhasa was violently suppressed, resulting in bloodshed. The Dalai Lama was forced to flee into exile, followed by some one hundred thousand Tibetans. The Chinese Army then proceeded to destroy the resistance in the monasteries and absorb Tibet into China—the territory, if not the people.

Hergé's timing is not what made this book remarkable, however. In fact halfway through it he almost abandoned the project. Rather than the news, he had been watching and listening to himself, obsessively, to the point of inhibiting all his creativity. In his sleep all his dreams were white; they were so powerful that he felt a need to write them down as soon as he awoke:

I was climbing up the stairs of a tower (the Hassan Tower in Rabat?) where everything, the ground, the walls, the ceilings were covered with dead leaves. (I was startled that my walking on this carpet of leaves made not a sound.) At every turn I expected something terrifying to leap out at me. Finally, filled with fear, I decided to walk down, and looking into the stairwell, I realized that I had reached the seventh or eighth floor. I continued walking down; on one landing lying on a platform was a dead body (white). As I touched the leg, it remained in my hand; it was a sort of cardboard tube, very light, and I threw it down the stairwell. At that moment on the lower landing a hole opened in the wall and out came a white skull, then a sort of demon, a large man, terrible and white, who threw the skull and piles of bones and other things into the stairwell. I was terrified he was also going to throw me into the void. I tried to pass by him by jumping over space, but he barred my way. I knew that I could not get past him, and that I had to climb back up again.[13]

Another dream:

A horse's head jutted out of a wall, like the shop sign of a butcher shop for horsemeat; the wall was all white, dazzling in the sunshine. On my left was a woman, and I approached the horse (perhaps to give it something to eat) but the trainer shouted at me: "No, don't come any nearer! You are wearing a white shirt. You mustn't. You're going to frighten him!" I thought that if he was afraid of white this wall must terrify him. Then I thought, he couldn't see the white because it was in back of his head jutting out of the wall. I thought that I must go change my shirt, perhaps into my green wool cardigan.[14]

The whiteness was not entirely new. Between the wars Hergé had thought of sending Tintin and Snowy on an adventure in Alaska. He drew them stranded on a melting ice floe. Later he returned to this project and set it in what looks like either Canada or Greenland. He had made lists of names of the characters—Eskimos, mounted policemen, seals, and bears—and drawn the accessories: sleds, icebreakers, and snowshoes. The story was inspired by the novels of Jack London. But it had gone nowhere.

Now, paralyzed by this vision of whiteness, he visited Professor Franz Ricklin, a Zurich disciple of Carl Jung. Hergé had read all Jung's works in French and believed in the collective unconscious, the interpretation of dreams, and the union of the individual, the species, and the cosmos.

Jung's shadow hovers over *Tintin in Tibet*. For years, on his own or with patients, Jung drew tankas on cloth as well as what he called European mandalas, inspired by the circles of colored sand representing the universe of a divinity in Tantric Buddhism.

Hergé's meeting with Professor Ricklin was brief and fruitless, however. He told Ricklin about his dreams and was stunned by the man's reply: "I don't want to discourage you but you will never complete your work," he told Hergé. "It's a crisis that you must face. If I were in your place, I would stop work immediately. You must exorcise your demons, your white demons. You must kill within yourself the demon of purity."[15]

The man was asking Hergé to choose between his inner well-being and his work. In the middle of publication of *Tintin in Tibet*, having to make a decision, Hergé decided not to see his psychoanalyst again and to finish the story on which he was working. He was determined to work through his book and his own problems. He returned to work feeling triumphant. "When in trouble a Scout smiles and whistles" became his mantra.[16] He knew that if he carried his story to its conclusion he would succeed in accepting himself as he was, not completely white but soiled. On that day he could turn the page. It would no longer be a crushing weight on him. He put the best of himself into *Tintin in Tibet*, a portrait of the artist at a turning point. Fortunately, at the instigation of his publishers, he dropped the original title of *The Cow's Snout* (which was the name of a fictitious mountain in Tibet).

His twentieth book stands alone among his work. There are no chases and pursuits, no villains, no family except for Captain Haddock. It's not a police investigation but a spiritual quest; the only conflict is between man and nature. Nothing really happens; the drama is internal. Hergé seems to have dropped all the traditional tools of an illustrator (though he did not give up visual gags, all instigated by Haddock).

Tintin is again the principal character. He is neither redressing wrongs nor bringing justice—is neither Don Quixote nor Zorro—which makes him all the more human. To find his lost friend he climbs to higher altitudes, surpasses his limits, and elevates himself. By sending Tintin into the mountains of Tibet, Hergé had retraced his own path as a troop leader in 1923 crossing the Pyrenees. Tintin, like Hergé, had become more of an individual, which paradoxically made his quest more universal. In the search for identity, an ideal, he illustrated the most universal of emotions: friendship.

Tintin in Tibet would remain Hergé's favorite. He thought it an ode to friendship, composed "under the double sign of tenacity and friendship."[17]

"It's the story of a friendship," he wrote in a letter, "the way people say, 'It's a love story.'"[18]

The personal significance of the work was symbolized by the size of the numbered deluxe edition. The first, naturally, went to King Baudouin, fifth king of the Belgians, on the throne for nearly ten years and on the eve of his marriage to the very popular Fabiola de Mora y Aragon. After the king, the members of the Palace at Laeken, then the editors of the Belgian and French *Tintin*, then Casterman, followed by the children of all his colleagues, coworkers, friends, politicians, notables, and writers. Not forgotten was a seventy-eight-year-old man: "To my young father, from his old son, very affectionately, Hergeorges."[19]

Publication coincided with the date of his formal separation from Germaine. He moved in with Fanny. With *Tintin in Tibet* he seemed to have come to terms with himself, as he wrote in an inscription, "the lovable abominable snowman?"[20]

11.

Finishing Touches
1960–1973

AT AGE FIFTY-FOUR, having just put the best of himself into his twentieth book, *Tintin in Tibet*, Hergé decided to take even greater risks.

He had searched for simple themes without being facile and would continue in this direction, renouncing even exoticism, the security net for an illustrator about to take the leap into the blank page. The new challenge appeared impossible: no bad guys, no violence, no detective novel suspense or intrigue. Any adventures would be internal. His idea was to show the world through the eyes of someone confined to a wheelchair. Hergé constructed a crazy story that held the reader purely through nontraditional graphic techniques.

Building on his new sense of freedom, Hergé followed what he believed were his most basic instincts: rebellion and nonconformism. He wanted to make fun of everything he had respected for so long. This side of his personality could occasionally be glimpsed in *Quick and Flupke* and in the rehearsed litanies of Captain Haddock, who in his moments of sobriety could raise understatement to a fine art. Hergé had become confident enough to consider undertaking a project that would make fun of himself. And through self-mockery he would satirize others—their codes of behavior and their rituals—less out of insolence than out of the desire to give himself over to satire, undermining the constraints he always imposed on his work. Incoherence would replace order.[1]

First came the Gypsies. For a change, it wasn't Tintin and his friends racing around the world, but the world coming to them. Hergé introduced the exotic by having the Gypsies make camp near Marlinspike Hall, and there on the periphery of the story they remained.

Marlinspike Hall is the unifying setting of the action. For the first time Hergé looked at the building from an architect's point of view; until now he had never drawn up a floor plan. The nature of the rooms and their layout were dictated by the ceaseless action and obeyed the demands of narrative rather than aesthetics. This explained why from one book to the next Professor Calculus doesn't always emerge from his room by the same staircase. This inconsistency hadn't escaped the attention of his young readers. A student from the Institut Polytechnique brought to his attention that the front entrance of the building had eight steps instead of the traditional nine. Hergé immediately corrected it, but he hoped that no one else had noticed.[2] To avoid any differences between the Marlinspike Hall of earlier volumes and this new one built on a more rigorous plan, Hergé opted for a compromise, part-surrealist castle and part–Chateau de Cheverny (the original model). It was a kingdom apart, a sort of "Western Syldavia."[3]

Finally, there was Blanche Chastefleur, known to the world as Bianca Castafiore. Hergé seemed determined to give her a major role, though he never took opera seriously and always saw the fat lady behind the singer.[4]

Despite his later taste for Debussy, jazz, and pop, Hergé usually thought of music as noise. In this he was influenced by comic film conventions. Castafiore made her entrance into Tintin's world with the theft of King Ottokar's scepter, in the series that appeared the same era as the Marx Brothers' *A Night at the Opera*. The picture of the young reporter looking stunned when the "Milanese Nightingale" started singing is reminiscent of one of the Marx Brothers pacing in front of the opera house, unsettled by the sounds coming from inside, and asking the porter, "They are paid to scream like that?"

Hergé was drawn to the suggestion of several of his readers that Captain Haddock marry, although he had in mind a fling rather than something more serious. Captain Haddock had become more of a stay-at-home, while Castafiore felt herself to be a spiritual traveler. This reconciliation of opposites seemed a reflection of his former wife, who was liked by one and all. Castafiore had won over everyone—everyone, that is, except Tintin and his friends.

For the first and only time a woman would be given the central part in one of Hergé's books. She would not emerge from it covered in glory. He would insist he wasn't misogynistic, saying that women were not exempt from satire. They appeared as rarely in his books as in the old silent films.[5] Tintin's world was clearly organized according to masculine bonds of

friendship. Bianca Castafiore justifies this with her outlandish exuberance, her ceaseless chatter, and her megalomania. In short, she drove everyone mad.

By the end of 1960 the major outline of Hergé's antistory was set down on paper. His main fear: "Difficulty: creating suspense, a semblance of danger."[6] Several somewhat prosaic titles were under consideration: *The Castafiore Affair, Castafiore's Sapphire, The Castafiore Jewels*. A spicier title was also considered: *The Captain and the Nightingale*. But *The Castafiore Emerald* slowly emerged as the favorite.

While walking with Tintin in the woods adjacent to Marlinspike, Captain Haddock comes upon a family of Gypsies picking through garbage. Disturbed by the sight, he invites them to set up camp in a meadow by the gardens at Marlinspike. Later the chief of the local police warns him that they are thieves, but Haddock does not change his mind. The chief of the Gypsies, Mateo, is also suspicious, seeing only contempt in the Captain's beneficence.

A fortune-teller reads Haddock's palm and predicts that he will soon encounter a great lady and be the victim of a robbery. On returning home afterward, he receives a telegram announcing the visit of Bianca Castafiore. The Milanese Nightingale has invited herself to stay with her "Sea Wolf," whom she calls, depending on the circumstances, Bartók, Fatstock, Drydock, Hopscotch, Stopcock, and even Balzac. In return he refers to her as "Signora Castoroili." She becomes unbearable when Haddock, having slipped on a broken step on the stairs, is confined to a wheelchair and unable to flee her. In the course of her stay she keeps worrying that her jewels will be stolen. Tintin begins to notice bizarre occurrences.

Characters float through the book; Nestor alone is the mainstay. Calculus, more inspired than ever, is concentrating on developing a new type of rose; the Thom(p)sons behave like carabinieris from an Offenbach operetta; and Jolyon Wagg is more exuberantly Belgian than ever. They are quickly followed by secondary characters, each of whom contributes surrealism to this story: Irma, Castafiore's maid; Igor Wagner, the suspicious pianist on the diva's tours; Arthur Bolt, the phlegmatic stonemason who repairs the stairs; Iago, the bel canto parrot; the ace reporters from *Paris-Flash*, Christopher Willoughby-Drupe and Walter Rizotto, who are on hand to cover the marriage of the century. Haddock falls into a rage when he reads in the pages of a magazine the details of his secret romance with Castafiore; the story's source is the partly deaf gardener. By the time champagne calms him down, a television team arrives and sets up microphones,

cameras, and monitors in the drawing room. Castafiore, interviewed about her international tour, does not need to be asked twice to sing the aria from *Faust* by Gounod that has made her famous. In Scene VI of Act III Marguerite discovers a casket of jewels, adorns herself with earrings, and, dazzled, looks in the mirror:

> Ah, I laugh to see myself
> So beautiful in this mirror!...
> Is it you, is it really you, Marguerite?
> ...Ah, if only he were here.

Suddenly the room is plunged in darkness, and in the confusion Castafiore's jewel case vanishes. A mysterious photographer has also disappeared. The Thom(p)sons arrive just in time to miss everything. The local police interview Castafiore about the theft, while she thinks about insurance. Then the jewel case turns up under a pillow on the sofa. However, soon afterward, the emerald, a gift from the maharajah of Gopal, disappears from its case, thus relaunching the investigation. Naturally the Gypsies are suspected and placed under surveillance, while Professor Calculus invents a revolutionary method for turning black-and-white television into color. In the end Tintin discovers the missing emerald in the nest of a thieving magpie.

Sixty-two plates and nothing occurs, but something does happen. It's a manic sequence of events swirling around a lethargic stonemason called in to repair the stairs but not eager to fix anything. Of all Hergé's works *The Castafiore Emerald* is the most deliriously absurd. Everyone is talking without ever communicating with one another. It's as if they don't speak the same language. This quid contra quo is not the exception but the rule. Hergé found the British edition, with its bubbles of evidently understated conversation, wonderfully delirious. "You really would think that this was originally written in English," he confided to his translator.[7]

Disorder, lapses, false leads, and dead ends dominate this unhinged book. Hergé put his talent into creating the confusion and his genius into organizing it. *The Castafiore Emerald* became a cult classic, appealing to intellectuals. In 1970, seven years after its publication, a long article on it appeared in the literary review *Critique*. Hergé became friends with its author, Michel Serres, a young philosopher who first introduced the subject of Hergé's work to the Sorbonne at the University of Paris.

The death of Walt Disney took place between the appearance of Barbarella, the first heroine of a comic strip for adults, and Georges Picard's first class on comic strips in the School of Applied Arts in Brussels. But if

progress had been made toward recognizing the art of illustration, the world of the comic book remained ghettoized, even for Tintin. The satiric French newspaper *Le Canard enchaîné*, for example, saw Hergé's work as a Boy Scout–Superman matinee, a bastion of conformism: "Parents, beware of this 'hero' for whom the whites are all white, and the blacks are all black. If your children must be picture-perfect, avoid the pictures by the illustrator Hergé."[8]

The Commission for the Surveillance and Control of Publications for Children and Adolescents had condemned *Mandrake the Magician* and threatened, in turn, *The Phantom* and *Flash Gordon*. Francis Lacassin, cofounder of the Club for Comic Books, along with the film director Alain Resnais, organized illustrators to protest by making a collective drawing of all their characters. A campaign of demonstrations, petitions, articles, and telegrams was launched against the censors. Hergé's reaction was characteristic. He joined with his colleagues in denouncing this attack on freedom of artistic creation, but he refused to add Tintin to the collective drawing. There was a limit to his solidarity.

By 1964 there were other clouds on the horizon, although sales remained robust. He continued to have a stormy relationship with the magazine he had cofounded. He remained its artistic director, but in name only. The periodical still had his name and the face of Tintin on its cover, but Tintin was no longer the main feature. He shared space with such new characters as Blake and Mortimer, Guy Lefranc, Dan Cooper, and Michel Vaillant, created by talented young illustrators.

In March he had yet another meeting with Raymond Leblanc to discuss things that he found wanting. They came away without resolving their differences; negotiations continued for months on end. Finally, tired of endless squabbling, Hergé took the high ground. "I don't have to justify in detail my decision to take up again the artistic direction of a weekly that bears the name of my hero," he wrote in a letter to a friend. "I don't think that I am De Gaulle, but I will say: 'Hergé doesn't have to submit to an examination to return to *Tintin*.'"[9]

In 1965, a year into this stalemate, Raymond Leblanc offered the position of editor in chief to Michel Régnier, better known as the illustrator "Greg," a friend who had worked on numerous publications and many series, including the scripts for animated film adaptations of the *Tintin* books. Greg would accept the offer only on one condition: "Let me put a little violence and sex in the weekly, young people being what they are. We're not in 1946 any longer."[10]

As soon as Greg arrived, so did a new set of values. Hergé had his reasons for keeping his distance; aside from the internal conflicts at the magazine, there was outside competition from a certain Astérix. Hergé was magnanimous, saying that the success of Tintin's rival was well deserved. Despite all evidence, Hergé refused to consider Astérix as competition for Tintin: "You can identify with Tintin but not with Astérix."[11]

Astérix was born in October 1959, along with the magazine that made him known, *Pilote*. The magazine had one rule: that *all* the characters in the weekly had to be French.[12] Such constraints seemed paradoxical because *Pilote* quickly became known internationally and was avant-garde in sensibility. This openness was partly due to the cosmopolitan nature of its trio of writers and illustrators: one Frenchman of Polish origin raised in Argentina (René Goscinny), one Frenchman of Italian origin (Albert Uderzo), and a Walloon, Jean-Michel Charlier.

Pilote, "the big illustrated magazine for young readers," was marketed to eight- to fifteen-year-olds, and though more expensive than comparable publications it quickly found its niche. Its originality lay in treating adolescents as adults and adopting the format of a newsmagazine. A link with Radio-Luxembourg assured its constant promotion. There were fewer comic strips. Five months after its launch it was bought out by Georges Dargaud, the publisher of the French edition of *Tintin*. Dargaud had a taste for power and an ability to delegate work to talented artists and competent people.[13]

In September 1966 *Astérix among the Bretons*, the eighth volume in the series, had an initial printing of six hundred thousand copies. Eight books in six years matched Hergé at his most productive. The *New York Times* devoted an article to this comic book hero who had "captured France's heart":

> Readers offer a variety of reasons for taking pleasure in Astérix. "Ah," said a Frenchwoman, "you would have to have lived under the Occupation. You see, the Romans are really the Germans...."
>
> Asked about this, Mr. Goscinny replied, indignantly, "It is not possible to joke about concentration camps."[14]

In France *L'Express* celebrated this new phenomenon, which was read by adults as well as children. It praised *Astérix* as being the standard of the West in the face of Communism.[15]

Hergé continued to reproach his publishers for their lack of aggressiveness. They had failed to take advantage of opportunities that had presented themselves: the newspapers' focus on comic strips, the exhibition "Tintin and 20 Years of Illustrated Comics," and a television special with *Tintin* animations. He even hired an expert to study the market in preparation to launch the next *Tintin* book in Europe and overseas. Casterman denied the criticism completely, pointing out that sales continued to increase annually. There could be no publicity without a new product to present. From Casterman's point of view, Hergé had broken the rhythm of sales: three-fourths of the books by Hergé were more than ten years old. As long as he was unable to produce a new book, his recriminations were unfounded.[16]

Hergé had been accumulating ideas, waiting until one of them jumped out at him. He wanted a conventional adventure, told in his classic mode but dealing with the possibility of life on other planets. He also wanted to settle accounts with the villains Roberto Rastapopoulos and Allan Thomson and their clique, not by finishing them off but by demystifying them, revealing the wretched beings beneath the criminal façade.

He was reading up on extraterrestrials in Robert Charroux's *The Book of Secrets Betrayed*. His team at the Studios, on the other hand, had their feet on the ground: Michel Demarets was studying the Brussels International Airport and the locking system on a Boeing 707, while Bob De Moor went to Ostende on the Belgian coast to study the bunkers from World War II. Readers from Jakarta were asked to send photos of the Kemajoran Airport (control tower, arrival building, terminals). In his mind Hergé was playing with a number of titles, revealing the range of possible stories: *Tintin and the Millionaire, The Downfall of Rastopopoulos, Were You Dreaming, Tintin?, The Jungle of the Great Secret, Tintin at the Frontier of the World, No Bone for Snowy, Stopover in Jakarta, Tintin and the People from Beyond, Travels Shape the Captain, Calling Dog Snowy, Tintin and the Titans, Venus from Venus....*

L'Express's claim that Astérix had left Tintin trailing in the dust and was enjoying the enormous success that was formerly Tintin's was a real spur.[17] Shortly afterward, *Tintin* magazine began publishing the first panels of *Flight 714*.

During a stopover in Jakarta on their way to Sydney, Tintin, Snowy, Haddock, and Professor Calculus discover an old acquaintance at the airport bar, the Estonian pilot Piotr Skut with whom they had shared a raft in *The Red Sea Sharks*. He is now working for the millionaire Lazlo Carreidas, a giant in the aeronautics industry, whom he is piloting to a congress in Australia. After being introduced to him they make such an impression that

Carreidas invites them all aboard his private jet to attend the Astronautical Congress. Haddock tries to resist the invitation. He and Tintin think Spalding, the secretary, and Paolo Colombani, the navigator, are shady characters. Their worst suspicions are confirmed when in midflight Spalding, with the help of some crew members, hijacks the plane to the obscure island of Pulau-Pulau Bomba. There Tintin discovers that the mastermind behind the plot is none other than Rastapopoulos. He wants to kidnap the millionaire in order to administer a truth serum that will make him reveal the secret code of his Swiss bank account. Rastapopoulos plans to liquidate the account. With the help of Snowy, Tintin manages to turn the tables on his captors and free the millionaire. In a scene of high comedy, Rastapopoulos accidentally injects himself with truth serum and confesses to his true nature, revealing all his evil machinations. A piqued Carreidas tries to match him crime for crime. Their trail is discovered by Rastapopoulos and his gang. With them in full pursuit, Tintin and his party flee into the jungle, where they find shelter in an underground cavern. There they discover a gigantic statue with a mechanism that opens it and permits them to hide inside, where they meet Mik Kanrokitoff, an expert in hypnotism and telepathy. Thanks to their newfound friend they escape the island's volcanic eruption by being taken up into a flying saucer. On their return to terra firma they are interviewed by a television reporter; they cannot explain what has happened to them because they have all been struck by amnesia (except for the shrewd Snowy). Yet in their statement there remains a question about the possibility of life on planets other than Earth.

The story ends where it began: at the departure gate of Kemajoran Airport, where our cast of characters catches the flight to Australia as originally planned. This stopover has been the strangest of dreams, the kind usually forgotten on awakening.

For the reader *Flight 714* may seem only another adventure, not an achievement on the same level as *Tintin in Tibet* and *The Castafiore Emerald*. Even with its undeniable graphic and technological accomplishments, the book did not incite the reader to dream in the same way as *Explorers on the Moon* had.

Hergé himself admitted that the Carreidas 160 jet, the plan, drawing, and model of the fuselage and the cabins, were the work of his colleague Roger Leloup.[18]

Nonetheless there are some new features. Not content with satirizing his cast of villains from previous works, Hergé also introduces new characters. Heading the list is Carreidas, a caricature of Marcel Dassault, the builder

of the Mirage and the Mystère airplanes. Hergé used his figure, his hat, his scarf, and his sensitivity to the cold; he was always sneezing. Horrified by tobacco smoke, Dassault was obsessed by germs to the point of avoiding shaking hands. He was also capable of buying paintings without having seen them simply to prevent their falling into the hands of others. Mik Kanrokitoff was inspired by the eccentric genius Jacques Bergier, passionate about the occult, parasciences, and the paranormal. Bergier was the coauthor of the best-seller *Morning of the Magicians* and was with the immensely successful spin-off review *Planète*.[19] Hergé was as fascinated by Bergier's intellectual curiosity as amused by his weirdness. But he took him seriously enough to use him as a major source for his work.

A touching aspect of the book involves a detail of which only Hergé and a few others were aware. Hergé was often asked by fans to depict them in his drawings for his next book (they all included photos, naturally). He systematically but courteously declined to do this. But one reader, more patient than the others, was rewarded for six years of effort.[20] Hergé was so touched by his letter that he decided to grant him the privilege. He is seen shaking the hand of Captain Haddock in the next-to-last panel in the book. Hergé's one condition was that no one know about it.

If the making of *Flight 714* was laborious—which sometimes comes through in the story—it was because Hergé struggled so painfully to get it right. Patches of eczema had invaded his hands to such an extent that for long periods he could hardly hold a pencil between his fingers. He complained to his English translator, Michael Turner, that he was tired of his hero. "In fact I can't stand the sight of him."[21]

And to Jacques Martin he confessed, "You can't imagine to what extent I hate Tintin."[22]

The five o'clock teas took on a deferential tone. The great illustrator had gradually become unapproachable. Few risked criticizing him. No one felt in a position to make him question what he was doing, or even to speak up. The reputation had overwhelmed the man.

For the time being, he continued to be in charge of the work produced in his name. To squelch any conjecture about inactivity, a few plates of a "future book," always the same, were kept on hand to be shown to visiting journalists and to the general public. Often filmed and photographed, they made the journalist believe he had a scoop, maintaining the illusion of intense activity in the laboratory on Avenue Louise.

Hergé took offense when the utility of keeping the Studios running was cast in doubt, and was even more insulted when it was said that its staff

could do very well without him. Nothing made him more furious than hearing certain rumors, such as that Bob De Moor was in charge of putting the finishing touches on the illustrations. He had assistance, he conceded, but no one else but he did the graphic work. He would never allow it to be said that he was no longer the author of his own books, though it was known that the updating of the early works and the beginning of *The Seven Crystal Balls* had been done by Edgar Jacobs, the lunar saga by Bernard Heuvelmans, the rocket and the airplanes by Roger Leloup, the character of Abdullah by Jacques Van Melkebeke, that of Jolyon Wagg by Alidor, and the visual gags of the last books by Bob De Moor and Jacques Martin. He refused to list the names of participants in any way at the beginning of the books. In his view their work belonged to him because they were paid to follow his directions. He found it normal to take credit for their ideas. He wouldn't even permit his books to be signed "Hergé Studios."

By the mid-1960s Casterman was selling more than a million and a half copies of Hergé's works per year. Three books had passed the million mark: *Tintin in America, Explorers on the Moon*, and *Red Rackham's Treasure*. Nine others were at 900,000, and five at more than 800,000 copies. A total of twenty million Tintin books were in circulation.[23] Never had Hergé needed his Studios as much as now. Though frustrated by not producing the new adventure expected of him, he had made it his duty to assure the continuity and permanence of the books already published. Updating, adaptations, modifications, and recasting of his earlier books were more than enough to justify the existence of his Studios.

No correction was ignored, not even those suggested by letters from readers. Sometimes Hergé made changes for his own shrewd reasons. In the new edition of *Cigars of the Pharaoh*, for example, a copy of *Destination Moon,* published decades later, can be seen in the sheik's tent. However, he didn't make changes simply for their own sake. When the magazine *Marie-Claire* informed him that in a survey 90 percent of their readers had voted not to make any changes in his hero's clothes, this pleased Hergé enormously. "All this confirms that Tintin's plus fours are one of the basic spiritual values of the West," he told them.[24]

The Black Island, on the other hand, underwent three revisions, a record in the annals of the comic strips. The total recasting of the work, which takes place in Great Britain, was at the instigation of its English publisher, Methuen. The editors found the book rife with misinformation and mistakes about England, 131 errors to be precise. Hergé agreed to the

revisions without reservation. He decided not to change the plot or the sequence, but to substantially revise the setting, the landscapes, and the accessories. It would entail two years' work. In a first draft Hergé and his team recast the book in pencil and submitted it in that state to the editors at Methuen. Only after their final corrections would it be inked in.[25]

He had always wanted to change anything that appeared out of date, old-fashioned, or, most important, prejudicial to the image of his hero. But nothing prepared him for the "suggestions" of the Methuen editors. They went over the book not with a magnifying glass but with a microscope. Their requests? Replace all the signs in train stations with those standardized by the British railroad system. Replace the Ford Consul with a "taxi" sign on it with a London taxi (which you would never find in the countryside). Modernize the clothes of the driver. Move from the right to the left side of the road a car that has stopped. Lower the height of trees in a landscape by the sea. Change the edge of the sidewalk to white stone. Transform the gates of a field to the English norm of five planks. Blacken the brown shoes of a policeman and replace his uniform with that of constabulary working for the commissioner in Sussex and not London. Rework the clothing of a gamekeeper. Make more of the fields planted with crops, because the number of fallow ones were monotonous. Update a telephone. Redo the uniforms, the colors of cars, and the system of fire alarms. Redraw the architecture of a house with wooden beams. Fix the collar on a doctor's uniform. Replace the old bills of the Bank of England with more recent ones. Draw a camper and a truck to conform to the rules of roadside safety. Replace a steam locomotive with a diesel. Review the size of the corridors in train compartments. Bear in mind that the rails are electrified in the south of England when Tintin walks along the tracks. Change the brand of whisky (the Scottish Johnny Walker would be replaced with the fictional Loch Lomond brand). The train conductor and mechanic had to be reclothed. Make one of the airplanes a Tiger Moth. Rethink all the costumes of the Scots, keeping in mind that they dislike green. Update the television, but don't forget that there was no color television in England at that time. Remove the helmets on the Scottish police officers. Replace their automatics with revolvers. Change the title of the newspaper to *The Daily Reporter* ... and on and on.[26]

The result of these changes was that the Belgian veneer of *Tintin* completely vanished. He had never been as universal. This definitive version of *The Black Island* exhibits great realism; the illustrators even made the pictures on the television screens black and white. The book lost in

spirit what it gained in exactitude, however. History took precedence over story, setting over action. Hergé had shown that he preferred clarity to mystery.

After *The Black Island* came *The Red Sea Sharks'* turn, but here the revisions were more limited in scope, concentrating on eliminating anything capable of incurring accusations of racism. Hergé had been accused of being racist and contemptuous of blacks and Arabs. The Paris bureau of Casterman suggested that he modify the faces of the pilgrims to Mecca that Rastapopoulos tried to enslave and whom Tintin and Haddock heroically set free.[27] Casterman advised him to lighten their complexion and features; not all Muslims are black. The second part was revising the language. In the new version of *The Red Sea Sharks* the blacks speak like New Yorkers. Hergé based his research on the detective novels of the expatriate writer Chester Himes; he thought their Harlem setting was more accurate.[28]

The revisions, particularly those of a political or ethnic nature, were never undertaken at Hergé's initiative, but always at that of the publisher. Hergé agreed in principle for commercial reasons and to cooperate with Casterman and Methuen even if it went against the artistic integrity of the work. The times had changed. Hergé was adapting. Which did not mean that he had evolved.

The sheer volume of pirated editions of his work troubled him, and he decided to take action. It was a recent phenomenon, and this form of flattery, which may have pleased others, only made him angry.[29] Casterman was in agreement with him, especially since they bore the brunt of the lost revenue.

At one point Hergé proposed reissuing *Tintin in the Land of the Soviets*. Casterman had thought of such a possibility, but in a limited edition. They would republish the integral text of the original black-and-white 1929 edition without revisions or additions, but it would be preceded by an editor's note to place the work in its original historical context. The project dragged on for years. Casterman was caught between Hergé, who threatened to publish this volume elsewhere, and his sales representatives, especially in Paris, who feared a virulent reaction from the leftist press. They thought it would harm their relations with booksellers and librarians because the winds of May 1968 had blown through schools, universities, and cafés. Casterman's representatives reminded him that in those days public opinion, of which Hergé was the faithful reflection, had been horrified at the martyrdom of the Romanovs and the massacre of the imperial family.[30]

When Casterman came around at last to Hergé's preferred version, they packaged it in such a way that its political content and provocative issues would be reduced and the criticism neutralized. Casterman gathered together the original black-and-white plates of *In the Land of the Soviets, Tintin in the Congo,* and *Tintin in America,* with *The Adventures of Totor* thrown in, and collected them in one volume published in 1973 under the title *Hergé Archives,* for collectors, purists, and nostalgia buffs. In other words, it was marketed as a curiosity, solving the problem of politics and race. It also eliminated the market for counterfeit books, to everyone's satisfaction.

This also appeared to resolve the thorny problems of *Tintin in the Congo,* which Casterman had refused to reprint, not out of consideration for the Congolese but out of fear of the pro-African French left.[31] The Usumbura publishing house in Rwanda had already published a Swahili edition of the book, numbering ten thousand, under the supervision of the Fathers of the Mission.[32]

However, in 1970 a revised edition in full color of *Tintin in the Congo* was published even before the original black-and-white volume was anthologized in the *Hergé Archives.* On the eve of that controversial publication, the editors of *Zaïre,* central Africa's most influential magazine, conducted a survey of Congolese readers between the ages of seven and seventy-seven. The results were edifying: not only did they consider Tintin part of their cultural heritage, but he was one of their national heroes. After all, he had gone to the Congo when he hadn't even set foot in Spain or Greece or Japan. Free of their colonial complex after a decade of independence, they were ready to enjoy Tintin's adventures without reservation. "If certain caricatures of the Congolese people in *Tintin in the Congo* made white people laugh, they also made the Congolese readers laugh because they found plenty to mock in the white man who saw them that way!"[33]

Hergé was deeply satisfied that *Tintin in the Congo* was published as a serial in *Zaïre.* His work had become part of the national consciousness. The day after the success of the Apollo moon mission, President Mobutu had congratulated President Nixon but pointed out that Tintin and Haddock had done it before the Americans.

Yet there remained one door barred to Hergé, and its symbolic importance was considerable. It was *Le Soir.* Hergé knew that his name and that of his hero had been anathema in the pages of the great francophone Brussels daily since 1945. This was not paranoia on his part; it was retribution for his collaboration on the "stolen" *Le Soir.*[34] Putting together a booklet

for *Le Soir* on the world's major comic strip creators, Marcel Vermeulen had naturally included Hergé. On reading the copy, the editor in chief, Charles Brisdorf, crossed out Hergé's name on the proofs with one word: "Traitor!"[35]

This ostracism lasted twenty-five years, until a young journalist, Henri Desclez, twenty-seven years old, took over direction of *Soir-Jeunesse*. A graduate of the École des Beaux Arts, Desclez was assigned to cover theater, youth, and comic strips. Naïvely ignorant of the tacit proscription of printing the name of the father of Tintin, he devoted his first article to Hergé. The copy was edited by Jean Corvilain, also new to the paper and equally unaware of this taboo, and the article was published. The old guard at *Le Soir* was scandalized. They called the young journalists to a conference, where they were informed that this was not done because the subject in question had been on a blacklist for a long time.[36] However, soon afterward Hergé's name was the lead in a review of an exhibition dedicated to *Explorers on the Moon* and the Apollo XII mission, and thereafter his name began to appear regularly in the columns of the newspaper.

Wanting to thank in person the man to whom he owed the lifting of this ban that had weighed so heavily on him, Hergé asked two friends to arrange a meeting with Desclez. It took place during an opening at an art gallery. Hergé told him of his gratitude and asked how he could repay it. Desclez replied that he would love to have an autographed copy of *Tintin in the Land of the Soviets*. He quickly received it.

In 1974, when the position of editor in chief of *Tintin* came open, Hergé backed Desclez, who got the job.[37] The moment Hergé was no longer banned from the pages of *Le Soir*, he felt he had closed the circle.

In New York in 1972, at the First International Comic Book Convention (Comi-Con), the whole profession unanimously paid tribute to the creator of *Tintin*. At the age of sixty-five, he was brimming with projects of all sorts: readings, meetings, travels, new books. The future lay before him.

12.

The End of a Life, the Culmination of His Work: 1973–1983

HAVING ATTAINED THE SUMMIT OF HIS CAREER, Hergé now became preoccupied with his legacy. He was tormented by the idea that he did not and could not measure up to the Tintin legend. The more scholarly analyses of his books that piled up on his desk, the more he feared that his characters would be lost beneath the tributes.

In 1975 a book was published that would feed and inform all future Tintin symposia, from the most sectarian to the most ecumenical. Entitled *Interviews with Hergé,* it was notable for lacking the usual banalities and repetitions. The idea for it was initiated by Numa Sadoul, a writer, actor, playwright, and fan; the interviews took place at both the Studios on Avenue Louise and at Hergé's home and lasted many days. This was the first time that Hergé had been questioned for so long and in such depth, and he was absorbed by it. Even when exhausted he asked to do more because his questioner showed such interest in his life and work. To his surprise, he found himself opening up more and more to this stranger; reserve had always been instinctive to him. Sadoul had arrived at the right moment in his life. Before, Hergé had never felt the need to speak so personally and so intimately about his work and his life. He had always insisted that he was amazed anyone was interested in his "little guys." On reading the typescript of the interviews, he couldn't believe that he had confided so many things.

The surprise was quickly followed by regret and retractions. For three years Hergé revised the successive versions, word by word, giving the manuscript the appearance of a first draft by Proust; pages were covered

with deletions and notations. On Casterman's advice Hergé attenuated his agnosticism and cut the passages about family life, as he was in the process of a divorce, as well as those revealing his politics, which sometimes came across as reactionary.[1]

In the end he became as invested in the book as if he were the author. A book of interviews had metamorphosed into something greater, something in which he felt he had found self-expression for the first and last time in a medium other than drawings; it was a profession of faith, even a sort of testament.

Self-editing was Hergé's standard procedure when dealing with interviews and questions about his life. When he was presented with the well-known "Proust Questionnaire," at first he had given the most spontaneous and least affected answers. Then, on second thought, he took them back, recasting almost everything. He added self-deprecating humor, which masked his modesty. Comparing the versions sheds light on certain aspects of his personality.

His greatest fear? Solitude, he first replied. Then he crossed it out and wrote, "Being sick, poor and alone." Where would he like to live? London or Rome, he initially replied, before adding that meanwhile he was very happy in Brussels. His idea of earthly happiness? He simply repeated, "Happiness." He then replaced it with "Mohamed's paradise on earth," and finally "To live in peace with myself and others." Avowed shortcomings? "Speling [sic] errors." His favorite characters from novels? Angelo, the hussar from Giono's novel *The Hussar on the Roof*, and Fabrice del Dongo, the young nobleman in Stendhal's *The Charterhouse of Parma*. Thinking this was not enough he added, "Heroes who are not heroes but ordinary human beings," before crossing that out. His favorite historical person? He pretended not to have known enough of them to be able to answer the question. He withdrew this bit of false modesty and chose Marcus Aurelius. Who was his favorite real-life heroine? At first he answered simply "women" without specifying, then crossed it out and wrote "nurses," the Sisters of the Poor. He crossed this out also and finally settled on "All the anonymous women who devote their lives to relieving the suffering of others." And fictional heroines? Madame de Mortsauf, the character in Balzac's *Lys dans la vallée*. He preferred Melanie to Scarlett in *Gone with the Wind*. His favorite painter? Botticelli among the old masters, Miró among contemporaries. His favorite musician? Debussy. On thinking it over he added Erik Satie and the Beatles, but on rereading withdrew the four boys from Liverpool. The quality he preferred in a man? Loyalty. And in women? Loyalty.

His favorite virtue? The same. His favorite occupation? Vacations in sunny places, he admitted, before crossing that out and saying he liked nothing better than "doing nothing, swimming, and lying in the sun." Who would he like to have been? "Nobody," then replaced this with Methuselah. His dominant characteristic? "Anxiety," he first replied, then added, "curiosity and perfectionism." What did he like most in his friends? Being natural. His main fault? He believed that he had them all. His dream of happiness? The sea, the sun, friends, paintings, music, and his cats. In revising this he kept the same order, but in place of sun and sea he wrote, "a woman." His greatest woe? Losing his eyesight. What would he like to be? A painter. The admission was glaring, he realized, and rejected it in favor of "I want nothing else than to be myself."

His favorite color? Red. His favorite flower? The rose. His favorite bird? The titmouse, then no, the robin. His favorite authors? Balzac, Stendhal, Dickens, Proust (except for his questionnaire!). His favorite poets? Villon and Verlaine. His heroes in real life? "Explorers, that is, the real explorers, like Haroun Tazieff and Paul Emile Victor." His heroine in history? After the toss-off "I haven't known any closely," he wrote, "Queen Elizabeth of England." Then he punned, "Heroine is very dangerous!" His favorite names? Northumberland, Beaugency, Samarkand. What does he despise above all else? Vulgarity. Historical people he despised the most? "Even the very worst, I wonder if I could have done better in their place." What action does he admire the most? "In all seriousness, the fact that the sun rises every day." The reform he most admires? He hesitated among several—eliminating slavery, the miniskirt, the construction of tram lines—without being able to choose any. Which natural gift would he like to have? "Being musical." How would he like to die? "Quickly and well. Or discreetly." After thinking about it: "peacefully and in good health." What is his present state of mind? "Relieved to have come to the end of the questionnaire." Finally, what is his motto? "Do your best." That struck him as insufficient, so he added the Chinese proverb "The courteous man avoids stepping on his neighbor's shadow."[2]

As for his philosophy, Hergé defined it five years later in a letter to the writer-priest Jean Toulat: "To accept the world as it is without wanting to change it; to accept myself as I am, trying all the same to improve myself here and there."[3] Hergé saw himself as both strong and vulnerable, capable of disarming humor yet devoured by anxiety, caught between willpower and resignation.

He always presented himself as someone who savored life. He loved good food and fine wine, with a predilection for Chateau La Lagune, one

of the finest Haut-Médoc. He had always enjoyed different and varied alcoholic drinks, and he smoked as well. Nevertheless he was the exact opposite of his brother, Paul, a bon vivant of robust physical strength and the morals of a Rabelaisian character. Paul Remi was an expert horseman, sardonic, intelligent, and cultivated, extroverted, generous, and with a certain nobility of character. He and Georges Remi did not speak the same language.

Hergé had retained the soul of a child and never had to put Tintin in perspective; they were the same age. He considered Che Guevara a hero of Scouting. He was superstitious, having his fortune read on the eve of making a major decision. He consulted fortune-tellers, believed in auguries and the evil eye, and was drawn to the esoteric and paranormal. He believed himself different from the ordinary, which is perhaps why he looked on the royal family with both respect and a secret sense of identification.

He felt more a native of Brussels than a true Walloon and above all else was francophone. When in an exuberant good mood he spoke the Brussels dialect with a strong accent. He worried about the future of his country; he believed in the unity of the Belgian nation and was distressed to see signs of its coming apart. He became increasingly critical of his fellow countrymen, in the same way that he would not stand for shoddy workmanship. He often used the uneven pavement of the alley behind Avenue Louise as a metaphor of this. He was too much of a perfectionist to love his country without reservation. And yet, paradoxically, he was the personification of Belgium.

He had always been haunted by the fear of ending up like his mother, locked in a home for the clinically depressed. She had languished there much of her life, her condition untreatable, in the clinic of Doctor Titeca, a name that could not be pronounced in Hergé's presence because it stirred up such painful memories. He was especially anguished by the specter of old age, easily becoming despondent about the future. His optimism hid a tragic vision of life. He did not have a vocation for happiness.

His friends did not know everything about him. Each knew only a portion of the truth, though he never compartmentalized his relationships. Rare were those to whom he opened himself up. There were certain subjects that were taboo and never mentioned in his presence, such as his mysterious grandfather and the last years of his mother. Another was children.

Officially, of course, he liked children. He even held them in high esteem, as his correspondence testifies. In the minds of most people, "Hergé" meant "children." The image of his hero was superimposed on his

own, and sometimes substituted for it. However, as his colleagues at the Studios knew, he systematically refused school visits. And it happened that he treated children who spontaneously came to greet him with impatience. One day, irritated by the noise of children playing in the courtyard of a special education school located just behind the Studios, he went to the police station and filed a complaint.

In all these cases these were other people's children. "What I dislike the most are all these little babies and these old ladies," he once said. When Numa Sadoul asked him if he thought of Tintin as his son, he answered, "That's possible. I nourished and raised him. But despite all that, I think that I am enough of an adult to do without adopted children." He erased these lines and replaced them with innocuous comments about being the father of Tintin.

In the early fifties, finding his brother Paul's behavior toward his family completely irresponsible, Hergé proposed to legally adopt Paul's two young children. He would see to their needs and give them a solid education, which they were missing, according to him. But their mother refused.[4]

Much later, in 1978, there appeared a surrogate son. Hergé had taken on a second secretary to assist with his daily tasks. Alain Baran, the son of his old friend Dominique de Wespin, was born in 1951 and had recently left the world of dance. Though two generations apart, Hergé and Alain worked so well together that the young man soon represented Hergé in business matters. Hergé trusted him as if he were a member of the family. Their relationship became filial. Hergé had watched Alain, who had lost his father at an early age, grow up, and there was even talk in the Studios of an adoption. Some wondered if Alain were an illegitimate son. Baran found this so flattering that he did not deny it.[5]

All this highlighted the fact that the only thing Hergé had not created was a real family. Twice married (he married Fanny in 1977), Hergé never had children. Germaine and Fanny both wanted to have a family. The problem was that Hergé was sterile due to the secondary effects of the use of radiation to treat a severe rash. It remained his secret. If he suffered from it, it was never enough to make him consult a doctor and seek treatment. Even with his intimate partners he avoided the subject.[6] Yet it makes it easier to understand what a number of his friends knew, without ever admitting it openly: the father of Tintin did not like children, didn't know how to behave toward them.

At the end of the forties, when the crisis that was tearing them apart seemed resolved, Georges had agreed to Germaine's insistent request that

they adopt. They adopted an orphan boy, seven or eight years old, from an overseas country. At the end of two weeks Hergé could not stand this addition, whose presence upset his daily routine. He forced Germaine to return the child.

Hergé remains an elusive figure. Most people expect his life to be as straightforward as the lines of his drawings. But it was full of complexity and contradictions, conflicts and paradoxes, of jagged peaks and crevasses. In his statements about himself, what is profoundly sincere has to be separated from his unswerving sense of duty. His quest for happiness was so naïvely intense that he was convinced that he had at last attained harmony and found the path to wisdom. The more he said he was finally reconciled with himself, however, the more visible was the specter of his anxiety.

If Hergé's literary sensibility had not changed much over the years, it had evolved. He did not renounce his intellectual roots, but he grew from them. When asked about the ten books that had most influenced him, his selection late in life was little different from what it had been decades earlier: *Without a Family, Robinson Crusoe, Treasure Island, The Three Musketeers, The Pickwick Papers, The Unknown Man, Cousin Bette, Great Expectations, The Charterhouse of Parma*, and *Remembrance of Things Past*.[7] Only works by Dickens appeared twice on this list from 1975. Thirty years earlier he had confided to a friend, "Like everybody I read one or the other of Proust's novels, but the truth is that this writer doesn't interest me very much; my work as an illustrator, which absorbs me more and more, doesn't allow me to devote much time to reading."[8]

Balzac and Simenon were always in his private pantheon. Soon they were joined by the works of his friend Félicien Marceau, the Belgian author who settled in France after the war; he was awarded the Prix Goncourt for his novel *Creezy*, to Hergé's great pleasure, and eventually elected to the Académie Française, on which occasion Hergé sent his warmest congratulations.[9] It was Marceau's famous study of Balzac and his time that may account for Hergé's continued love of this writer.

In the sixties Hergé became interested in literature that led him toward distant horizons. After having long believed that he was a sincere Catholic, he discovered that in fact he was not. From his Catholic upbringing he mainly retained, as we've seen, the sense of duty and of sin. These were the cause of a profound guilt complex in the depth of his being, one from which he would devote his life to free himself.

Books rather than men played the decisive role in his attraction to Eastern philosophy. Initially Hergé retained the apparent simplicity of the

principles, learning to be rather than to have. He enjoyed the lucidity and naturalness of *The Path of Wisdom* by Arnaud Desjardins, and above all the *Tao Te Ching,* the treatise by the Chinese philosopher Lao-tzu, that drew him irresistibly toward Taoism, not as a religion but as a way of life. From the precept of action without acting, so symbolic of the spirit of Tao, he would seek a detachment about the practical consequences of his deeds and the ability to focus on the cause rather than the effect.

Representing the world as incarnated in two complementary energies suited him completely. Convinced that wisdom was a demanding task-master, he became completely preoccupied by the nature of the balance between the yin and the yang, rest and activity, hot and cold. His ambition was not to gain wisdom, but to become wise.[10]

When not absorbed in the works of Lao-tzu or Carl Jung, Hergé was immersed in the heady essays of the English philosopher Alan Watts, who called himself a "celestial hobo." Watts was one of the guiding lights of 1960s American counterculture, who formulated a synthesis of Emerson and Thoreau and had sought God in Nature, combining the religious psychology of Jung with the principles of Taoism, the whole done up in the libertarian spirit that was in the air in those days. It's easy to under-stand that the hippies and the beatniks were seduced by such a guru, but Hergé? Yet when he saw the musical comedy *Hair* he pronounced it "marvelous."[11] In fact he was discovering himself in hyperindividualism, the criticism of the state, and the total detachment and epicurianism distilled in Watts's books. They contained a poetic and mystical element that made them all the more relevant.

Through Watts, Hergé had learned to live again. Since he began his relationship with Fanny, he had changed, and *Tintin in Tibet* was the first external sign of this. Rather than a passing phase, the lure of the Orient was the symptom of a more enduring metamorphosis. In taking up his new life, punctuated by a long-delayed divorce in 1975 and his remarriage two years later, Hergé had transformed his way of life. He worked less, seized the present moment, and began a frantic schedule of travel: Italy, Great Britain, Sweden, Greece, Denmark, Nationalist China, the United States.

He no longer withheld his judgment of his colleagues in the profession, though he preferred to praise them rather than to criticize. He believed Sempé to be the social moralist of the twentieth century.[12] Claire Bretécher's panels for *Frustrés* (Frustrated) had a ferocity and a pathos he thought wonderful, and he found the book a pleasure to read both for the dialogues

and the drawings.[13] Besides the work of men such as Jacobs, Cuvelier, Charles Schulz, and Johnny Hart, which he already considered classic, Hergé praised the works of artists such as Jean Giraud, called "Gir," as well as Moebius, Hermann Huppen, Gégé (Gérard Cousseau, "who is full of talent"), André Franquin ("prodigious illustrator"), Marcel Gotlib, and Raymond Macherot, the creator of *Anthracite* and *Chlorophille,* whom he deemed the equal of Walt Disney in his way of camping up his animal characters. He read in one sitting *The Six Voyages of Lone Sloan,* a hero compared to whom he found Tintin very bourgeois and rational. The author, Philippe Druillet, was one of those rare artists able to bring a new dimension to the comic strip, closer to dreams than fantasy. As for Jean-Claude Mézière, whom he had known since the age of fifteen, Hergé was impressed by his capacity for invention and his powerful compositions. After reading *Ambassador of Shadows, The Birds of the Master, The Country without Stars,* and *Empire of a Thousand Planets,* he would compare him to Hieronymus Bosch and Gustave Doré.

But in his eyes, Fred (Frédéric Othon Aristidès), the mainstay of *Pilote,* stood way above the rest for his ability to remain independent of American influence, for the poetic dimension and clarity of his drawing, his satire, his ability to make the unbelievable completely credible, and for his unique combination of surrealism, absurdity, suspense, comedy, and logic.[14]

While trying to remain open to a new generation of illustrators, he nevertheless was not willing to accept just anything. He was neither youth-oriented nor a demagogue, but he could apply brakes to his enthusiasm. Hergé would always make a distinction between creators and manufacturers, distinguishing artists from the rest of the purveyors. In fact only vulgarity, sloppy work, and confusion really offended him. Sent a package of underground comic strips from Amsterdam, he did not dismiss them out of hand because he appreciated the drawings of Robert Crumb and even found the pornographic comic strips interesting for their humor and fierceness.[15] These artists, more or less young and daring, had in common that they told stories through pictures. For Hergé, this was the first criterion for belonging to the club. The rest—clarity, readability, and simplicity—was a matter of choice, taste, and sensibility.

Art had become increasingly important in his life, and his new involvement with it was the surest sign of his inner transformation. Until then Hergé was classical in his taste. His inclination and his curiosity seemed inhibited. He allowed himself to write about the Belgian watercolorist Henri Cassier (1858–1944), whose talent as a poster designer had had a

great influence on his developing "the clear line." Other than Ingres, whose genius in drawing he admired wholeheartedly, Hans Holbein was his primary reference. He had a reproduction of one of his sketches pinned on the wall of the Hergé Studios, next to a reproduction of *Dutch Interior* by Joan Miró. These artists were his two poles. His friends understood that something was happening to Hergé the day copies of Belgian Expressionist artists went up alongside Holbein and Miró. He eventually moved away from these new artists in favor of artists who were more reserved, meditative, and dreamlike. Referring to the drawing from *The Crab with the Golden Claws* so dear to him (in the foreground it has pirates lying down resting; they are getting up in the middle ground, and fleeing in the background), he surprised himself by describing it as a deliberate imitation of *Nude Descending a Staircase* by Marcel Duchamp.

Hergé had set himself free of the rigid categories of his taste. Henceforth he no longer hesitated to equate painters, sculptors, and illustrators of comic strips, focusing on what they had in common: creativity, originality, the search for a balance. On learning about the Renaissance principles of the golden mean and divine proportions, Hergé realized that he had instinctively used them in composing his work. He was convinced that his best drawings (such as Sir Francis Haddock defending his ship with saber blows and pistol shots against the pirates in *The Secret of the Unicorn*) were examples of those principles.

Excited by the links between painting and the world of comic book illustration, Hergé did not simply make timid allusions to the works of Braque, Renoir, and Picasso in *Flight 714*. He was among those who wondered whether Picasso had been inspired by the American comic strips that Gertrude Stein gave him when he was painting *The Dream and the Lies of Franco* in 1937.

By the end of the sixties, when asked to name his three favorite artists, he responded with Miró, Jean Dewasne, and Victor Vasarely. Hergé cleared his house of superfluous works, eliminating those that reminded him too much of the Germaine years. Several classical works were mixed in with those from the Fanny period. When briefly in Paris, he purchased two Song Dynasty vases, and later that day a large Calder mobile, whose grace, lightness, and poetry dazzled him as much as the porcelain.

He collected modern classics, such as Kasimir Malevitch's *White Square on White Ground*; works by American artists from the generation born in the twenties, Kenneth Noland, Robert Rauschenberg, and Roy Lichtenstein;

French artists such as Jean Dewasne; Belgian artists such as Pierre Alechinsky; and Dutch artists such as Karel Appel. These formed the core of his imaginary museum. Their works hung alongside those by David Hockney, Frank Stella, and Andy Warhol, and their elders, Alexander Calder, Constant Permeke, Victor Vasarely, Jean Dubuffet, Lucio Fontana, Serge Poliakoff, and Mark Rothko. These were the artists whose works he continued to follow, and they were sometimes joined by sudden infatuations with the work of young artists of promise, such as his fellow Belgian Jean-Pierre Maury or the Dutch Pat Andréa, the Spanish sculptor Miguel Berrocal, or the French Jean-Pierre Raynaud.

Animated by the fervor of the newly converted, Hergé was not simply a daring collector interested in the neon sculptures of Dan Flavin or the earthworks of Dennis Oppenheim, who traced circles in the snow of New England. He was there before others were interested. He wanted to make his own way as a collector and to develop his personal relationship to the artist and the work; he did not collect to accumulate nor to speculate, but to contemplate the art and to live surrounded by paintings. He never bought with the intention of reselling, though he never hesitated to exchange one work for a new one he was obsessed by. Hergé purchased frantically: African art, Chinese ceramics, and always paintings. Sometimes he acquired out of friendship and purchased works out of weakness, but in retrospect the thirty works that made up the core of his collection showed that he was rarely mistaken in his choices.

It is a collection with an astonishing coherence and openness of spirit, neither systematic nor excessive, which is surprising in a member of his generation. Despite his fortune he kept a cool head, all the more so since he was not someone who could bargain. In London in 1978 he saw a remarkable vase, Chun Yao from the Song Dynasty, of a blue he found unforgettable, but when told the price of 75,000 pounds sterling (current equivalent: $466,053), he walked away. However, when in 1973 he was offered a Rothko painting for 9 million Belgian francs (current equivalent: $1,234,976), he chewed his nails for eight days before deciding against acquiring it.

Two men played a key role in his development as a collector. First was Marcel Stal, whom he met in 1935 through his brother, Paul, when they were in artillery school. Stal was a career officer stationed in Germany after the war who quit the army in 1960 as a colonel. Paintings were his passion. He purchased his first picture as a teenager when his peers were collecting stamps. To give him the necessary boost and convince him to become an art dealer, Hergé forced his hand: he offered to pay the first

trimester of rent for his gallery, Carrefour (Crossroads), located at 170 Avenue Louise in the center of Brussels, just a few houses down from the Studios at 162. The proximity was not accidental; it became Hergé's favorite hang-out. Every day he would be there precisely at 12:05 to discuss the current show with critics, collectors, and artists passing through over a glass of "French," a local cocktail (one-third gin, two-thirds Noilly Prat dry). There he made friends with Stéphane Janssen, an indefatigable promoter of the COBRA artists at the gallery La Balance (The Scale), just a few steps away. (COBRA is an acronym for a group of postwar painters from Copenhagen, Brussels, Amsterdam.) Through Stal and his circle Hergé became acquainted with Lucio Fontana, whose perforated and lacerated monochromes made a profound impression on him. He interpreted certain slashes as haikus in the paintings and infused them with a Zen dimension that nonetheless may have been their true context. It was at the Carrefour gallery that Hergé acquired numerous works that populated his imaginative universe.

The other influence on Hergé was the critic and art historian Pierre Sterckx, who gravitated in the same circles around the Carrefour gallery. When he was a child in Brussels at the end of World War II, Sterckx discovered, in one fell swoop, painting, comic books, and literature the day his father brought him a copy of *The Blue Lotus* and had the whole family color it in. Sterckx was a critic, a professor of aesthetics at the Saint-Luc School, a writer, and a playwright. Everything that he was involved in brought him back to painting. And jazz was his great unrequited passion; he was convinced that his life was a failure because he had not become a professional double-bass player.

At the Carrefour gallery Hergé approached him. "I've read your articles," he told Sterckx, "and I have heard of you. I would like to invite you, say every Thursday at noon, to discuss painting. I will pay you for it." Sterckx burst out laughing. It seemed an incongruous proposal. He did not yet know that it corresponded perfectly to Hergé's temperament, because he needed not so much a guide as a preceptor.

Sterckx agreed, and soon a friendship developed. They met regularly at Hergé's home in Uccle, delving more and more deeply with each meeting into the ethics and aesthetics of art. Together they visited exhibitions and met artists in their studios in Belgium and elsewhere. Hergé attended Sterckx's lectures on Piero della Francesca and Uccello and started reading the ideas of Roland Barthes. Their friendship went beyond art; Sterckx also helped him discover music. After attending a concert by

the twenty-three-year-old jazz pianist Keith Jarrett, Hergé said, completely dazzled, "It was as if Debussy had not died."[16]

Hergé not only collected paintings; during one period he believed himself a painter. Other illustrators had believed that they were artists—Rodolphe Töpffer and Simon Christophe, to cite only two. Some, such as Lyonel Feininger, went from illustration to painting. Georges Remi first wanted to be the journalist Albert Londres, then Joan Miró. In retrospect it might be said that in his covers for *Boy-Scout* at the end of the twenties the young illustrator was making Warhols before Warhol, publishing the same portrait every month but changing the background colors each time.[17]

The painter Pierre Alechinsky, who had confronted Hergé for his anti-Semitic caricature, grew up on the works of Hergé from his earliest age. He never forgot the comic strips of *Quick and Flupke* that marked his adolescence at the end of the thirties. One of them in particular, "Occultation I," was about an exhibition of Flupke's paintings, "Brussels at Night," at the Thétis Gallery. Having first seen those black monochrome canvases as reminiscent of Dada and Alphonse Allais, Alechinsky would in retrospect see them as prefiguring the works of Yves Klein.[18]

Hergé had an irrepressible need to surround himself with paintings. At different times his environment consisted of masterworks by Serge Poliakoff, Lucio Fontana, James Rosenquist, Jean Dewasne, Miguel Berrocal, Frank Stella, and Kenneth Noland. He also had his famous portrait in four parts done in 1977 by Warhol, who compared him to Walt Disney in terms of an influence on him. This portrait became useful promotionally in the distribution of *Tintin* in the American market. Roy Lichtenstein was also important to Hergé, especially his prints of the cathedral after Monet and the proximity of his work to the universe of comic strips. His use of comic book images and the graphic clarity of his work inspired in Hergé a sincere sense of affinity.[19]

All of this raises the question of whether Hergé had missed his vocation as a painter, as he himself often said was the case, particularly in his bouts of depression. At the height of his upheaval, questioning everything, he quietly set aside his drawing board for the easel. He had met Louis Van Lint at the Carrefour gallery and asked him for private lessons. The same age as Hergé, Van Lint, a lyrical abstract painter who had participated in the founding of the COBRA group, came to his home each week to teach him the basic techniques.

Hergé started painting abstract canvases of medium size, with two exceptions, which were portraits of Fanny. His early work, as might be

expected, was influenced by Van Lint, but eventually his long-held interest in the works of Miró ("Snowy" in Japanese!) predominated. Obviously he was searching for something.

When it became known that he had started painting, people began questioning what he was doing. They wondered whether he had an inferiority complex about the comic strip in general and Tintin in particular. His friend Robert Poulet pushed this line of reasoning even further. He believed that this new direction corresponded with Hergé's discovery of contemporary art and his attending avant-garde gallery openings. Poulet was persuaded that this whole painting thing was a "snobbish phase." Hergé had temporarily renounced being himself.[20]

One day Hergé asked an old friend, the lawyer Gaston Duval, to arrange a meeting with Duval's father-in-law, a critic he knew only by reputation and whose opinion he believed would be decisive. Léo Van Puyvelde was the director of the Royal Museum of Beaux Arts of Belgium. Hergé went to his villa in Uccle with five or six canvases under his arm that he wanted to submit for an expert opinion. He was warmly greeted by this eminent expert in Flemish painting who had collected all the books of *Tintin* in the original black-and-white editions. The judgment was courteous but decisive: "It's not bad, not bad at all. But it would be so much better if you would devote yourself to comic strips."[21] Hergé could not hide his great disappointment. He continued to paint for several weeks, but his enthusiasm had deserted him. One day he stopped completely: "I'll never be more than a Sunday painter," he told Fanny.[22]

He also feared being consumed by this devouring passion and not being able to draw when he decided to tackle his next book. "I felt that if I continued, I would lose my pencil," he confided to Marcel Stal.[23]

Despite his pride and his vanity, he was not deceived about his limitations. That was one of his strengths. Painting had haunted him since earliest childhood; he now knew it was inaccessible. Not only did he not have the dedication, but he had nothing to say in the medium. It was not the time to forge a new artistic career, especially on such an uncertain basis—not when one is Hergé and cannot bear mediocrity.

All in all he produced thirty-seven paintings. They were never shown in public and remained the property of Fanny, except for two, which he signed "Hergé," the pseudonym he had originally chosen for drawings, saving his real name for his future paintings.[24] Stal owns these two paintings. One, titled *Person in a Dream*, was obviously influenced by Miró and could only be ripped from the artist's hand in exchange for a small Fontana

that the gallery owner had just brought back from Italy and for which Hergé would have sold his soul.[25] The other, influenced by Van Lint, was sold for one million Belgian francs (current equivalent: $143,360) in 1995. It is now in the home of the actor Stéphane Steeman, a *Tintin* collector.

The day that Hergé abandoned his easel to return to the drawing board he was inspired. This painting adventure had at least taught him that when you have done something that can be done by no other person in the world, you stay with it for life, even if it sometimes seems like a life sentence. His bouts of depression were now over, and he could celebrate his "happy fifty years of work."

SINCE 1962 Hergé had been planning to write a story about the rivalry between the generals Alcazar and Tapioca, assiduous practitioners of serial coup d'états, fraternal enemies of the revolution and the counterrevolution since *The Broken Ear*. The path to fruition was not smooth. Hergé put the project aside, then returned to it, hesitating as much over details as the broad outline of the plot. He wondered whether Tintin shouldn't be a victim, even imagined having him imprisoned for political reasons.[26]

For the moment his provisional title was *Tintin and the Bigotudos*. Reintroducing the name of his hero in the title was Casterman's idea; he insisted on it for commercial reasons. Hergé agreed with reaffirming the primacy of Tintin, although many of his readers were bigger fans of Haddock. As for the word *bigotudos,* it is a Latin American term for "mustachioed."

Current events intervened in his plot. The young French intellectual and radical Regis Debray filled headlines. Having taken the side of the Bolivian revolutionaries, he joined the guerrillas and their legendary leader, Che Guevara. Apprehended by the troops of General-President Barrientos and put on trial, he was sentenced to thirty years in prison. After three years he was set free as the result of a massive public opinion campaign and behind-the-scenes diplomatic pressure.

Despite the romantic allure of Debray's story, it wasn't what Hergé had in mind. Tintin was no dreamy radical. His motivation would be to help a friend in distress. The rest was in place: an imaginary country in Latin America, with downtrodden Indians, a ruthless dictator, the grim-faced guerrillas, the shameful exploitation of resources by the multinationals.[27] For documentation Hergé had only to read the newspapers, though he also used Jean Lartéguy's *The Guerrillas*, which retraced the footsteps of Che through a dozen countries in South America. The photographs accompanying the text proved useful, illustrating the uniforms of the revolutionaries

that served as models for the Tapiocan soldiers' attire. For the title of the book Hergé finally settled on *Tintin and the Picaros*, introducing the notion of the picaresque.

Tintin and Haddock learn through the press that La Castafiore has been arrested in Tapiocapolis, capital of San Theodoros, one of the numerous stops on her tour of Latin America. Accused of having conspired to overthrow the regime of General Tapioca, she has been imprisoned, along with the Thom(p)sons. The San Theodoros newspaper *The Truth* (*Pravda* in Russian) identifies Marlinspike Hall as the tactical headquarters of a conspiracy hatched by Tintin, Haddock, and Professor Calculus, complicit with the International Banana Company. Asked to explain himself by the government of San Theodoros, Haddock takes up the challenge and sets off for Latin America accompanied by Professor Calculus. Tintin refuses to walk into what he sees clearly as a trap. It doesn't take long for the old sea wolf to learn that his young friend had been right; they are indeed in a trap, although it is a gilded cage, the palace of Colonel Alvarez.

Feeling guilty about letting his friends set off by themselves, Tintin immediately follows them. He is shadowed by the familiar face of Colonel Sponsz, former chief of police of Szohod in *The Calculus Affair*. Forewarned that an attack by fake Picaros has been planned as a pretext to eliminate them, Tintin, Haddock, and Calculus flee into the jungle, where they fall into a trap but are saved by General Alcazar, another old acquaintance, who is the head of the guerrillas. They take refuge in a village held by the rebels, who are under the influence of the Loch Lomond whisky that General Tapioca sends down to them by parachute in generous quantity. The trio makes the acquaintance of Peggy, the "sweet dove" of General Alcazar but in reality a shrew who henpecks her husband. Tintin offers to help Alcazar train his men but refuses any payment, asking only that the general promise a bloodless coup. He agrees. But first Tintin has to detoxify the guerrillas from their alcoholic fog, both to help them overthrow the dictator and to secure the release of their friends, Castafiore and the Thom(p)sons. Professor Calculus throws pills of his own concoction into their cooking pot; the troops sober up quickly and take up arms again.

Just then a tour bus arrives in the middle of the jungle with the dreaded Jolyon Wagg and his Jolly Follies on board. They are on their way to the carnival in Tapiocapolis. The guerrillas don masquerade costumes and, commandeering the bus, infiltrate the city. Taking advantage of all the delirious festivities, they overthrow the old dictator. It's a palace coup rather than a full-blown civil war; the citizens are completely oblivious.

Tapiocapolis becomes Alcazaropolis, and our friends depart for home and Marlinspike. The new San Theodoros they leave behind is no different from the old.

Published in 1976, the twenty-third in the series, the adventure would be the last one Hergé completed. The charm was gone. It is a book made "in the manner of" Hergé, and though he remained nominally in charge of the work, he feels absent.[28] The revelation by Captain Haddock that his first name is Archibald offers meager consolation for his readers: after years of faithfully waiting they deserve better. Tintin is no longer recognizable: whereas he was fourteen or fifteen for the first forty years of his life,[29] he is older now. He travels by automobile, a concession to the times and an outrage to purists. Worse, Hergé has exchanged Tintin's plus fours for blue jeans. If Tintin was formed by his time, it was never obvious. Updating his appearance in his adventure among the Picaros was done to satisfy film producers, who wanted to make Tintin less old-fashioned-looking to the wide American public.[30] To maintain visual continuity the jeans would not be a washed-out blue, but brown, a halfway solution for the worse.

However, not everything was lost. The character of Peggy is original. Hergé discovered her while watching a television program about the Ku Klux Klan. On seeing the secretary of the public relations man for the organization, he leaped out of his armchair: "There's Alcazar's wife! That's her completely!"[31] He grabbed a pencil and paper and made a sketch from life. Though he had always refrained from drawing at home, this time the urge was too strong. He could not resist the idea: a terrifying dictator has an even more terrifying wife, who leads him by the nose.[32]

The masks and floats in the parade were inspired by the Carnival in Nice—sculptures of Marcel Arnould and the paintings of Poliakoff—while the interior of houses came out of the pages of *Maison Française*, which gave the story a tonality that differentiated it from other books. Bob De Moor did his work well: not a detail is missing from any of the cars. Jolyon Wagg's tour bus of happy travelers is an exact replica, inside and outside, of a Volvo bus. The decor and accessories obey the same principles of accuracy. But this is not enough to give soul to the work.

When Professor Calculus meets Colonel Alvarez he says, "I am sorry, soldier, but I refuse to shake a hand that tramples on inalienable human rights." It's a funny moment, and representative of the time. A few years later, in 1982, Hergé would be solicited to join an international campaign for the defense of Hector Oesterheld, a leftist Argentinean author and comic book editor. The author of a graphic biography called *The Life of*

Che, Oesterheld was kidnapped from his home in 1976 by a paramilitary group linked to the regime and had been missing for five years. At the request of Amnesty International, Hergé wrote a letter to General Leopoldo Galtieri, asking for a thorough investigation. However, Oesterheld was never seen again.[33]

The publication of *Tintin and the Picaros* unleashed a wave of articles and broadcasts. Many were more than simply filler articles, as in the past, but often carefully argued critiques. The interest seemed in inverse proportion to the quality of the work in question. In Belgium the reviewers fell into three categories: those who focused on the work, those who wanted to judge Hergé according to his political views, and those who defended him out of respect for past work.[34]

Politics dominated. One journalist who had written about the African adventures of Tintin judged Hergé's work paternalistic, reactionary, and, in sum, racist. "Enough!" he concluded his article. "It's poisoning our children. Hergé has to be burned."[35] Hergé defended himself in an interview: "People say that [*Tintin and the Picaros*] was political, which is not the point at all. It takes place against a political backdrop. Obviously everyone brings to it what they carry within them.... Both of the Picaros' leaders are dictators," he added. "Tintin is carried along by events, rather than driving them."[36]

AT SEVENTY Hergé was becoming more frail. His resilience, on which he had so often counted, now failed him. Stricken with an ailment whose exact nature remains unknown, he became extremely tired. Yet traveling, painting, reading, his friends, and Fanny, above all, had given him a vision of what earthly happiness could be. He had perhaps never been so close to achieving inner harmony.

On his list of unfinished business, however, finding his old friend Chang figured prominently. Since that day in 1935 when they last saw one another on the platform of the train station in Brussels, Chang had married and had four children. For thirty years he had directed a school of painting and sculpture he founded in Shanghai. A committed Communist, he had also used his brush to serve the regime. In 1966 the Cultural Revolution destroyed everything; his school was looted and he was sent to a reeducation camp. He was later put to work planting rice and then in a steel mill, picking up nails.

Having had no news of Chang for years, Hergé nonetheless never lost hope of seeing him again. He knew what he owed to him and never missed

an opportunity to acknowledge it. He mentioned him in all his interviews; it was his way of searching for him. In 1974 he thought that he had located Chang and sent him the two works in which he appears, *The Blue Lotus* and *Tintin in Tibet*. The Chinese customs officers returned them shortly afterward with the notice "Forbidden Mail. Import Refused." Convinced his friend was still alive, living somewhere in China, he did not abandon his search. He systematically went through the list of Chinese restaurants in Brussels, starting with the one called The Blue Lotus (it was actually Vietnamese). In each establishment he asked the proprietor whether they knew a certain Chang Chong-Chen. Every time a shake of the head signifying "sorry." His Chinese pronunciation doubtless made things worse. One day a restaurateur on Avenue Louise made him repeat the name several times: "Ah! You mean Chang Chong-Chen." It was like a conversation between Haddock and Professor Calculus.

Hergé eventually learned that Chang was living in Shanghai, on Hei Fei Street, the same address as forty years before. Shortly after this discovery, a neighbor came knocking on Chang's door in Shanghai. It was Wei Su Kong, the son of the Chinese ambassador to Belgium and a friend of the restaurant owner. He found Chang bedridden—still recovering from his treatment by the Red Guard—and gave him Hergé's address. "He has been looking everywhere for you over the last few years. Write him."[37]

Chang soon received a long letter from Hergé, along with several books, including *Tintin and the Picaros*.[38]

Despite the progress made since Nixon's visit to China in 1976, the political climate there was not propitious for travel. Two figures would play a decisive role in the historic reunion of Hergé and Chang. One was Gérard Valet, a radio, television, and film producer, who took advantage of an official visit by King Baudouin and Queen Fabiola to the Great Wall to find Chang and persuade the authorities to allow him to travel. Valet was the coauthor of a documentary on Hergé; he knew that nothing would give him greater pleasure. The other was Han Suyin, the Chinese Belgian doctor who had become a best-selling novelist. Passing through Brussels in 1977, she agreed to intercede on Hergé's behalf and deliver a letter to Huang Cheng, the Chinese minister of culture. In Brussels she was joined by Serge Pairoux of the China-Belgium Friendship Association in putting pressure on the Chinese cultural attaché to the embassy to grant Hergé a visa. Even Joseph Schoumaker, the director of foreign affairs, was put to the task to use all his influence as a former ambassador to China. Years passed with no results.[39]

One day Hergé received a letter from Chang, asking him to help his second son, Shieu Jen. He had grown up during the Cultural Revolution and wanted to continue his education. He would be able to study in Belgium on the condition that a school invited him, which would perhaps accelerate the procurement of a visa for him. "If this could be done, I would feel relieved of an enormous burden. I am in a cave in Tibet, but Tintin is not with me.... I don't know how high the sky is, nor how low the earth. But I can do nothing for my son."[40]

Finally, on March 1, 1981, at the airport in Zaventem, a crowd of journalists and fans converged to await the arrival of a flight from Paris. Rather than the traditional banner of welcome there was a huge poster from *Tintin in Tibet*. In the general surge of the crowd, the little man accompanied by the indispensable Gérard Valet appeared. Hergé and Chang rushed toward each other with open arms. They couldn't keep back the tears, especially Hergé, considerably weakened and thin from his illness. It had been forty-six years since they had seen one another. During the press conference Chang was too moved to speak. Even Hergé, more used to public exposure, could not find words.[41]

Chang was introduced to Queen Fabiola of Belgium on the occasion of her visit to the Hergé Studios. Everyone looked after Chang. Claude de Valkeneer, the press attaché to the king, worked behind the scenes to extend his stay in Belgium as long as possible. In France Régis Debray had become an advisor on foreign relations to President Mitterrand and extended an offer to Chang to take up residence in France. The minister of culture, Jacques Lang, seconded it with an official invitation. Chang learned that a whole country had read the two books of which he was a hero. Young readers felt they now had proof that Tintin was a living person. If Chang was real, so too must be Tintin.

Chang was everywhere, winning over one and all, wordlessly. In the School of Graphic Research in Brussels journalists and students watched him trace the calligraphic characters with his brush in an almost religious silence. Asked what it meant, he replied, "Work gives work and produces patience. Patience gives patience and produces strength." Impassively Chang added, "It's a quote from Rodin."[42]

Chang spent several months in Belgium before returning to China, where he and his family made preparations to settle in the Paris suburbs.

By finding Chang, Hergé had finally realized one of his fondest wishes. But he had other wishes as well, one of which he dreaded so much that he avoided doing anything until events forced his hand.

At issue was whether to give film rights to Hollywood. If he accepted, he felt he was rushing headlong into a commitment without any guarantee of control over the final result. To refuse, however, would shut off an opportunity to rejuvenate his creation.

Hergé now rarely went to the movies, aside from the occasional Chaplin or John Ford classic, and he rarely referred to major directors. Yet his work was intimately involved with the cinematic. The influence of silent films on his work has been widely noted—on the visual gag, the pacing, the rhythm; the birth and appearance of Tintin was contemporaneous with talkies. Without knowing any, as an illustrator he felt an affinity with film directors. Like them, he created the sequences in total chronological disorder, going from one plate to another, from the end to the beginning and back again. The magic came from the editing. Everyone working with images shared common issues, such as how to create the feeling of duration without sacrificing the rhythm. In addition, writing a story line was like writing a film script: both used the present tense and had short sentences, a telegraphic style, and minimal descriptions. In short, Hergé's technique was cinematographic; the art lay in joining one sequence to the next. The techniques were similar: close-ups, shot/reverse shot, bird's-eye view, ground angle shot, and depth of field. And, of course, there was the jump cut, the most difficult to manage because it heightens the tension of the action or accentuates the comical.[43]

When Hergé's effort to contact Walt Disney after the war failed, Raymond Leblanc undertook with his company, Belvision, to produce a series of seven animated shorts adapted from the adventures of Tintin and Snowy, each lasting five minutes, which were distributed to television stations around the world. Belvision then launched into producing two animated feature films: *Tintin and the Temple of the Sun* (which combined *The Seven Crystal Balls* and *Prisoners of the Sun*) and, three years later, in 1972, *Tintin and the Lake of Sharks*. Hergé worked on the adaptation of the first, but the second feature was entirely out of his hands.

Nevertheless Hergé remained guarded about taking the comparison between comic strips and films too far. He rejected the argument that watching a film and reading an illustrated book took approximately the same amount of time.

More than that, however, Hergé doubted that film could ever be compatible with his sensibility.[44] From the time he started trying to extend his work with Tintin into an audiovisual dimension he felt closer to movie-making than animation. "Tintin is not Alice in Wonderland!" he insisted.[45]

"What if the living Tintin, the Tintin in the film, didn't come close to resembling the Tintin in the books?" he wrote to one young reader. "If you and all the spectators refused to recognize 'your' Tintin in the actor portraying him, I am sure that after calling him out on it (you're going to say, 'we want the real person!'), you'll chase him off as an impostor."[46]

Starting in the fifties he had received a constant stream of offers for the film rights, some absurd, others serious, but nothing came of any one of them. There was even a suggestion that Jacques Cousteau film *Red Rackham's Treasure*. Hergé did meet with the Hollywood producer Larry Harmon, who had expressed his desire to bring Tintin to the screen. Things developed far enough that Hergé began to offer advice: "I'm asking you, my dear Larry, not to reduce my characters to stereotypes; they have to remain human. I ask you not to reduce their adventures to a series of mechanical gags; they have to remain human adventures." If the films turned out too "slow" for Americans, "that [would] be fine."[47]

Two feature films by the French producer André Barret were made in the sixties with flesh-and-blood actors: *Tintin and the Mystery of the Golden Fleece*, directed by Jean-Jacques Vierne from a script by Remo Forlani, and *Tintin and the Blue Oranges*, directed by Philippe Condroyer, with yet another script by Remo Forlani.

Hergé was initially unconvinced that they needed to use an original script. He thought the story should be taken from one of his books. It was explained to him that the similarities between illustrations and cinema held up only to a certain point, but he claimed that a story that had matured over years had to be superior to a script dashed off in a few months, whose gags and plots seemed mediocre to him.[48] Finally he had to accept the arguments of professionals and give his consent that another person write the script. However, he maintained the right to veto the final project and darkened innumerable pages with drawings and suggestions. It wasn't his text, but it was his "child," and he was not abandoning him. In his line-by-line criticism he applied the techniques of one art to another, never doubting for a moment that he would help the film succeed.[49] The misunderstanding was complete because Hergé and Barret did not speak the same language. In the final scene of *Prisoners of the Sun* Professor Calculus is convinced that he was an extra in an epic production when he was almost burned alive at the stake: "I'll never act in another film no matter how much gold Hollywood throws at me."[50] When Casterman published the books based on these two films, Hergé refused to let his name appear on the cover.

The lukewarm reception of the first film in 1962 confirmed his original suspicions. His friend Robert Poulet put into words what Hergé felt without being able to express it. The film lacked poetry. The voices were too commonplace. The film stripped Tintin of everything that makes him magical; what is left is simply a remarkably resourceful adolescent. "The film makers didn't dishonor the legend: they were satisfied to make it bourgeois and turn it into prose."[51]

From then on Hergé did not want to hear about film options. His position was expressed in a letter he wrote to a young reader unhappy after having seen the animated *Temple of the Sun*: "I don't like Captain Haddock in the film. He doesn't have the same voice as in the book."[52]

This remained Hergé's stance in 1982 when he received one of those offers that seemingly could not be refused. At thirty-six Steven Spielberg already had an impressive filmography; *Duel*, *The Sugarland Express*, *Jaws*, *Close Encounters of the Third Kind*, *1941*, and *ET* had all been international successes with record-breaking attendance and receipts. Despite his reservations Hergé was impressed enough to give Spielberg's proposal serious consideration and be flattered by the project.

Negotiations went on for months. Spielberg was European only in his passion for François Truffaut. In everything else he remained completely American. The contracts went back and forth between Los Angeles and Brussels and between their respective lawyers. Hergé was anxious lest Spielberg Americanize his story too much and lose the spirit of his books. These fears were premature, because it was not at this point a question of the script nor of adaptation, but only about *business*.

As Spielberg was to be both producer and director of the film, Hergé conceded more and more on the commercial level to give the project the best chance of succeeding at the artistic level. Making less money was less important than making sure Tintin came out triumphant. Alain Baran, his private secretary, and Eric Osterweil, his lawyer in Brussels, did everything possible so that the Americans, represented by Kathleen Kennedy, would advance the project.

Spielberg's demands were draconian. He wanted total control of the merchandising of the film, thus of the characters created by Hergé; he wanted to keep for himself the rights from the comic strips and any television series derived from them; and he wanted sole artistic and commercial control of the whole project. Hergé agreed.

At the moment of signing the contract for a thirty-month option, Hergé's advisors realized that the Americans had added a new clause,

stipulating that in case the screenplay ordered by Steven Spielberg from his collaborators was unsatisfactory, Spielberg reserved the right to assign the directing of the film to someone else. For Hergé such an eventuality was unacceptable. He had made all the financial concessions because Spielberg himself would be in charge of the film.[53] It had been difficult enough for him to accept the fact that Tintin, Snowy, and Haddock would appear on hundreds of millions of objects, articles of clothing, and gadgets without Hergé's receiving any benefit. But it was unthinkable that he would consent to allowing anyone else to make the film. Both parties went their separate ways. However, the business would not be a total loss.

Twenty years earlier, right after Philippe de Broca abandoned the idea of bringing Tintin to the screen, he had made *That Man from Rio,* which had an extraordinary success. The director had collaborated on the screenplay with Jean-Paul Rappeneau, Ariane Mnouchkine, and Daniel Boulanger, all avid readers of *Tintin,* judging from the plot of the film. It opened with the theft of a statue from the Amazon currently at the Musée de L'Homme in Paris, followed by the mysterious kidnapping of Professor Catalan, the discovery of two more statues similar in every detail, the intervention of a soldier on leave who braves all dangers before the magical properties of the statues reveal the treasure of the Maltèques. Jean-Paul Belmondo, who played the lead, is not Tintin and *That Man from Rio* is not *The Broken Ear,* but it has the same plot and rhythm.

When Spielberg gave up pursuit of *Tintin,* he made *Indiana Jones and the Temple of Doom;* set in 1935, it involves a cabaret in Shanghai, a daring archaeologist who is unconscious of danger, ritual human sacrifices practiced in a volcano, and a magical diamond. The resemblance to *Cigars of the Pharaoh, The Blue Lotus, Prisoners of the Sun,* and *The Red Sea Sharks* is not purely coincidental. Spielberg had never hidden what his imagination owed to Hergé's world: the nostalgic quest for the lost paradise of childhood.

In any event, this was not the end of Spielberg's quest for Tintin. Although the original negotiations between Spielberg and Hergé had failed, after Hergé's death Spielberg obtained an option on Tintin from the estate, which he continued to renew on and off for roughly two decades. In 2002 Spielberg, joined by director Peter Jackson and Kathleen Kennedy as coproducers, successfully concluded an option to make three *Tintin* films. The first, to be directed by Spielberg, will be *The Secret of the Unicorn,* due for release in 2011. Jackson's New Zealand–based WETA, a digital special-effects company, will supply photorealistic "performance capture" techniques, as were used in part of *The Lord of the Rings,* in an

effort to retain Hergé's line drawing techniques (the clear line) and adapt them to the screen.

HERGÉ WAS GROWING increasingly weary of Tintin and tired of comic strips. He had exhausted the genre at the very moment his work was being consecrated as a classic of children's literature and part of the European cultural heritage. He still had a great deal he wanted to say but sought other means of expression.[54] Yet he always came back to the comic strip.

For several years he sketched out a number of projects, but only a few stood out. One was called simply "Airport"; its origins date from the period between the world wars. In 1973 during a stopover at the Rome-Fiumicina Airport, his obsession returned. In his mind an airport was always the geometric center of all sorts of encounters, of unexpected situations, the core of the nervous system radiating outward in concentric circles. It was like a miniature city—cosmopolitan, lively, exotic, and picturesque. Love and tragedy, adventure and comedy were permanently there side by side. Anything could happen. It contained unsuspected human wealth, the whole world gathered in a few thousand square yards.[55]

In 1976 he filled fifteen pages with drawings and scripts, mixing elements from a story line with sketches under the heading "A winter day at a certain airport." From the beginning strange things occur (fog, fuel shortages), and the place fills up with people who are forced to spend several hours together, the airplanes being unable either to depart or to land. Tintin and Haddock are there to accompany Professor Calculus to a congress of inventors, while the Thom(p)sons had intended to take a flight for an international convention of detectives. That's when they are joined by the rest of the family: Emir Ben Kalish Ezab, looking to buy a chateau to house the unbearable little Abdullah; King Muskar IV, pursued by extremists; General Alcazar on his way to Switzerland to check his numbered accounts; the diva Castafiore, who creates a commotion because she will not be able to sing; the Bird brothers, involved in trafficking hashish on being released from prison; the intrusive and irritating Jolyon Wagg; Mull Pascha, alias Dr. Mueller; the shivering billionaire Lazlo Carreidas; Señor Oliveira da Figueira, ever ready to deal in arms; the maharajah of Gopal; and Arabs, Jews, Indians, Japanese, Americans, all readily identifiable by their outfits. Among them a Pakistani appears regularly to ask questions (no one knows why)—What time is it? Where is the toilet?—until the very end of the story.

Everything becomes complicated to the point of confusion, yet Hergé gave himself over to it joyfully, introducing new characters, such as the

boring traveler always ready to relate adventures no one wants to hear, and the intellectual with his all-inclusive philosophical system. Hergé noted that Haddock was in a somber mood, Professor Calculus having made him abstain from whisky. In the end Hergé asked himself, "What is Tintin doing in all this? He is the link, but he is no longer a hero!"[56] He put the story away in a drawer and moved on to other things.

Two years later he would confide to Alain Baran, "I have an idea. I want to return to Tintin's beginnings. The reporter detective, the mystery, to put it in a few words."[57] During the summer of 1978 he was inspired by a case that had been in the media eleven years earlier. Fernand Legros, a Parisian art dealer with a comical if slightly over-the-top appearance (cowboy hat, dark sunglasses, necklaces, chauffeur-driven Rolls), had sold to the American collector Algur Hurtle Meadows, an oil magnate, several dozen Derains, Vlamincks, Modiglianis, and Marquets at prices defying all competition. Following an auction Legros was exposed: his masterpieces were forgeries. The scandal had repercussions because Legros had sold works to many people.

Hergé's idea was to combine the Legros case with that of the false Vermeers by the Dutch painter Hans Van Meegeren. Around Tintin and his pals Hergé gathered new characters: Endaddine Akass, a phony priest; Ramo Nash, a conceptual artist who copies works in his spare time; the art expert Jacques Monastir and Yvon Fourcart, gallery owners inspired by his friend Marcel Stal; and Zolotas, a shady dealer reminiscent of Paul Pétrides, the Parisian expert on Maurice Utrillo.

Hergé put aside the project, took it up again, and then forgot about it. He thought of investigating the world of religious sects. A feature in *Paris-Match* on the guru Maharishi Magesh had fascinated him. He sketched out forty-two pages. In the last one Tintin is in serious danger. Hergé even called his friend Stéphane Janssen, an art dealer from Brussels, and asked whether it would be all right if Tintin died on the terrace of his house in Beverly Hills. Trapped by villains, Tintin is threatened with being compressed into a sculpture by the French artist César, which would naturally be called *Reporter*. His fate was to end up incorporated and transformed into a work of art.[58] Unless . . . We will never know. Hergé stopped looking at the file of *Tintin and Alph-Art*, the working title of the book.

In 1983, at the age of seventy-five, Hergé was at the end of his strength and decided, at least for the time being, to stop working. The last painting he purchased was by Stephan Dejaeger, a young artist from Brussels.

Composed of Polaroids on a panel that formed the outline of a figure, it was titled *Le Tricheur* (The Cheater).

Four years earlier, all the festivities in Brussels and Paris celebrating the fiftieth anniversary of the birth of Tintin had taken a toll. Ever since, Hergé hadn't felt well. He had stopped smoking years before but still drank, less now, but enough to worry about cirrhosis of the liver. The doctors confirmed that he had osteomyelofibrosis; he was no longer producing white corpuscles. The word "leukemia" could not be spoken, though it was on the tip of everyone's tongue. Hergé knew it but wanted to remain optimistic, counting on advances in medicine. When Chang learned of it, he consulted the three most renowned Chinese specialists.

Every two weeks, then every week, Hergé went to the hospital for a transfusion. "I have a full tank," he told the friend who accompanied him.[59]

Hergé would turn up at the Studios periodically. The mood there had darkened. He followed from his home the course of the little work that was carried on. More than ever now, Alain Baran orchestrated everything, and he became the conduit to Hergé. Together they had looked at a building not far from his house, as Hergé was making plans for the near future in the light of his state of health. He thought of moving the Studios and installing them closer to him so that it would require less of an effort to "go to work." It was an unrealistic plan, naïve and pathetic, but it sustained him, and even made him want to return to *Tintin and the Alph-Art*.[60]

He who had loved driving fast now allowed himself to be driven by Alphonse Slachmuylders, his chauffeur. He worked only intermittently and watched the news with detachment. Great conflicts between countries worried him less than civil wars between armed bands. After he underwent a prostate operation, his travels were planned with the greatest caution. A rest cure at the Hotel Eden Roc of Ascona on Lake Maggiore temporarily put him back on his feet. But shortly afterward, during a stay in the mountains, he had to be evacuated to a hospital, having contracted double pneumonia.

Because of his age and his state of health, the future disposition of his work was of course an issue. He had often made it known that his characters would disappear with him. There would be no more Tintin without Hergé because Hergé was not Walt Disney. Despite his success and fame, his genius and his scope, he had remained in his own way an honest artisan. Some of his colleagues at the Studios hoped for a sign from him that they would be invested with the responsibility of carrying the torch. Hergé didn't disabuse them. Bob De Moor, whom everyone believed to be his natural successor, was convinced that this lack of resolve was in his favor. The day he

understood that Hergé had in fact never wanted a spiritual heir to continue with Tintin in his place he would be all the more saddened and bitter.

It was not a question of technical or artistic competence, but of spirit. Hergé was convinced that he was the only one who could bestow a soul on his character.

This position forced Hergé to confront a seemingly insoluble problem: how to keep alive a work that is finished. To his way of thinking, Tintin meant the books, and not the objects, the posters, and postcards that would continue as grist for the financial mill when he was no longer there. The products derived from his work interested him only financially. Alain Baran was no longer satisfied with being the important secretary of the Studios, dealing with Éditions du Lombard and Casterman. Because of their close relationship, he was authorized to speak more and more often in the name of Hergé. He wanted Hergé to restructure his relation to the merchandising in order to bring the major Tintin products under the direct control of the Studios.

It became all the more difficult once Hergé started looking on his business with detachment and complacency. It caused problems when he seemed unconcerned about not having a say in these matters. When someone came to propose a new license, Hergé would comment sarcastically, "Here's someone else on the verge of bankruptcy who wants to reinvent himself!"[61]

By contrast the adventures of Tintin and Snowy were his life. "These are my lungs, these are my very guts!"[62] He didn't dare say that they were his life's blood. He rarely evoked death; the word was absent from his vocabulary. For him it was only a rite of passage.

Although feeling increasingly ill, Hergé wanted desperately to recover. He was not thinking of the future, but of living fully in the present, faithful to his Taoist teaching. This did not prevent him from planning ahead. Three months before his death he made Fanny his sole heir.

The blood transfusions became more difficult. The word "leukemia" was no longer taboo. Those who worried about him spoke of it openly.[63]

His cheeks were hollow, he was swimming in his clothes, his hands trembled; only his gaze remained steady. Increasingly weakened by the disease, he remained optimistic in his own way. If he must leave, then let it be as a sage. This superior state corresponded to his most profound aspirations. Now if he encountered in the street his old English professor from Saint-Boniface College, the one who always asked him, "So, are you still making your little doodles?" Hergé would no longer become enraged.[64]

Wisdom was not to react, but to continue on his way with a smile. He was neither in revolt, nor anguished, nor resigned, nor bitter. He had nothing more to hide. In his last interview, granted to Benoît Peeters two months before he died, he said, "What if I told you that I put my whole life into Tintin?"[65]

He still had the strength to visit Germaine every Monday at their home in Céroux-Mousty. He wanted to stroll in the garden by himself, but Germaine quickly joined him. She told him he looked tired. He replied that he was.[66]

These were the last words they exchanged. He returned home and almost never left it again. In January he had to give up the idea of attending the fiftieth birthday party for his friend Stéphane Steeman. But to be present in spirit at the home of his most faithful collector, he asked Bob De Moor to bring Steeman two Chinese editions of *The Black Island* accompanied by this note: "Happy Birthday. Sorry I can't be with you tonight, curse this enforced idleness. Your friend, Hergé."[67]

Elegant to the last, he adhered to the dictum that humor is the courteous expression of despair. On February 25, 1983, Hergé was rushed to the emergency room at Saint-Luc Clinic in Brussels for heart failure. The transfusions threw him into a state close to unconsciousness, but he would have been worse off without them. Fanny and Alain Baran were at his side. They were the only two people authorized to be with him until the end.

After reading a letter from an Indian boy thrilled with his books, he expressed his amazement to his colleagues: "I don't understand how a child from such a different culture can feel such interest in my characters." If he marveled at this, he was still living, his capacity to be moved intact. Even thinking back to the Spielberg business, he said that he had been ready to give him the freedom to create even if what he created was no longer recognizably Tintin. He considered Spielberg a genius.[68] When he exhausted himself by talking, they asked him to stop. He was unaware that the end was so close until the doctors rushed him to the intensive care unit. "It will pass or it will break," murmured one of them. Lying on the trolley, Hergé had the strength to take Fanny's hand and say, "I love you."[69]

These were his last words before falling into a coma. On March 3, 1983, at ten o'clock in the evening, he died.

IT WAS AS IF TINTIN HAD GONE as well. That day the seismographs of the heart registered universal grief among those between seven and seventy-seven. In the memory of his readers, no one had ever seen anything like it.

abbreviations used in notes

AAGCM	Archives of the General Auditor to the Military Court (Brussels)
ABH	Bernard Heuvelmans Archives (Le Vésinet, France)
AFH	Hergé Foundation Archives (Brussels)
AFR	Fanny Rodwell Archives (Brussels)
AGK	Germaine Kieckens Archives (Louvain, Belgium)
AGM	Gabriel Matzneff Archives (Paris)
AJM	Jacques Martin Archives (Lausanne, Switzerland)
AN	National Archives (Paris)
ARL	Raymond Leblanc Archives (Brussels)
BCR	Chamber of Representatives Library (Brussels)
BN	National Library (Paris)
CBBD	The Belgian Center for Comic Strips (Brussels)
CREHSGM	Center for Historical Research and Study of the Second World War (Brussels)
IHTP	Institute of Contemporary History (Paris)

notes

Preface

1. Joël Kotek, "Tintin: A Belgian Myth of Replacement," in *The Great Myths in the History of Belgium, Flanders and Wallonia*, ed. Anne Morelli (Brussels: Vie ouvrière, 1995), pp. 281–82.

Chapter 1. A Life in Gray: 1907–1925

1. Hergé, interviewed by Numa Sadoul, unpublished version, second interview, 1971, p. 15. Sadoul's typescript.
2. Marie-Louise Degand-Remi, as told by Jacques Martin to the author.
3. Hervé Springael, *Avant Tintin: Dialogue with Hergé* (Self-published, Brussels, 1987), p. 11.
4. Oscar Coomans de Brachène, *État present de la noblesse Belge*, Annuaire de 1988, 1re partie; Geneviève Hanquet van Roye, as told to the author.
5. Dominique de Wespin, *Teilhard, Béjart, Hergé: Trois hommes pour une vie* (Lasne: Agendart, 1993), pp. 176, 177.
6. Hergé, interview with Pierre Ajame in *Les Nouvelles Littéraires*, June 1963. See also Pierre Ajame, *Hergé* (Paris: Gallimard, 1991), p. 22.
7. Hergé, interview in *La Libre Belgique*, Dec. 30, 1975.
8. Hergé, letter to a reader, 1957, AFH.
9. Hergé, interviewed by Sadoul, p. 22.
10. André Buisseret, "Notre Hergé," *Revue de Saint-Boniface*, June 1983.
11. Réginald Hemeleers, "Hergé, le père de Tintin," *Revue de Saint-Boniface*, June 1939.
12. Buisseret, "Notre Hergé."
13. Ibid.
14. Numa Sadoul, *Entretien avec Hergé* (Tournai: Casterman, 1989), p. 1.

Chapter 2. Scoutmaster in the Twentieth Century: 1925–1929

1. Charles d'Ydewalle, "Robert Poulet ou l'inestimable," Archives du CREHSGM, cote PP, 9.

2. Alexis Hennebert, nephew of Father Wallez, as told to the author.

3. Erik Defoort, "Le courant réactionnaire dans le catholicisme franco-phone belge, 1918–1926," *Revue belge d'histoire contemporaine* 8 (1977): 99, 100; Eugen Weber, *L'action française* (Paris: Fayard, 1985), pp. 533–38, IHTP.

4. Thierry Smolderen and Pierre Sterckx, *Hergé: Portrait biographique* (Tournai: Casterman, 1988), pp. 65.

5. *Revue Catholique des idées et des faits*, Nov. 2, 1923.

6. Francis Balace, "Fascisme et catholicisme politique dans la Belgique francophone de l'entre-deux-guerres," in *Handelingen van het xxxiie Vlamms filogencongres* (Leuven, 1979), pp. 154, 155.

7. Raymond De Becker, *Le Livre des morts et des vivants* (Brussels: Editions de la Toison d'or, 1942), p. 72.

8. Norbert Wallez, *Belgique et Rhémanie: Quelques directives d'une politique* (Brussels: Albert Dewit, 1923), pp. 25–36.

9. Hergé, interviewed by Numa Sadoul, unpublished version, second interview, 1971, pp. 10, 16. Sadoul's typescript.

10. Charles Chaplin, *The Story of My Life* (Paris: Robert Laffont, 1964), p. 176.

11. Hergé, interview in *La Libre Belgique*, Dec. 30, 1975; Hergé, interviewed by Sadoul, p. 20.

12. Hergé, interviewed by Numa Sadoul, unpublished version, third interview, 1971, pp. 2, 3. Sadoul's typescript.

13. Hergé, interview in *Les Cahiers de la bande dessinée* 14–15 (1978), CBBD.

Chapter 3. The Many Births of Tintin: 1929–1934

1. Hergé, letter to a reader, Nov. 15, 1966, AFH.

2. Hergé, letter to a reader, Sept. 10, 1982, AFH.

3. Hergé, interview in *La Libre Belgique*, Dec. 30, 1975.

4. Hergé, letter to a reader, Nov. 10, 1965, AFH.

5. Hergé, letter to Pierre Fresnault-Deruelle, July 28, 1970, AFH.

6. Peter Avis, in *The Observer*, Aug. 8, 1993.

7. Hergé, letter to a reader, Aug. 11, 1966, AFH.

8. Baudouin van den Branden de Reeth, letter to Daniel Pinchon, Mar. 19, 1970, AFH.

9. Germaine Kieckens, as told to the author.

10. Hergé, letter to a reader, Oct. 13, 1966, AFH.

11. Alexis Hennebert, nephew of Father Wallez, as told to the author.

12. Hergé, letter to Raymond Buren, June 4, 1975, AFH.

13. Frédéric Soumois, *Dossier Tintin* (Brussels: Éditions Jacques Antoine, 1987), p. 22.

14. Hergé, *In the Land of the Soviets*, p. 154.
15. Ibid., pp. 44, 56, 123, 163.
16. Hergé, interviewed by Numa Sadoul, unpublished version, third interview, 1971, p. 40. Sadoul's typescript.
17. Hergé, interviewed by Numa Sadoul, unpublished version, second interview, 1971, p. 20. Sadoul's typescript.
18. Hergé, interviewed by Pierre Boncenne, in *Lire*, Dec. 1978, p. 29.
19. Francis Beauvais and Didier Robrieux, "Hergé et Jules Verne: Des parentés insolites," authors' typescript.
20. Serge de Waesegger, "Tintin et les homme-léopard," *Les Amis de Hergé*, no. 13 (June 1991): 6–8.
21. Hergé, interviewed by Sadoul, third interview, pp. 2, 3.
22. Germaine Kieckens, as told to the author.
23. Hergé, letter to a reader, Oct. 5, 1977.
24. Pol P. Gossiaux, "L'Afrique nue de Simenon," *Traces*, no. 1, Université de Liège, 1989, pp. 100, 103, 117.
25. *Voilà*, nos. 81–86, Oct. 8 to Nov. 12, 1932.
26. Interview by Alain Saint-Ogan for *La Dépêche du Midi*, May 30, 1973.
27. Georges Duhamel, *Scènes de la vie future* (Paris: Mercure de France, 1930), p. 58.
28. Charles Chaplin, *The Story of My Life* (Paris: Robert Laffont, 1964), p. 185.
29. Hergé's personal notebook, 1931, AGK.
30. Germaine Kieckens, as told to the author.
31. Paul Jamin, as told to the author.
32. Hergé, letter to E. Dejardin, July 11, 1932; E. Dejardin, letter to Hergé, July 12, 1932, AFH.
33. Jules d'Hermann, "Au Vingtième chez Hergé," *L'Effort*, Jan. 1930. Article discovered by Hervé Springael.
34. Atelier Hergé, contract of Jan. 3, 1934; letter of agreement for dissolution of Atelier Hergé, July 13, 1934, AFH.
35. *Le Petit Vingtième*, Jan. 15, 1931.
36. *Le Petit Vingtième*, Apr. 4, 1934, p. 14.
37. *Le Petit Vingtième*, May 17, 1934.
38. *Le Petit Vingtième*, June 21, 1934, p. 5.
39. *Le Petit Vingtième*, May 18, 1933, p. 5; Apr. 27, 1933, p. 5; May 11, 1933, p. 5.
40. *Le Petit Vingtième*, May 10, 1934, p. 14.
41. Paul Jamin, as told to the author.
42. *Le Petit Vingtième*, Apr. 26, 1934.
43. *Le Petit Vingtième*, Feb. 1, 1934, p. 4.
44. Alexis Hennebert, nephew of Father Wallez, as told to the author.
45. Hergé, letter, Feb. 3, 1934, AFH.
46. Contract dated Nov. 1, 1934, AFH.
47. Charles Lesne, letter to Georges Remi, Apr. 4, 1932, AFH.
48. Georges Remi, letter to Charles Lesne, Apr. 7, 1932, AFH.

49. Georges Remi, letter to Charles Lesne, Apr. 14, 1932, AFH.
50. Charles Lesne, letter to Georges Remi, Jan. 21, 1933, AFH.
51. Charles Lesne, letter to Georges Remi, Feb. 26, 1934, AFH.
52. Rodolphe Töpffer, *L'Invention de la bande dessinée*, texts réunis et présentés par Thierry Groensteen et Benoît Peeters (Paris: Hermann, 1994), p. 27.
53. Hergé, letter to a reader, Nov. 10, 1973, AFH.
54. Marie-Louise Degand-Remi, as told to the author.
55. Quoted in Numa Sadoul, *Entretien avec Hergé* (Tournai: Casterman, 1989), p. 148.
56. Casterman, letter to Georges Remi, Mar. 4, 1934, AFH.
57. Charles Lesne, letter to Hergé, Apr. 16, 1934, AFH.
58. Hergé, letter to Charles Lesne, June 18, 1936, AFH.
59. Pierre de Vos, "La mort de Léon Degrelle," *Le Monde*, Apr. 4, 1994.

Chapter 4. What Chang Taught Hergé: 1934–1936

1. Hergé, letter to a reader, Dec. 3, 1975, AFH.
2. *The Exploits of Quick and Flupke*, "Some Music …,"Aug. 3, 1933, in Hergé Archives 2 (Tournai: Casterman, 1978), pp. 166–67.
3. Hergé, letter to Father Édouard Neut, Feb. 20, 1973, AFH.
4. Hergé, letter to Father Édouard Neut, May 3, 1934, AFH.
5. Father Édouard Neut, letter to Hergé, May 11, 1934, AFH.
6. Chang Chong-Chen, letter to Hergé, Apr. 25, 1934, AFH.
7. Chang Chong-Chen, as told to the author.
8. Ibid.
9. Hergé, letter to Chang Chong-Chen, Mar. 28, 1976, AFH.
10. Chang Chong-Chen, as told to the author.
11. *Tchang au pays du Lotus Bleu* (Séguier, 1990), pp. 128–36.
12. Charles Lesne, letter to Hergé, Feb. 11, 1936, AFH.
13. Hergé, letter to Charles Lesne, Feb. 12, 1936, AFH.
14. Ibid.
15. Charles Lesne, letters to Hergé, Feb. 15 and 21, 1936, AFH.
16. Hergé, letters to Charles Lesne, Apr. 7 and 16, 1936, AFH.
17. Hergé, letter to Charles Lesne, Oct. 8, 1936, AFH.

Chapter 5. Eye of the Storm: 1936–1940

1. Chang Chong-Chen, letter to Hergé, Aug. 6, 1937, AFR; Chang Chong-Chen, as told to the author.
2. Charles Lesne, letter to Hergé, Nov. 3, 1936, AFH.
3. Charles Lesne, letter to Hergé, Mar. 11, 1937, AFH.
4. Hergé, letter to Charles Lesne, Nov. 23, 1936, AFH.
5. Norbert Wallez, *Belgique et Rhémanie: Quelques directives d'une politique* (Brussels: Albert Dewit, 1923), p. 78.

6. Hergé, interviewed by Numa Sadoul, unpublished version, second interview, p. 30; Hergé, interviewed by Benoît Peeters and Patrice Hamel, *Minuit*, Sept. 1977.

7. Félicien Marceau, *Les Années courtes* (Paris: Gallimard, 1968); paperback reprint, Folio, 1973, pp. 281, 282.

8. Hergé, *The Black Island*, p. 35.

9. Hergé, letter to Charles Lesne, Nov. 22, 1938, AFH.

10. Hergé, letter to Charles Lesne, Oct. 29, 1936, AFH.

11. Bernard Pourpris, "Lecture politique de Mickey," *Économie et Société*, no. 199 (May–June 1971).

12. Adelin Van Ypersele, letter to Hergé, Aug. 9, 1939; Hergé, letter to Adelin Van Ypersele, Aug. 12, 1939, AFH.

13. Hergé, notebook from the 1930s, AFH.

14. Hergé, letter to a reader, Apr. 7, 1982; Hergé, letter to a reader, Oct 5, 1978, AFH.

15. Hergé, interviewed by Sadoul, p. 36; Numa Sadoul, *Entretien avec Hergé* (Tournai: Casterman, 1989), p. 110.

16. Hergé, letter to Jean-Paul Chemin, Mar. 22, 1973, AFH.

17. Hergé, letter to Charles Lesne, June 12, 1939, AFH.

18. Pierre Ickx, letter to Hergé, Sept. 15, 1939, AFH.

19. William Ugeux, as told the author.

20. Dominique de Wespin, as told to the author.

21. Hergé, letter to Father Neut, Jan. 3, 1940, AFH.

22. Hergé, letter to M. Tong, minister of propaganda in Chunking, Dec. 19, 1939, AFH.

23. Speech of Oct. 27, 1939, quoted in Jacques Willequet, *La Belgique sous la botte: Résistances et collaborations, 1940–1945* (Paris: Édition universitaires, 1986), p. 42.

24. Quoted in Willequet, *La Belgique sous la botte,* p. 43.

25. Willequet, *La Belgique sous la botte,* pp. 43, 44.

26. Jules Gérard-Libois and José Gotovitch, *L'An 40: La Belgique occupée* (Brussels: Centre de recherches et d'information socio-politique [CRISP], 1971), p. 44.

27. Jules Gérard-Libois and José Gotovitch, p. 48; *Courrier hebdomadaire* 497–98 (Brussels: CRISP, Oct. 30, 1970), p. 2.

28. Colonel Servais, letter to Charles de Bus de Warnaffe, Feb. 21, 1940, AFH.

29. *Le Vingtième Siècle*, letter to Hergé, Feb. 26, 1940, AFH.

30. Hergé, interviewed by Numa Sadoul, unpublished version, third interview, p. 14. Sadoul's typescript.

31. Paul Struye, *L'Évolution du sentiment publique en Belgique sous l'occupation allemande* (Brussels: Édition Lumière, 1945), p. 16.

32. William Ugeux, as told to the author.

33. Hergé, letter to Chang Chong-Chen, Feb. 15, 1977, AFH.

34. Hergé, letter to Colonel Rémy, Nov. 19, 1976, AFH.

35. Hergé, interviewed by Sadoul, third interview, p. 15.
36. Willequet, *La Belgique sous la botte,* p. 60.
37. William Ugeux, as told to the author.
38. Hergé, interviewed by Sadoul, third interview, p. 11.
39. Hergé, letter to Charles Lesne, Aug. 10, 1940, AFH.

Chapter 6. The Golden Age: 1940–1944

1. Hergé, interviewed by Numa Sadoul, unpublished version, third interview, p. 15.
2. Quoted in Numa Sadoul, *Entretien avec Hergé* (Tournai: Casterman, 1989), p. 130.
3. *Le Vingtième Siècle,* letters to Hergé, Oct. 30, 1940, Jan. 21, 1941, AFH.
4. Hergé, letters to Louis Casterman, July 23, Aug. 6, 1940, AFH.
5. Hergé, letter to M. Van den Eynde, Oct. 28, 1940; Hergé, letter to M. Van Acker, Sept. 13, 1940, AFH.
6. Hergé, letter to Charles Lesne, Sept. 12, 1940, AFH.
7. Hergé, interviewed by Numa Sadoul, unpublished version, second interview, p. 25.
8. J. L. Charles, "Les services allemands de propagande et de contrôle de l'information en Belgique occupée," *La Communication sociale et la guerre,* Institut de Sociologie Bruylant, Brussels, 1974, p. 245; Els de Bens, "La presse au temps de l'occupation en Belgique," *Revue d'histoire de la Seconde Guerre mondiale* 20 (1970): 27, 28; Paul Struye, *L'Evolution du sentiment publique en Belgique sous l'occupation allemande* (Brussels: Édition Lumière, 1945), p. 45.
9. Dossier JB 41, Archives du CREHSGM.
10. Paul Jamin, as told to the author.
11. Hergé, letter to Charles Lesne, Sept. 5, 1940, AFH.
12. *Le Journal de Mickey,* no. 297 (Sept. 22, 1940).
13. *Le Journal de Mickey,* no. 309 (Dec. 15, 1940).
14. *Le Soir-Jeunesse,* Oct. 24, 1940.
15. Anonymous, letter to Hergé, Oct. 16, 1940, AFH.
16. Hergé, letter to Charles Lesne, Oct. 18, 1968, AFH.
17. Hergé, *The Crab with the Golden Claws,* p. 8.
18. Hergé, interviewed by Sadoul, third interview, p. 4.
19. Germaine Kieckens, as told to the author; Hergé, letter to Pierre Fresnault, May 7, 1968, AFH.
20. Hergé, *The Crab with the Golden Claws,* pp. 37, 38.
21. Hergé, letter, Aug. 28, 1974, AFH.
22. Jacques Willequet, *La Belgique sous la botte: Résistances et collaborations, 1940–1945* (Paris: Édition universitaires, 1986), pp. 53, 54; Hergé, interviewed by Sadoul, third interview, p. 16.
23. Thierry Crépin, *Un journal pour enfants sous l'occupation: Coeurs Vaillants 1940–1944* (Bordeau: Université de Bordeau-III, 1984–85), pp. 15, 33, 34.
24. Hergé, interviewed by Sadoul, third interview, p. 16.

25. Marcel Vermeulen, "Cinquante ans dans les coulisses du 'Soir,'" unpublished typescript, cote 06/BE, Bibliothèque du Soir, 1995, pp. 78, 79.

26. Ibid., p. 81.

27. "Affaire 'Le Soir,'" Archives du CREHSGM, cote JB 41.

28. Liste du 9 juillet 1941, Archives du CREHSGM; Pascal Fouché, "L'Édition française sous l'occupation" I, IHTP, Université de Paris-VII, pp. 39, 40.

29. Program of the "Parti des Provinces Romanes de Belgique," May 19, 1941, cote PD9, Archives du CREHSGM.

30. Martin Conway, *Degrelle, les anneés de collaboration, 1940–44* (Ottignies: Quorum, 1994), p. 96.

31. Program of the "Parti des Provinces Romanes de Belgique"; Conway, *Degrelle,* p. 98.

32. L'abbé Varzim, letter to Hergé, Nov. 2, 1942; Hergé, letters to abbé Varzim, Feb. 23, 1943, June 12, 1944, and June 10, 1945, AFH.

33. Hergé, letter to Charles Lesne, Sept. 15, 1941, AFH.

34. Hergé, letters to Charles Lesne, Dec. 18, 20, 1941; Hergé, letter to M. Bremisch, Dec. 18, 1941; Charles Lesne, letters to Hergé, Dec. 19, 23, and 31, 1941, AFH.

35. Charles Lesne, letter to Hergé, Aug. 13, 1941; Hergé, letter to Charles Lesne, Aug. 11, 1941, AFH.

36. Hergé, letter to Charles Lesne, Aug. 11, 1941, AFH.

37. Charles Lesne, letter to Hergé, Nov. 20, 1941, AFH.

38. Maxime Steinberg, *L'Étoile et le fusil: La Question juive, 1940–42* (Brussels: Vie ouvriére, 1983), pp. 16, 17.

39. Dominique Manaud, "Un regard sur la folie à travers les aventures de Tintin," medical thesis, no. 265, Université de Bordeaux-II, 1980, pp. 1, 6; François Flahaut, "Le plaisir de la peur: 'LÉtoile mystérieuse' et l'araignée géante," *Communications,* no. 57 (1993): 157–90.

40. Hergé, interviewed by Sadoul, third interview, p. 39.

41. Robert Mochkhovitch, in *Télérama,* July 26, 1995, p. 45.

42. Steinberg, *L'Étoile et le fusil,* p. 17.

43. *Le Soir,* Mar. 4, 1941.

44. Ibid.

45. Hergé, letters to Charles Lesne, Jan. 29, Feb. 15, 1942, AFH.

46. André Colard, "With Tintin and Snowy," a radio interview with Hergé, Radio-Brussels, Mar. 5, 1942, recording no. 1961, transcription, Archives du CREHSGM, 1B3, AIII42.

47. Sadoul, *Entretien avec Hergé,* p. 110.

48. Hergé, letter to Charles Lesne, May 18, 1942, AFH.

49. Pascal Ory, "Le Petit nazi illustré," in *Le Téméraire* 1943–1944 (Paris: Albatros, 1979), p. 25.

50. Hergé, letter to Louis Casterman, Mar. 15, 1942, AFH.

51. Hergé, notes, July 24, 1942; M. Thiéry, letter to Hergé, July 24, 1942; "Affaire Thiéry-Remi," AFH.

52. Hergé, letter to Louis Casterman, Feb. 15, 1942, AFH.

53. Contract, 1942, AFH.
54. Hergé, letter to Lucien Fonson, Mar. 31, 1941, AFH; Vermeulen, "Cinquante ans dans les coulisses du 'Soir,'" p. 81; "Hergé au Théâtre des Galeries," *Les Amis de Hergé*, no. 2 (Dec. 1985).
55. Hergé, letter to Edgar P. Jacobs, Feb. 10, 1942, AFH.
56. Gérard Liger-Belair, "La Licorne," *Les Amis de Hergé*, no. 9 (June 1989).
57. Hergé, letter to Charles Lesne, Nov. 21, 1942, AFH.
58. Hergé, letter to Jean-Claude Lemineur, Aug. 8, 1979, AFH.
59. *Le Soir*, Apr. 1941, cited in Steinberg, *L'Étoile et le fusil*.
60. Hergé, letter to Charles Lesne, Oct. 1, 1942, AFH.
61. Raymond De Becker, "En marche vers l'unité," *Le Soir*, Oct. 27, 1942.
62. *Le Soir*, Oct. 26, 1942.
63. Hergé, letter to Dominique Labesse, July 1, 1969, AFH.
64. Raymond De Becker, letter to Léon Degrelle, Jan. 18, 1943, Archives du CREHSGM, PD9.
65. Vermeulen, "Cinquante ans dans les coulisses du 'Soir,'" pp. 82, 83.
66. Georges Beatse, "À propos d'une conference," *Le Soir*, May 1942.
67. Guy Lebrun, "L'abbé Norbert Wallez, découvreur du talent d'Hergé," *L'âge d'o r*, no. 18 (Jan. 1991).
68. Charles Lesne, letter to Hergé, Nov. 26, 1943; Hergé, letter to Charles Lesne, Dec. 1, 1943, AFH.
69. Frédéric Soumois, *Dossier Tintin* (Brussels: Éditions Jacques Antoine, 1987), p. 192.
70. Hergé, letters to readers, Mar. 13, 1964, Feb. 16, 1971, AFH.
71. Hergé, letters to Pierre Fresnault, May 7, 1968, Dec. 8, 1971, AFH.
72. Benoît Denis, *Les Avatars de Tintin: Stratégie thématique, idéologique, et formelles dans l'oeuvre d'Hergé* (Liège: Université de Liège, 1991–92), pp. 100–103.
73. Hergé, *Red Rackham's Treasure*, p. 36.
74. Hergé, letter to Charles Lesne, Sept. 6, 1943, AFH.
75. Raymond De Becker, "Conférence rédactinelle au 'Soir,'" Sept. 3, 1943, Fonds Léo Lejeune (756) PL1, No. 416–419, Archives du CREHSGM.
76. Robert Poulet, letter to José Streel, May 27, 1942, Fonds Streel, PS16 III No.23, Archives du CREHSGM.
77. Paul Kinnet, "Dupont et Dupond, Détectives," *Les Amis de Hergé*, no. 12 (Dec. 1990): 34, 35.
78. Alexis Peclers, letters to Hergé, Jan. 18, 20, 1943; Hergé, letter to Alexis Peclers, Jan. 20, 1943, AFH.
79. Charles Lesne, letter to Hergé, Sept. 1, 1943, AFH.
80. Hergé, letter to Charles Lesne, Sept. 6, 1943, AFH.
81. Camille Joset, "Présentation du faux 'Soir,'" in *Histoire du faux "Soir" du 9 Novembre 1943*, brochure du Comité nationale du Front de l'indépendance, Brussels, 1993, p. 3.
82. Jean Pihan, *Merci pour le passé* (Paris: Fleurus, 1985), pp. 80, 81; Crépin, *Un journal pour enfants sous l'occupation*, p. 45.

83. Crépin, *Un journal pour enfants sous l'occupation*, cites Alain Saint-Ogan's letter of Dec. 22, 1943, to the secretary general of propaganda.
84. Henry Coston, "Les Corrupteurs de la Jeunesse," *Bulletin d'information antimaçonniques*, undated (1943): 24.
85. Christian Delporte, *Les crayons de la propagande: Dessinateurs et dessin politique sous l'Occupation* (Paris: CNRS Éditions, 1993), pp. 44, 45.
86. "Contre l'exitation à la haine et au désordre," liste des ouvrages retires de la circulation et interdits en Belgique, July 9, 1941, Archives du CREHSGM.
87. Hergé, letter to Pierre Fresnault, Dec. 19, 1972, AFH.
88. Charles Lesne, letter to Hergé, Nov. 8, 1943, AFH.
89. Hergé, letter to Charles Lesne, Nov. 16, 1943, AFH.
90. Hergé, letter to Charles Lesne, Nov. 25, 1943, AFH.
91. Hergé, interview in *La Libre Belgique*, Dec. 30, 1975.
92. Étienne Pollet, "Phénomène et édition," in *Tintin patrimoine des imaginaries* (Paris: IESA/Economica, 1992), pp. 72, 87.
93. Sadoul, *Entretien avec Hergé*, p. 89.
94. Jacques Chancel, interview with Hergé, Jan. 29, 1970, "Radioscopie," France-Inter.
95. Soumois, *Dossier Tintin*, pp. 30, 31, 35.
96. Hergé, letter of contract to Edgar P. Jacobs, Dec. 30, 1943, AFH.
97. Hergé, letter to Charles Lesne, June 19, 1944, AFH.
98. Hergé, letter to *Het Laatste Nieuws*, June 19, 1944; *Het Laatste Nieuws*, letter to Hergé, June 21, 1944, AFH.
99. Vermeulen, "Cinquante ans dans les coulisses du 'Soir,'" p. 93
100. Charles Lesne, letter to Hergé, July 1, 1944, AFH.
101. "La Bête est morte!" reprinted by Gallimard, 1995; Patrick Gaumer and Claude Moliterni, *Dictionnaire mondial de la bande dessinée* (Paris: Larousse, 1994), p. 64.

Chapter 7. The Plight of the *Inciviques*: 1944–1946

1. *L'Insoumis* (The Undefeated), Sept. 1944.
2. Dossier Georges Remi, opened by the general prosecutor under the case number 3065, 1944, AAGCM.
3. Hergé, interviewed by Numa Sadoul, unpublished version, second interview, 1971, p. 25; Robert Poulet, "Hommage à Hergé," *Rivarol*, Mar. 18, 1983.
4. *Le Soir,* Sept. 8, 1944.
5. *La Patrie*, no. 1 (Sept. 3–10, 1944).
6. *La Patrie*, no. 2 (Sept. 10–17, 1944).
7. *La Patrie*, no. 3 (Sept. 23–30, 1944).
8. Hergé, letter to Charles Lesne, Sept. 19, 1944, AFH.
9. Luc Huyse and Steven Dhondt, *La Répression des collaborations* 1942–52: *Un passé toujours present* (Brussels: Centre de recherches et d'information socio-politique [CRISP], 1993), p. 65.

10. Annales parlementaires, Chambre des représentants (BCR), Brussels, Nov. 14, 1946, pp. 2–6.
11. Ibid., pp. 8, 9.
12. Huyse and Dhondt, *La Répression des collaborations,* p. 43.
13. M. Vinçotte, confidential letter to the general auditor, Mar. 8, 1945, AAGCM.
14. Raymond Leblanc, *Dés pipés* (Brussels: André Gilbert, 1942); Raymond Leblanc, as told to the author.
15. Albert Debaty, interview with Hergé in *Vlan,* Dec. 3, 1986, p. 79.
16. Raymond Leblanc, as told to the author.
17. Ibid.
18. Ibid.
19. Pierre Ugeux, as told to the author.
20. William Ugeux, as told to the author.
21. Étienne Pollet, "Phénomène et édition," in *Tintin patrimoine des imaginaries* (Paris: IESA/Economica, 1992), pp. 72, 87.
22. M. Vinçotte, letter to the general auditor, Nov. 12, 1945, Dossier Georges Remi, no. 3065–44, AAGCM; Pierre Ugeux, as told to the author.
23. William Ugeux, as told to the author.
24. William Ugeux, letter to the Service communal de la Participation de la ville d'Ottignies, May 31, 1989, AFH.
25. Walter Ganshof van der Meersch, letter to the minister of justice, Feb. 2, 1947, administrative dossier on Georges Remi, joint o/566, AAGCM.
26. Raymond Leblanc, as told to the author.
27. Two certificates of good citizenship, dated June 25 and Oct. 4, 1946, ARL.
28. Bernard Thiéry, letter to the Société Les Beaux Films, July 3, 1946, AFH.
29. Quoted in Benoît Peeters, *Le Monde d'Hergé* (Tournai: Casterman, 1983), p. 210.
30. Hergé, interviewed by Sadoul, p. 17.
31. Pierre Ickx, letter to Hergé, Aug. 16, 1946; Hergé, letter to Pierre Ickx, Sept. 24, 1946, AFH.
32. Hervé Springael, "Tintin retrouvé," *Les Amis de Hergé,* no. 7 (June 1988): pp. 4–8.
33. Hergé, letter to Charles Lesne, Feb. 8, 1945, AFH.
34. Robert Poulet, interview on Channel 1, Belgian Radio Television (BRT), a program on Belgium under the occupation, May 16, 1982.
35. Henri Roanne-Rosenblatt, as told to the author, in the course of a documentary in collaboration with Géerard Valet, 1974–75.
36. Jacques Martin, as told to the author.
37. Numa Sadoul, *Entretien avec Hergé* (Tournai: Casterman, 1989), pp. 90, 135.
38. Henry de Montherlant, *Essais* (Paris: Bibliothèque de la Pléiade, 1963), p. 729.
39. Robert Poulet, "Hommage à Hergé," *Rivarol,* Mar. 18, 1983.
40. Hergé, letter to Maurice Bardèche, Feb. 17, 1959, AFH.

41. *Le Soir*, June 21, 1946.
42. *Le Soir*, June 26, 1946.
43. Maurice Duwaerts, "À propos des process de presse," *Le Soir*, July 6, 1946, p. 1.
44. Hergé, interviewed by Sadoul, p. 17.
45. Yves Duval, as told to the author.
46. *Le Soir*, July 25, 1946.
47. BCR, Brussels, Oct. 29, 1947, p. 6.
48. Raymond Leblanc, as told to the author.

Chapter 8. The Dark Years: 1946–1950

1. Hergé, interviewed by Numa Sadoul, unpublished version, second interview, 1971, p. 18.
2. Hergé, notes for a preface for a book by Philippe Goddin about Cuvelier, AFH.
3. Philippe Goddin, *Corentin ou les chemins du merveilleux* (Brussels: Éditions du Lombards, 1984).
4. Hergé, interviewed by Sadoul, p. 18.
5. Stanislas Faure, *L'Univers du "Journal de Spirou,"* 1946–1968, mémoire de maîtrise d'histoire, Université de Paris-X, Oct. 1993, p. 20.
6. Thierry Crépin, *Un journal pour enfants sous l'occupation: Coeurs Vaillants 1940–1944* (Bordeau: Université de Bordeau-III, 1984–85), pp. 129, 130.
7. Alain Saint-Ogan, *Je me souviens de Zig et Puce et de quelques autres* (Paris: La Table ronde, 1961), p. 181.
8. Gilles Picard, "Du côté des Communistes: *Vaillant* contre les Américains," in *Le Temps de la guerre froide* (Paris: Institut du temps présent, 1995), pp. 131–34.
9. Raymond Leblanc, as told to the author.
10. "Chronique de l'incivisme," *Le Quotidien*, Sept. 28, 1946.
11. Fernand Demany, "Presse pourrie, journalists marrons," *Drapeau rouge*, Sept. 30, 1946.
12. *Le Soir*, Sept. 29, 1946.
13. *La Cité nouvelle*, Oct. 6, 7, 1946.
14. Raymond Leblanc, as told to the author.
15. *Le Rouge et le Noir*, Nov. 4, 1936.
16. Hergé, letters to his readers, Sept. 27, 1969, Dec. 8, 1979, AFH.
17. Hergé, interviewed by Numa Sadoul, unpublished version, third interview, p. 39; Hergé, *Red Rackham's Treasure,* p. 24.
18. Gérard Lenne, *L'Affaire Jacobs* (Saint-Germaine-en-Laye: Megawave, 1990), pp. 31, 115.
19. Dominique de Wespin, as told to the author.
20. Hergé, letters to Germaine Remi, no place or date [Notre-Dame-de-Scourmont, 1947–48], AGK; Hergé, letter to R. P. Hupperts, Mar. 18, 1948, AFH; Affaire Hergé-Bernard Thiéry, May–June 1947, AFH.

21. Marijac, "Mon ami Hergé," *HAGA,* no. 53 (1983): 11.

22. J. G. Londos, "Le problème des inciviques," *Le Soir,* June 21, 1946, p. 2.

23. Hergé, letter to Jeanne Cappe, Mar. 4, 1947, AFH.

24. *Le Phare,* July 20, 1947.

25. *Annales parlementaires,* Chambres des représentants, séance of Oct. 29, 1947, Brussels, p. 8.

26. Raymond Leblanc, as told to the author.

27. Hergé, letter to the consul from Argentina, Jan. 23, 1948, AFH.

28. Hergé, letter to Nestor Orsi, Feb. 5, 1948, AFH.

29. Hergé, letter to Louis Casterman, Apr. 8, 1948, AFH.

30. Louis Casterman, certificate signed by him dated Apr. 12, 1948, AFH.

31. Hergé, letter to a Belgian friend not identified (J. Guerome?), resident of Buenos Aires, Apr. 10, 1948, AFH.

32. Hergé, letter to Charles Lesne, Apr. 9, 1948; Hergé, letter to Walt Disney, Apr. 9, 1948; Gil Souto (from Walt Disney), letter to Hergé, June 2, 1948, AFH.

33. Guy Dessicy, as told to the author; Frans Jageneau, as told to the author.

34. Bernard Heuvelmans, as told to the author.

35. Bernard Heuvelmans, letter to Hergé, Sept. 14, 1947; Hergé, letter to Bernard Heuvelmans, Feb. 21, 1949, AFH.

36. Hergé, letter to Louis Casterman, May 10, 1943, AFH.

37. Raymond Leblanc, as told to the author.

38. Germaine Remi, personal note, Aug. 10, 1948, AGK; Hergé-Jacobs, correspondence, undated, 1947–49, AFH.

39. Gérard Liger-Belair, "La Licorne," *Les Amis de Hergé,* no. 9 (June 1988), p. 11.

40. Hergé, letter to E. P. Jacobs, Aug. 20, 1949, AFH.

41. Thierry Smolderen and Pierre Sterckx, *Hergé: Portrait biographique* (Tournai: Casterman, 1988), p. 232.

42. Jean Libert, "Le souvenir de mon ami Hergé," unpublished ms, 1995.

43. Hergé, letter to Germaine Remi, July 3, 1948, AGK; Jean Libert, as told to the author.

44. L'abbé Wallez, letter to Germaine Remi, Aug. 1, 1949; Hergé, numerous letters to Germaine Remi, 1948–49, AGK.

45. Hergé, interviewed by Sadoul, second interview, p. 19.

46. Hergé, letter to Pierre Ickx, Apr. 22, 1947, AFH.

47. Hergé, letter to Paul Cuvelier, Oct. 15, 1948, AFH.

48. Hergé, letter to Paul Cuvelier, Jan. 31, 1949, AFH.

49. Hergé, letter to Evany, Mar. 31, 1953, AFH.

50. Report retracing the history of the business, drawn up by Casterman for the lawyers, undated (probably July 1951), AFH; Hergé, letter to Casterman Publishers, May 5, 1951, AFH.

51. Note sent to the editors, Mar. 10, 1947, AFH.

52. Hergé, copy of a manuscript letter written to Raymond Leblanc, Nov. 1 or 2, 1949, AFH.

53. Raymond Leblanc, letter to Hergé, Nov. 5, 1949, AFH.

54. Hergé, letter to Raymond Leblanc, Nov. 12, 1949, AFH.

Chapter 9. Toward Fulfillment: 1950–1958

1. Robert Lanquar, *L'Empire Disney* (Paris: PUF, 1992), pp. 28, 29.

2. Guy Dessicy, as told to the author.

3. Jean Libert and Paul Jamin, as told to the author.

4. Hergé, letter to Raymond De Becker, Jan. 8, 1954, AFH.

5. Guy Delfosse, "Au secour des droits de l'homme" (Helping Human Rights), in *La Conférence*, Brussels, 1995–96, no. 2, pp. 11, 12; Raymond De Becker, letter to Hergé, Nov. 12, 1959, AFH.

6. Jacqueline van den Branden de Reeth, as told to the author.

7. Dominique de Wespin, *Teilhard, Béjart, Hergé: Trois hommes pour une vie* (Lasne: Agendart, 1993), p. 174; Hergé, letter to a reader, Oct. 26, 1965, AFH.

8. Guy Dessicy, as told to the author; Bob De Moor, "Une curieuse victoire," *Le Vif-Magazine*, special ed., Apr. 22, 1983, pp. 22–24; Bob De Moor, interviewed in *Les Amis de Hergé* 2 (Dec. 1985): 23.

9. Hergé, letters to Jacques Martin, Dec. 16, 1949, Oct. 28, 1954, AJM; Jacques Martin, interviewed in *Les Amis de Hergé*, no. 10 (Dec. 1989).

10. Hergé, interviewed by Numa Sadoul, unpublished version, fourth interview, 1971, pp. 24, 25.

11. Jacques Martin, as told to the author.

12. Philippe Goddin, *Comment Naît une bande déssinée: Par-dessus l'épaule d'Hergé* (Tournai: Casterman, 1991); Philippe Goddin, *Hergé et Tintin reporters: Du* Vingtième Siècle *au* Journal Tintin (Brussels: Éditions du Lombard, 1986), pp. 123–25; Benoît Peeters, *Case, planche, recit: Comment lire une bande dessinée* (Tournai: Casterman, 1991), pp. 26, 27; *Le Musée imaginaire de Tintin* (Tournai: Casterman, 1980); Hergé, interviewed by Sadoul; Hergé, letter to Chang Chong-Chen, Mar. 28, 1976, AFH; Hergé notebooks manuscript, AFH; Guy Dessicy and Frans Jageneau, as told to the author; Hergé, letters to his readers, July 26, 1978, Feb. 18, 1971, Jan. 16, 1971, Nov. 3, 1967, May 12, 1960, Jan. 16, 1975, AFH; draft of reply never sent to an inquiry from the Faculty of Human Science and Letters at the University of Nice, AFH.

13. Hergé, letter to Father Gosset, Mar. 17, 1945; Hergé, letter to a reader, June 18, 1975, AFH.

14. Frédéric Soumois, *Dossier Tintin* (Brussels: Éditions Jacques Antoine, 1987).

15. Hergé, letter to Pierre Servais (his representative at Casterman after the death of Charles Lesne in 1950), Jan. 12, 1956, AFH.

16. Soumois, *Dossier Tintin,* p. 68.

17. Hergé, letter to a reader, Jan. 21, 1972, AFH.

18. D. Leroux, V. Thepot, and E. Hispard, "Tintin et l'alcool," *Aujourd'hui l'alcoologie*, ADRIA, no. 48 (May–June 1991): 8–12.

19. Pierre Servais, letter to Baudouin van den Branden, Apr. 24, 1959, AFH.
20. Hergé, letter to a reader, June 22, 1960, AFH.
21. Hergé, letter to a reader, July 25, 1958, AFH.
22. Thomas Hines et Cie, letter to Casterman, Apr. 25, 1958; Hergé, letter to the director of Tho. Hines et Cie, May 14, 1958, AFH.
23. Hergé, letter to Louis-Robert Casterman, Dec. 14, 1956; Louis-Robert Casterman, letter to Hergé, Dec. 22, 1956, AFH.
24. Hergé, letter to Casterman, Dec. 10, 1953; R-L. Casterman, letter to Hergé, Aug. 11, 1954, AFH.
25. Mme. B., letter to Hergé, Mar. 1, 1954; Hergé, letter to Mme. B., Mar. 17, 1954, AFH.
26. Hergé, letter to Louis-Robert Casterman, June 18, 1954, AFH.
27. Hergé, interviewed by Sadoul, p. 41; Maurice Einhorn, "L'antisémitisme dans la bande dessinée," *Regards*, no. 24 (Apr. 17–30, 1981); "L'antisémitisme en bulles," *Regards*, no. 99 (Aug. 26, 1983).
28. Pierre Alechinsky, as told to the author; Hergé, letter to Pierre Alechinsky, Oct. 13, 1977, AFH; Pierre Alechinsky, *Far Rockaways* (Montpellier: Fata Morgana, 1977), p. 122.
29. "Relevé des corrections à faire dans les albums Tintin," Jan. 1959, AFH.
30. Hergé, interviewed by Numa Sadoul, unpublished version, second interview, 1971, p. 11.
31. Hergé, letter to a reader, May 17, 1955, AFH.
32. F41bis 920 181/1, AN.
33. Jacques Perret, "On veut museler la presse enfantine," *La Bataille*, Jan. 21, 1948.
34. Alain Saint-Ogan, *Je me souviens de Zig et Puce et de quelques autres* (Paris: La Table Ronde, 1961), pp. 184, 185.
35. Pascal Ory, "Mickey go home! La déaméricanisation de la bande déssinée 1945–1950," *Vingtième Siècle, revue d'histoire*, no. 4 (Oct. 1984): 82, IHTP.
36. Loi No. 49-956, votée le 2 juillet 1949, publié le 16 dans le *Journal officiel* et modifié par le loi du 29 novembre 1954, AN.
37. Rapport de la commission de censure, 1950, p. 32, AN; *Combat*, Dec. 6, 1954.
38. Armand Lanoux, in *L'Éducation nationale*, Apr. 27, 1950, IHTP.
39. Bertrand Caillé, *Analyse du contenu du journal "Pilote" de 1959 à 1974*, mémoire de maîtrise d'histoire, Université de Paris-X, 1991, p. 71; G. Craenhals, *Les Préjugés et stéréotypes raciaus et nationaux dans les principales bandes dessinées belges*, Université catholique de Louvain, 1970, p. 173.
40. Stanislas Faure, *L'Univers du "Journal de Spirou," 1946–1968*, mémoire de maîtrise d'histoire, Université de Paris-X, Oct. 1993, p. 66.
41. Marcel Dehaye, letter to Hergé, Dec. 12, 1951, AGK.
42. ARL.
43. "*Journal Tintin*. Note Hergé," manuscript text, 1952, AFH.
44. Ibid.

45. Hergé, *Destination Moon*, p. 14.
46. Hergé, letter to a reader, Sept. 25, 1974, AFH.
47. Hergé, letter to Louis Brouwet, Nov. 4, 1953, AFH.
48. Hergé, letter to Max Hoyaux, Aug. 20, 1950; Max Hoyaux, letter to Hergé, Jan. 18, 1951, AFH.
49. Hergé, letter to Max Hoyaux, Jan. 29, 1951, AFH.
50. Hergé, letter to a reader, Nov. 14, 1954, AFH.
51. Benoît Peeters, *Le Monde d'Hergé* (Tournai: Casterman, 1983), pp. 94–97.
52. Hergé, interviewed by Benoît Peeters, in ibid.; Hergé, letters to Bernard Heuvelmans, Nov. 29, 1949, June 6, 1950, July 2, 1951, Jan. 22, 1959, Apr. 19, 1962, Feb. 22, 1974, AFH; Bernard Heuvelmans, letter to Hergé, June 14, 1950, AFH; Jacques Martin, as told to the author.
53. Bernard Heuvelmans, as told to the author.
54. Hergé, letter to a reader, Dec. 18, 1951, AFH.
55. Compte rendu des travaux de la Commission de surveillance et de contrôle des publications destinées à l'enfance et à l'adolescence au cours de l'année 1950, Mars 1951, F41bis 920 181/1, AN.
56. *Tintin*, no. 45 (Nov. 11, 1953).
57. Hergé, *Explorers on the Moon*, p. 55; Hergé, letter to a reader, Jan. 10, 1970, AFH; Hergé, interviewed in *La Libre Belgique*, Dec. 30, 1975.
58. Hergé, letter to Louis-Robert Casterman, Aug. 24, 1954, AFH.
59. Proceedings Congrès de psychiatrie et de neurologie, Poitiers, 1983, pp. 75–77.
60. Jean Meeus, letter to Hergé, Apr. 19, 1982, AFH.
61. Peeters, *Le Monde d'Hergé*, p. 99.
62. Hergé, letter to Louis-Robert Casterman, Jan. 11, 1956, AFH.
63. Pascale Bieri, "La boîte aux lettres du professeur Tournesol," *La Suisse*, Feb. 10, 1994, p. 23.
64. Gérard Métron (linguiste), "Éléments de langue bordure," *Les Amis de Hergé*, no. 15 (June 1992): 12, 13.
65. Hergé, letter to a reader, Sept. 3, 1976, AFH.
66. Frédéric Pomier, "L' affaire Tournesol, 'Torn Curtain': Essai d'analyse comparative," unpublished memoire, 1986.
67. Hergé, letter to a reader, Mar. 13, 1958, AFH.
68. Hergé, letter to Éditions Julliard, May 9, 1957, AFH.
69. List dated Oct. 1958, AFH.
70. Paul-Emile Victor, letter to Hergé, Mar. 29, 1961, AFH.
71. Hergé, interviewed by Sadoul, unpublished version, fourth interview, p. 132.
72. Fanny Rodwell, as told to the author, AFR.
73. Hergé, letter to Louis-Robert Casterman, Sept. 20, 1956, AFH.
74. Marguerite Duras, "L' Internationale Tintin," *France-Observateur*, no. 373 (July 4, 1957): 13.
75. Jacques Borgé, "Premier au depart pour la lune: Tintin," *Paris-Match*, no. 493 (Sept. 20, 1958).
76. Baudouin van den Branden de Reeth, letter to Félicien Marceau, Dec. 22, 1958, AFH.

77. Pol Vandromme, *Le Monde de Tintin*, collection "La petite vermillion" (Paris: La Table ronde, 1994), p. 60.
78. Roger Nimier, "Tintin fait son entrée dans la literature," preface to ibid. (also published in the collection/anthology by Roger Nimier, *Les écrivains sont-ils bêtes?* [Paris: Rivages, 1990]).
79. Pol Vandromme, as told to the author; Hergé, letter to Éditions Gallimard, Nov. 26, 1959; Roger Nimier, letter to Hergé, Dec. 8, 1959, AFH.

Chapter 10. The Demon of Purity: 1958–1960

1. Jacqueline van den Branden de Reeth, as told to the author.
2. Numa Sadoul, *Entretien avec Hergé* (Tournai: Casterman, 1989), pp. 14, 134, 135; Hergé, interviewed by Numa Sadoul, unpublished version, fourth interview, 1971, pp. 8, 22.
3. Hergé, letter to Olivier Todd, Nov. 19, 1958, AFH.
4. Guy Dessicy, as told to the author.
5. Germaine Kieckens, as told to the author; Fanny Rodwell, as told to the author.
6. Projects, undated (probably 1957), AFH.
7. Hergé, letter to Father Gall, Nov. 13, 1957; Father Gall, letter to Hergé, Dec. 22, 1957, AFH.
8. Benoît Peeters, "Hergé, une longue route vers le Tibet," in *Au Tibet avec Tintin, Catalogue de l'exposition* (Brussels: Fondation Hergé, 1995), p. 47.
9. Hergé, letter to Richard Lannoy, July 23, 1958, AFH.
10. Bernard Heuvelmans, letter to Hergé, Feb. 1, 1958, AFH.
11. Hergé, letter to Bernard Heuvelmans, Feb. 4, 1958, AFH.
12. Sadoul, *Entretien avec Hergé*, p. 180.
13. Hergé, letter to Dr. Roland Cahen, Nov. 5, 1965, AFH. Quoted in Thierry Smolderen et Pierre Sterckx, *Hergé: Portrait biographique* (Tournai: Casterman, 1988), p. 323.
14. Quoted in ibid.
15. Quoted in Sadoul, *Entretien avec Hergé*, pp. 57–59.
16. Hergé, interviewed by Sadoul, p. 14.
17. Quoted in Sadoul, *Entretien avec Hergé*; Hergé, inscription in Raymond Leblanc's copy of *Tintin in Tibet*, Oct. 1960.
18. Hergé, letter to Jean Toulat, Jan. 16, 1975, AFH.
19. "Hommage to *Tintin in Tibet*," Oct. 1960, AFH.
20. Inscription on the copy for Bernard Heuvelmans, ABH.

Chapter 11. Finishing Touches: 1960–1973

1. Numa Sadoul, *Entretien avec Hergé* (Tournai: Casterman, 1989), pp. 70, 83; Hergé, letter to a reader, Mar. 22, 1973, AFH.

2. Hergé, letter to a reader, Sept. 12, 1967, AFH.
3. Hergé, letter to a reader, Aug. 20, 1963; Hergé, letter to a reader, Jan. 11, 1972; Hergé, letter to a reader, Apr. 20, 1976, AFH.
4. Sadoul, *Entretien avec Hergé,* pp. 46, 47.
5. Hergé, letter to a reader, May 14, 1976, AFH.
6. Preparatory project for *The Castafiore Emerald,* Dec. 7, 1960, AFH.
7. Hergé, letter to Leslie Lonsdale-Cooper, Feb. 25, 1965, AFH.
8. *Le Canard Enchaîné,* no. 2360 (Jan. 12, 1966), quoted in Claude Stoller, *L'Univers politique de Tintin* (Strasbourg: Université de Strasbourg, 1966), p. 58.
9. Hergé, letters to Jean Favart, July 29, Oct. 1, Dec. 4, 1964, AFH.
10. Raymond Leblanc, as told to the author.
11. Hergé, interview in *Tendances,* no. 47 (Mar. 22, 1978): 25.
12. *Astérix, Journal exceptionnel des 35 ans,* Nov. 1994, p. 8.
13. Bertrand Caillé, *Analyse du contenu du journal "pilote" de 1959 à 1974,* mémoire de maîtrise d'histoire, Université de Paris-X, 1991.
14. *New York Times,* Sept. 12, 1966.
15. René Goscinny, Jean-Michel Charlier, and Jean Ache, letter to Hergé, Nov. 30, 1964; Hergé's reply, Dec. 5, 1964, AFH; *L'Express,* no. 796 (Sept. 19–25, 1966): 24–26.
16. Hergé, letter to Louis-Robert Casterman, June 29, 1967, AFH; Casterman, notes on the "Promotion of Tintin," July 4, 1967, AFH.
17. Jacques Martin, as told to the author.
18. Hergé, letter to a reader, Jan. 5, 1972, AFH; Jean-Claude Quinart, "Progrès tous azimuts," *Athena,* no. 72 (June 1991): 24–29.
19. Umberto Eco, *La Guerre du faux* (Le livre de poche, 1985), pp. 119–25.
20. Hergé, letters to Jean Tauré de Bessat, Nov. 6, 1962, Dec. 14, 1967, AFH; Jean Tauré de Bessat, letter to Hergé, Nov. 8, 1962, AFH.
21. Harry Thomson, *Tintin: Hergé and His Creation* (London: Hodder and Stoughton, 1991; reprint Sceptre, 1992), p. 191.
22. Jacques Martin, as told to the author.
23. Hergé, letter to a reader, June 15, 1867, AFH.
24. Hergé, letter to a reader, Nov. 13, 1964; Hergé, letter to Gabriel Matzneff, Nov. 10, 1964, AFH.
25. Hergé, letter to Leslie Lonsdale-Cooper, Oct. 6, 1961, AFH.
26. Changes suggested for the revision of *The Black Island,* 1965, AFH.
27. Pierre Servais, letter to Hergé, Dec. 29, 1966, AFH.
28. Hergé, interviewed by Numa Sadoul, unpublished version, fourth interview, 1971, p. 40.
29. Hergé, letter to Louis-Robert Casterman, July 24, 1961, AFH.
30. Hergé, letter to Louis-Robert Casterman, Nov. 17, 1972, AFH.
31. Hergé, letter to Claude Stoller, Feb. 8, 1966, AFH.
32. Cobel-Presse, letters to Casterman, Feb. 29, Mar. 15, 1952, AFH.
33. "Tintin revient au Congo" (Tintin Returns to the Congo), *Zaïre,* no. 73 (Dec. 29, 1969): 3.

34. Hergé, interviewed by Numa Sadoul, unpublished version, second interview, 1971, p. 9.

35. Ibid., p. 59; Walter Schwilden, secretary general of *Le Soir*, letter to Stéphane Steeman, Aug. 7, 1991, Bibliothèque du *Soir*.

36. Henri Desclez, as told to the author; *Le Soir*, Nov. 9, 1969 (p. 9), Nov. 26, 1969 (p. 12), Dec. 3, 1969 (p. 11), Dec. 24, 1969 (p. 10).

37. Henri Desclez, as told to the author; Hergé, interviewed by Sadoul, second interview, p. 29.

Chapter 12. The End of a Life, the Culmination of His Work: 1973–1983

1. Numa Sadoul, *Entretien avec Hergé* (Tournai: Casterman, 1989), pp. 11, 12.

2. Hergé, "Questionnaire de Proust," Oct. 1970, AFH.

3. Hergé, letter to Jean Toulat, Jan. 16, 1975, AFH.

4. Georges Remi Jr., as told to the author.

5. Alain Baran, as told to the author; Dominique de Wespin, *Teilhard, Béjart, Hergé: Trois hommes pour une vie* (Lasne: Agendart, 1993), p. 117.

6. Germaine Kieckens, as told to the author; Fanny Rodwell, as told to the author.

7. Hergé, answer to Plon-Comodo, Jan. 16, 1975, AFH.

8. Hergé, letter to Peter Ickx, Apr. 22, 1947, AFH.

9. Hergé, telegrams to Félicien Marceau, Nov. 17, 1969, Nov. 10, 1976, AFH.

10. Wespin, *Teilhard, Béjart, Hergé*, p. 151; Hergé, postcard to Gabriel Matzneff, Sept./Oct. 1979, AGM.

11. Hergé, letter to Michael Turner, May 13, 1969, AFH; document, AFH.

12. Hergé, letter to Gabrielle Rolin, July 16, 1966, AFH.

13. Hergé, letter to Claire Bretécher, Apr. 11, 1979, AFH.

14. Hergé, interviewed by Numa Sadoul, unpublished version, second interview, 1971, p. 6; Sadoul, *Entretien avec Hergé,* p. 89; Hergé, letters to Fred, Apr. 4, Oct. 17, Nov. 27, 1973, June 5, 1979, AFH; Hergé, "Hommage à Raymond Macherot," Apr. 1975, AFH; Hergé, letters to Jean-Claude Mézière, Feb. 23, 1954, Nov. 13, 1975, AFH; Hergé, letter to Philippe Druillet, Nov. 23, 1972, AFH.

15. Hergé, letter to Win N., Feb. 16, 1971, AFH.

16. Marcel Stal, Pierre Sterckx, and Stéphane Janssen, as told to the author; Hergé, letter to M. Lambert, June 7, 1963, AFH; Hergé, letter to Chang Chong-Chen, Feb. 15, 1977, AFH; Hergé, letter to Pierre Fresnault, May 10, 1969, AFH; Hergé, letter to Francis Boseret, Jan. 3, 1978, AFH; Pierre Sterckx, "Une Molécule pour pseudonyme," *Le Vif-Magazine*, Apr. 22, 1983, pp. 36, 37; "De Holbein à Kichtenstein," in (À suivre), hors series, *Spécial Hergé*, 1983, pp. 90–92; "Chang, Hergé et la peinture," in *Chang Revient!* (Brussels: Magic Strip, 1981); Hervé Springael, "Trois images de

Hergé," *Les Amis de Hergé*, no. 6 (Dec. 1987): 6–11; Sadoul, *Entretien avec Hergé*, pp. 44, 94, 227; Hergé, interviewed by Numa Sadoul, unpublished version, second interview, pp. 2, 14; third interview, pp. 37, 38; Frédéric Brébant, "Hergé et l'art contemporain," *Le Viv/l'Express*, June 17, 1994, pp. 15–17; Michel Daubert, "Les toiles mystérieuses," *Télérama*, no. 2388 (Oct. 18, 1995).

17. Benoît Peeters, *Hergé 1922–1932: Les débuts d'un illustrateur* (Tournai: Casterman, 1991), p. 43.

18. Pierre Alechinsky, as told to the author.

19. Hergé, interviewed by Thierry Smolderen, 1975, in *Les Amis de Hergé*, no. 13 (June 1991): 12–13.

20. Robert Poulet, "Hommage à Hergé," *Rivarol*, Mar. 18, 1983.

21. Yves Duval, as told to the author.

22. Fanny Rodwell, as told to the author.

23. Marcel Stal, as told to the author.

24. Hergé, interview in *La Libre Belgique*, Dec. 30, 1975.

25. Marcel Stal, as told to the author.

26. Philippe Goddin, *Hergé et les Bigotudos: Le roman d'une aventure* (Tournai: Casterman, 1990), pp. 10, 11, 62, 136.

27. Sadoul, *Entretien avec Hergé*, pp. 62, 192.

28. Philippe Goddin, *Hergé et Tintin reporters: Du* Vingtième Siècle *au journal* Tintin (Brussels: Éditions du Lombard, 1986), pp. 285, 287.

29. Hergé, letter to a reader, Jan. 21, 1976, AFH.

30. Benoît Peeters and Patrice Hamel, "Entretien avec Hergé," *Minuit*, no. 25 (Sept. 1977).

31. Fanny Rodwell, as told to the author.

32. Goddin, *Hergé et Tintin reporters*, p. 269.

33. Amnesty International, letter to Hergé, Mar. 25, 1982; Hergé, letter to General Galtieri, May 11, 1982, AFH.

34. *La Relève*, Apr. 10, 1976; *La Libre Belgique*, May 5, 1976; *Pourquoi pas?* Apr. 29, 1976; *Spécial*, May 12, 1976; *Pour*, Oct. 1, 1975, Apr. 21, 1976; *Hebdo 76*, Apr. 14, 1976; *Notre Temps*, Apr. 15, 1976; *Le Monde*, Apr. 26, 1976; *Notre Jeunesse*, May 20, 1976; *Pilote*, no. 27, 1976; *Charlie-mensuel*, Aug. 1976; *Révolution*, Apr. 23, 1976; *Sud-Ouest*, May 16, 1976; *Témoignage Chrétien*, May 20, 1976; *L'Humanité rouge*, May 16, 1976; *Minute*, Sept. 10, 1975; *La Croix*, Aug. 24, 1975; *Paris-Normandie*, May 5, 1976; *La Presse de la Manche*, Apr. 27, 1976; *France-Soir*, Apr. 16, 1976; *Critique*, no. 358 (Mar. 1977).

35. Michèle Nieto, "Tintin à la loupe," *Le Point*, no. 15 (Jan. 22, 1973).

36. *Les Nouvelles Littéraires*, May 13, 1976.

37. Chang Chong-Chen, as told to the author.

38. Hergé, letter to Chang Chong-Chen, Mar. 28, 1976, AFH.

39. Han Suyin, letter to Hergé, Dec. 11, 1977, Feb. 15, 1978; Hergé, letter to Chang Chong-Chen, Dec. 26, 1977; Hergé, letter to Han Suyin, Feb. 25, 1978; Hergé, letter to Serge Pairoux, Feb. 28, 1978; Hergé, letter to

Hermann Liebars, June 2, 1978, AFH; "Une evolution vers le Tao," *Le Vif-Magazine*, Apr. 22, 1983.

40. Chang Chong-Chen, letter to Hergé, July 1980, AFH.

41. Anonymous, *Chang au pays du Lotus Bleu* (Brussels: Séguier), 1990.

42. Pierre Sterckx, "Chang, Hergé et la peinture," in *Chang revient!* (Brussels: Magic Strip, 1981).

43. Paul-Dominique Labesse, "Repères biographiques," *Schtroumpf, les cahiers de la BD,* spécial Hergé, nos. 14–15, pp. 191–97, CBBD; Hergé, interviewed on Radio-Brussels, Mar. 4, 1942; Hergé, reply to Michel Verger's questionnaire, Jan. 9, 1970, AFH.

44. Réginald Hemerleers, "Hergé, le père de Tintin," *Revue de Saint-Boniface,* June 1939.

45. Hergé, letter to a reader, Jan. 1973, AFH.

46. Hergé, letter to a reader, June 17, 1955, AFH.

47. Hergé, letter to Larry Harmon, June 18, 1959, AFH.

48. Hergé, letter to André Barret, Nov. 13, 1958, AFH.

49. Hergé, letter to André Barret, May 23, 1958, AFH.

50. Hergé, *Le Temple du Soleil*, p. 61.

51. Robert Poulet, letter to Hergé, Jan. 5, 1962, AFH.

52. Quoted in Sadoul, *Entretien avec Hergé*, p. 82.

53. Alain Baran, as told to the author; Dossier, "1983. Projet U.S.A. Négotiations," AFH.

54. Fanny Rodwell, as told to the author.

55. Sadoul, *Entretien avec Hergé*, p. 202; Hergé, interviewed by Thierry Smolderen, *Les Amis de Hergé*, no. 13 (June 1991): 12, 13.

56. Hergé, "Un jourd'hiver, sur un aeroport" (A Winter's Day at an Airport), unpublished project, 1976, AFH.

57. Alain Baran, as told to the author.

58. Hergé, *Tintin et L'Alph-art* (Tournai: Casterman, 1986); Fanny Rodwell, as told to the author; Stéphane Janssen, as told to the author; Jean-Paul Morel, "Tintin et l'album inachevé" (Tintin and the Unfinished Book), *Le Matin de Paris*, Oct. 8, 1986.

59. Sterckx, "Une Molécule pour pseudonyme."

60. Alain Baran, as told to the author.

61. Ibid.

62. Hergé, interviewed by Sadoul, second interview, p. 27.

63. Stéphane Janssen, as told to the author; Gabriel Matzneff, as told to the author.

64. Hergé, interviewed by Sadoul, second interview, p. 2.

65. Quoted in Peeters, *Hergé 1922–1932*.

66. Germaine Kieckens, as told to the author.

67. Stéphane Steeman, as told to the author; Stéphane Steeman, *Le Livre de Steeman* (Brussels: Éditions Le Livre, 1995), p. 172.

68. Alain Baran, as told to the author.

69. Fanny Rodwell, as told to the author.

select bibliography

Books

Ajame, Pierre. *Hergé*. Paris: Gallimard, 1991.

Au Tibet avec Tintin, Catalogue de l'exposition. Brussels: Fondation Hergé, 1995.

Baetens, Jean. *Hergé écrivain*. Brussels: Labor, 1989.

Benton, Mike. *The Comic Book in America*. Dallas: Taylor, 1989.

Blake, Bell. *Strange and Stranger: The World of Steve Ditko*. Seattle: Fantgraphics Books, 2008.

Bourdil, Pierre-Yves, and Bernard Tordeur. *Bob De Moor: 40 ans de bande dessinée, 35 ans aux côtés d'Hergé*. Brussels: Éditions du Lombard, 1986.

David, Michel. *Une psychanalyse amusante: Tintin à la lumière de Lacan*. Paris: Épi/La Méridienne, 1994.

Delporte, Christian. *Les crayons de la propagande: Dessinateurs et dessin politique sous l'Occupation*. Paris: CNRS Éditions, 1993.

Eisner, Will. *Comics and Sequential Art*. Tamarac, FL: Poorhouse Press, 1985.

Farr, Michael, trans. *The Adventures of Hergé, Creator of Tintin*. San Francisco: Last Gasp, 2008.

———. *Tintin: The Complete Companion*. San Francisco: Last Gasp, 2002.

Filippini, Henri. *Dictionnaire de la bande dessinée*. Paris: Bordas, 1989.

Fouché, Pascal. *L'Édition française sous l'occupation, 1940–1944*. Paris: BLFC, Université de Paris-VII, 1987.

Fournet, Éric. *Quand Tintin découvrait l'Amérique*. Brussels: Didier-Hatier, 1992.

Gabler, Neal. *Walt Disney: The Triumph of the American Imagination*. New York: Knopf, 2006.

Gaumer, Patrick, and Claude Moliterni. *Dictionnaire mondial de la bande dessinée*. Paris: Larousse, 1994.

Goddin, Philippe. *Hergé et Tintin reporters: Du Vingtième Siècle au journal Tintin*. Brussels: Éditions du Lombard, 1986.

———. *Hergé, Ligne de vie*. Brussels: Éditions Moulinsart, 2007.

Goddin, Philippe, and Michael Farr, trans. *The Art of Hergé, Inventor of Tintin*. Vol. 1: 1907–1937. San Francisco: Last Gasp, 2008.

Hadju, David. *The Ten-Cent Plague: The Great Comic-Book Scare and How It Changed America.* New York: Farrar, Straus and Giroux, 2008.

Hergé: Correspondance. Lettres choisies, presentées et annotées par Edith Allaert et Jacques Bertin. Brussels: Duculot, 1989.

Hergé by Hergé. Catalogue of exhibition celebrating the 100th anniversary of his birth. Centre Pompidou. Brussels: Éditions Moulinsart, 2007.

Huyse, Luc, and Steven Dhondt. *La Répression des collaborations 1942–52: Un passé toujours present.* Brussels: CRISP, 1993.

Jacobs, Edgar P. *Un opéra de papier: Les mémoires de Blake et Mortimer.* Paris: Gallimard, 1981.

Lambert, Pierre. *Le Cartoon à Hollywood.* Paris: Librairie Séguier, 1988.

Lerman, Alain. *Histoire du journal Tintin.* Brussels: Éditions Jacques Glénat, 1979.

McCarthy, Tom. *Tintin and the Secret of Literature.* London: Granta, 2007.

McCloud, Scott. *Understanding Comics.* Amherst, MA: Kitchen Sink Press, 1993.

Michalis, David. *Schulz and Peanuts: A Biography.* New York: Harper, 2007.

Mozgovine, Cyrille. *De Abdallah à Zorrino: Dictionnaire des noms propres de Tintin.* Tournai: Casterman, 1992.

Le Musée imaginaire de Tintin. Album de l'exposition. Tournai: Casterman, 1980.

Nyeberg, Amy Kriste. *Seal of Approval: The History of the Comics Code.* Jackson: University Press of Mississippi, 1998.

Ory, Pascal. "Le Petit nazi illustré," *Le Téméraire 1943–1944.* Paris: Albatros, 1979.

Peeters, Benoît. *Case, planche, récit: Comment lire une bande dessinée.* Tournai: Casterman, 1991.

———. *Hergé, Fils de Tintin.* Paris: Flammarion, 2002.

———. *Hergé 1922–1932: Les débuts d'un illustrateur.* Tournai: Casterman, 1991.

———. *Le Monde d'Hergé.* Tournai: Casterman, 1983.

———. *Tintin and the World of Hergé.* London: Methuen, 1999.

Raphael, Jordan, and Tom Spurgeon. *Stan Lee and the Rise and Fall of the American Comic Book.* Chicago: Chicago Review Press, 2003.

Ro, Ronin. *Tales to Astonish: Jack Kirby, Stan Lee, and the American Comic Book Revolution.* New York: Bloomsbury, 2004.

Sabin, Roger. *Comics, Comix, and Graphic Novels.* London: Phaidon Press, 2000.

Sadoul, Numa. *Entretien avec Hergé.* Tournai: Casterman, 1989.

Smolderen, Thierry, and Pierre Sterckx. *Hergé: Portrait biographique.* Tournai: Casterman, 1988.

Soumois, Frédéric. *Dossier Tintin.* Brussels: Éditions Jacques Antoine, 1987.

Springael, Hervé. *Avant Tintin: Dialogue with Hergé.* Self-published, Brussels, 1987.

Sterckx, Pierre, and Benoît Peeters. *Hergé, Illustrator: Sixty Years of the Adventures of Tintin.* Catalogue. Translated by Michael Farr. Tournai: Casterman, 1988.

Thomson, Harry. *Tintin: Hergé and His Creation.* London: Hodder and Stoughton, 1991; reprint Sceptre, 1992.

Tisseron, Serge. *Tintin chez le psychanalyste.* Paris: Aubier, 1985.

———. *Tintin et les secrets de famille.* Paris: Aubier, 1992.

——. *Tintin et le secret d'Hergé*. Paris: Hors collection, 1993.

Vandromme, Pol. *Le Monde de Tintin*. Paris: Gallimard, 1959; reprint, La Table ronde, 1994.

Willequet, Jacques. *La Belgique sous la botte: Résistances et collaborations, 1940–1945*. Paris: Édition universitaires, 1986.

Journal

Les Amis de Hergé (Soignies, Belgium). Published twice yearly.

Information of Interest

On June 2, 2009, the Hergé Museum, designed by Christian de Portzamparc, opened in Louvain-la-Neuve, Belgium, just outside of Brussels. See www.museeherge.com

works by hergé

Comic Strips (other than "Tintin")

"Les Aventures de Jo, Zette et Jocko" (The Adventures of Jo, Zette, and Jocko)

"Les Aventures de Popol et Virginie au Far West" (The Adventures of Popol and Virginia in the Far West)

"Les Aventures de Totor C.P. des hannetons" (The Adventures of Totor, Troop Leader of the June Bugs)

"Cet aimable M. Mops" (The Loveable Mr. Mops)

"Les Exploits de Quick et Flupke" (The Adventures of Quick and Flupke)

"Popol et Virginie chez les Lapinos" (Popol and Virginia among the Lapinos)

"La Vallée des cobras" (The Valley of Cobras)

Tintin Books

All of Hergé's works were published by Casterman (Tournai, Belgium).

The date given is of the first publication of the Tintin stories in book form.

The English translations are by Leslie Lonsdale-Cooper and Michael Turner.

Tintin in the Land of the Soviets (1930)
Tintin in the Congo (1931)
Tintin in America (1932)
Cigars of the Pharaoh (1934)
The Blue Lotus (1936)

The Broken Ear (1937)
The Black Island (1938)
King Ottokar's Scepter (1939)
The Crab with the Golden Claws (1941)
The Shooting Star (1942)
The Secret of the Unicorn (1943)
Red Rackham's Treasure (1945)
The Seven Crystal Balls (1948)
Prisoners of the Sun (1949)
Land of Black Gold (1951)
Destination Moon (1953)
Explorers on the Moon (1954)
The Calculus Affair (1956)
The Red Sea Sharks (1958)
Tintin in Tibet (1960)
The Castafiore Emerald (1963)
Flight 714 (1968)
Tintin and the Picaros (1976)

acknowledgments

Without the cooperation, assistance, and goodwill of Fanny Rodwell, this book would not have been feasible. The widow of Georges Remi not only confided in me her own experiences, but she also gave me unlimited access to the archives of the Fondation Hergé, including certain private documents, without setting conditions of any sort. To her, my infinite gratitude.

I am completely indebted to Philippe Goddin, whose advice, erudition, and support were invaluable all during my research, and I am grateful as well for the equally valuable assistance of Bernard Tordeur, without forgetting the friendly efficiency of Madame Alain Berenboom, who never failed me.

I want to pay tribute to the memory of Germaine Kieckens, recently deceased, and to express my gratitude to her nephew, Georges Remi, for her assistance.

I would also like to thank Nick Rodwell for his patience and discreet help with my research for this book.

In several circumstances old friendships were combined with work, to my great advantage. The vigilant efforts of my agent, François-Marie Samuelson, were again indispensable from beginning to end, as well as the support of my editors, Olivier Orban, who enabled me to pursue my research to its conclusion, and Anthony Rowley, who followed my work step by step until I finished. His critical spirit was to my great benefit, for which I am very grateful. The manuscript of this book, like the preceding ones, was made much better by the attentive eye of Stéphane Khémis, who lets nothing get by him.

I would like to express my warmest thanks to numerous people in France and Belgium who met and spoke with me and sent written comments, giving generously of their time: Jacqueline van den Branden de Reeth, Katherine Canivet, Marie-Louise Degand-Remi, Yaguel Didier, France Ferrari, Agnès Guérin, Geneviève Hanquet, Gabrielle Rolin, Nicole Thenen, Dominique de Wespin;

Pierre Alechinsky, A. Andries (premier avocat general près la Cour militaire), Alain Baran, Jean-Pierre Bertin-Maghit, Chang Chong-Chen, Martin Conway, Albert Debaty, Pierre Delville, Benoît Denis, Henri Desclez, Guy Dessicy, Paul Dirkx, Yves Duval, Maurice Einhorn, Roger Faligot, Michel Fernez, Louis Gérard, Jean Godin, Bernard Goorden, Laurent Greilsamer, Alexis-Jean Hennebert,

Bernard Heuvelmans, Luc Huyse, Frans Jagueneau, Paul Jamin, Stéphane Janssen, Raymond Leblanc, Jean Libert, Arnould de Liedekerke, Félicien Marceau, Jacques Martin, Gabriel Matzneff, Maurice Mességué, M. Meyers, Pascal Ory, Benoit Peeters, Henri Plard, Didier Platteau, Étienne Pollet, Henri Roanne-Rosenblatt, Charles Ronsac, Numa Sadoul, Pierre Sissman, Marcel Stal, Stéphane Steeman, Pierre Sterckx, Pierre Ugeux, William Ugeux, Claude de Valkeneer, Pol Vandromme.

Friendships were made in the course of my research. I hope that they will not end with the reading of this work.

Finally, a thank-you to Angela, who has reason to hate biographies, and to Meryl and Kate, who still prefer comic books. They followed my work from the first to the last minute and always gave me their support. They still do, despite everything. This book is for the three of you.

The revised PLON edition, corrected, enriched, and improved, owes much to the suggestions and comments sent by attentive readers, namely, Daniel du Bois de Vroylande, Jean-Yves Brouard, Gustave Dessers, Philippe Destatte, Pierre Deligny, Bruno Dufresne, Philippe Goddin, Bernard Heuvelmans, Pierre Logié, Thierry Martens, Didier Pasamonik, Dominique Petitfaux, and Désiré Roegiest.

Pierre Assouline

I would like to dedicate this translation to Alex Ruas Nelson. This book belongs especially to the next generation of *Tintin* readers: Zoey and Olga Ruas, Shawn Orrico, Isobel McBride, Henry, Lucy, and Chloe Ainley, and Polly, Rose, and William Allingham, as well as Jacques Zhai Wu Zhou, who knew Tintin as Ding Ding in China. I also want to express my gratitude for the always unfailing support of Rob Wynne through this process, the generous assistance of Irene Skolnick, without whom this translation would not exist, the razor-sharp editing of Tim Bent, and, in particular, the extraordinary and patient support of Joellyn Ausanka, who lets nothing slip by her.

Charles Ruas

Index

Printed in the United States
By Bookmasters